KEEPING
FAITH

by Cornel West

Prophesy Deliverance! An Afro-American Revolutionary Christianity (1982)

Theology in the Americas: Detroit II (1982) (*co-editor*)

Post-Analytic Philosophy (1985) (*co-editor*)

Prophetic Fragments (1988)

The American Evasion of Philosophy: A Genealogy of Pragmatism (1989)

Out There: Marginalization and Contemporary Cultures (1990) (*co-editor*)

The Ethical Dimensions of Marxist Thought (1991)

Breaking Bread: Insurgent Black Intellectual Life (1991) (*with bell hooks*)

Beyond Eurocentrism and Multiculturalism. Volume One: Prophetic Thought in Postmodern Times (1993)

Beyond Eurocentrism and Multiculturalism. Volume Two: Prophetic Reflections: Notes on Race and Power in America (1993)

Race Matters (1993)

Cornel West

KEEPING FAITH

Philosophy and Race in America

Routledge

New York London

Published in 1993

Paperback edition published in 1994 by

Routledge
29 West 35th Street
New York, NY 10001

Published in Great Britain by

Routledge
11 New Fetter Lane
London EC4P 4EE

Library of Congress Cataloging-in-Publication Data

West, Cornel.
    Keeping faith : philosophy and race in America / Cornel West.
      p.   cm.
    Includes bibliographical references and index.
    ISBN 0-415-90486-2 (HB)—ISBN 0-415-91028-5 (PB)
    1. Afro-Americans—Intellectual life. 2. Afro-Americans—Politics
and government. 3. United States—Race relations. I. Title.
E185.615.W427 1993
305.896'073—dc20   93-19377
                                                                    CIP

British Library Cataloguing-in-Publication Data also available.

To the love of my life,
my precious wife

Elleni Gebre Amlak

heir of a great family and civilization of faith
and harbinger of hope to come

Contents

Law and Culture

Explaining Race

Preface: The Difficulty of Keeping Faith

In Ethiopia

As I sit and watch the sun rise over the mountains of Addis Ababa, Ethiopia, my mind recalls the powerfully moving ceremony of two days past—a ceremony in which my loving mother (I reject the term 'in-law'), Harigewain Mola, transferred her house to my wife Elleni and me.

This extraordinary woman was born into one of the great families of Ethiopia. She is a direct descendant of Bulo, leader of the Oromo people, who wedded the sister of Menelik II, the nineteenth-century creator of modern Ethiopia; three days before the Italian invasion in 1935, she married into another grand Amhara family, Gebre Amlak. She owned thousands of acres of land (estimated to include significant portions of Addis Ababa itself), lost all but one house through the uncompensated confiscation of lands and properties under the communist regime, and now lives with dignity and Christian humility in one of the most culturally rich yet economically impoverished countries of the late twentieth century.

The ceremony lasted five tearful and rip-roaring hours. With my brothers and sisters, Gasha Milliard, Sewasew, Sirak, Tselat and Elleni, we shared personal stories interwoven with national narratives that highlighted the courage and integrity as well as the failures and farewells of the matriarchs and patriarchs of my Ethiopian lineage. We concluded by kissing the feet of our beloved mother, whose unselfish life of giving and living embraces both loss and love.

This ceremony, with its outpouring of deep feelings, echoes my wedding of exactly one year earlier. The wedding, organized by a committee of leading Ethiopian citizens, was a unique religious ceremony in the grand Coptic cathedral known as Haile Selassie Church; two thousand people attended the celebration at the Addis Ababa Hilton. But if the event is etched in the recent memory of many Ethiopians it is because of the incredible depths of joy and ecstasy, of love and happiness experienced by so many from sunrise to curfew. The fact that my father, mother and only brother (my best man) made the trip from California to Addis Ababa indeed added to these depths—as did my new Ethiopian name, Fikre Selassie.

My initiation into Ethiopian life raises urgent issues of inheritance and rootlessness, tradition and homelessness. What is my relation to my African heritage and Ethiopian house? How do I understand my African American tradition and sense of black homelessness in America? Who is the "I" or "me" that has emerged out of a particular black family, church and neighborhood, a white academy, a multicultural American mass communication network, and a set of progressive political organizations? And, to put it bluntly, why do I have the urge to leave America and live in Ethiopia? Is this the urge of an émigré, an expatriate or an exile?

In America

As I reflect on these complex questions, I realize that they sit at the core of my intellectual vocation and existential engagement: a profound commitment to what I call a prophetic vision and practice primarily based on a distinctly black tragic sense of life. On the one hand, this commitment looks the inescapable facts of death, disease and despair in the face and affirms moral agency and action in our everyday, commonplace circumstances. On the other hand, it is rooted in a certain view of the Christian tradition that is so skeptical about our capacity to know the ultimate truths about our existence that leaps of faith are promoted and enacted because they make sense out of our seemingly absurd conditions. The tragicomic vision of Anton Chekhov—the most illuminating and empowering vision put forward in our ghastly century—encourages me to put a premium on garnering resources from a vanishing past in a decadent present in order to keep alive a tempered hope for the future, a hope against hope that human empathy and compassion may survive against the onslaught of human barbarity, brutality and bestiality. It is the love ethic of Christian faith—the most absurd and alluring mode of being in the world—that enables me to live a life of hope against hope without succumbing to a warranted yet paralyzing pessimism or to an understandable yet miserable misanthropy.

How then does a black philosopher keep faith as he, or she, focuses on the pain and paranoia in America's chocolate cities and on Africa's sense of impending catastrophe? What are the sources for brave thought and courageous action in this frightening moment of global cynicism and fatalism? My feeble attempt to put forward a prophetic criticism for our times is a direct response to these grave questions.

Prophetic criticism rests on what I understand to be the best of Euro-American modernity—the existential imperative to institutionalize critiques of illegitimate authority and arbitrary uses of power; a bestowal of dignity, grandeur and tragedy on the ordinary lives of everyday people; and an experimental form of life that highlights curiosity, wonder, contingency, adventure, danger and, most importantly, improvisation. These elements constitute a democratic mode of being in the world inseparable from democratic ways of life and ways of struggle. Prophetic criticism is first and foremost an intellectual inquiry constitutive of existential democracy—a self-critical and self-corrective enterprise of human 'sense-making' for the preserving and expanding of human empathy and compassion. Chekhov's drama of the everyday and Kierkegaard's unique Christian perspective, are exemplary European expressions of the personal aspects of existential democracy. John Dewey's pragmatism (and democratic socialism) is a leading American example of the political aspects of existential democracy.

Yet prophetic criticism is the product of not only Euro-American modernity, but also New World African modernity. New World African modernity consists of degraded and exploited Africans in American circumstances using European languages and instruments to make sense of tragic predicaments—predicaments disproportionately shaped by white-supremacist bombardments on black beauty, intelligence, moral character and creativity. New World African modernity attempts to institutionalize critiques of white-supremacist authority and racist uses of power, to bestow dignity, grandeur and tragedy upon the denigrated lives of ordinary black people, and to promote improvisational life-strategies of love and joy in black life-worlds of radical and brutish contingency. New World African modernity radically interrogates and creatively appropriates Euro-American modernity by examining how "race" and "Africa"—themselves modern European constructs—yield insights and blindnesses, springboards and roadblocks for our understanding of multivarious and multileveled modernities. Prophetic criticism rests on the best of New World African modernity by making explicit the personal and political aspects of existential democracy implicit in the visions, analyses and strategies of American African victims of Euro-American modernity. Billie Holiday's artistic sensibilities and Howard Thurman's religious sentiments are exemplary New World African expressions of the personal aspects of existential democracy. W. E. B. Du Bois's early pragmatism (and democratic socialism) is a leading New World African example of the political aspects of existential democracy.

Prophetic criticism suffers from a kind of Du Boisian double-consciousness—of *being* deeply shaped by Euro-American modernity but not *feeling* fully a part of it. New World African modernity—quite distinct from, yet continuous with, Old World African modernity—is what we get when Africans in the Americas, confronting their exclusion from the human family by white supremacists, use this as an occasion to remake and recreate themselves into a distinctly *new* people—a world-historical and monumental process in which oppressed and degraded people invent themselves in alien circumstances and with alien languages and products. If modernity is measured in terms of newness and novelty, innovation and improvisation—and not simply in terms of science, technology, markets, bureaucracies and nation-states—then New World African modernity is more thoroughly *modern* than any American novel, painting, dance or even skyscraper.

Similarly, New World Africans are deeply modern in the sense of being exiles, banished from their native lands and forced to live lives as perennial "outsiders," finding a "home" only in a dynamic language and mobile music—never in a secure land, safe territory or welcome nation. The fundamental theme of New World African modernity is neither integration nor separation but rather migration and emigration. This is why Marcus Garvey not only led the largest mass movement among New World Africans, but also exemplifies the basic orientation in New World African modernity: to flee the widespread victimization of Euro-American modernity, to escape the absurdity of white-supremacist treatment and to find a "home" in a safe and "free" space. But there are few emancipatory options, and this space is never reached.

So New World African moderns become a people of time, who constitute a homebound quest in offbeat temporality, a quest found in the timing of our bodies in space (how we walk and gesture rhythmically), the timing of our voices in ritual and everyday practices (the syncopation and repetition in speech, song, sermon and prayer)—in short, the timing of our communal efforts to preserve our sanity and humanity in Euro-American modernity. Garvey's genius was neither his nationalism (based on European models) nor his pessimism (based on Euro-American systemic racist treatment of Africans). Rather it resides in his wedding of black misery in America to transnational mobility to Africa, forging a sense of

possible momentum and motion for a temporal people with few
spatial options. In the space-time of New World African modernity,
to hope is to conceive of possible movement, to despair is to feel
ossified, petrified, closed in. This is why decolonization in the New
World for Africans is more a matter of self and mind than masses
and land, and hence much more subject to delusion and deception
in the New World than in the Old.

This is also why the fundamental frontier myth of North
America rings false for New World Africans. The idea that outward
migration breeds progress and moral regeneration worked only for
those who could credibly conceive of themselves as owners of land
and full participants in the governance of that land. Again, the
spatial option is closed for New World Africans. The brief yet
gallant struggle to make Oklahoma an all-black (and red) state
bears witness to this homebound quest for space—a failed quest
that produced Chief Sam's back-to-Africa movement (a model for
Garvey years later), and the legendary "free mind" of black Oklaho-
mans associated with black towns like Muskogee, Boley and Langston, and with such black natives as Ralph Ellison, John Hope
Franklin, Charlie Christian, the Gap Band and, I humbly add,
myself.

In this sense, the *doubleness* and *modernness* of New World
African modernity is reflected in the *exilic* and *experimental* character of prophetic criticism. By exilic, I mean unhoused in regard
to academic discipline; estranged, to some degree, from American
society; marginal, to some extent, in black culture; and suspicious
of any easy answers, quick fixes or dogmatic routes to reach "home."
By experimental, I mean radically historicist and unrelentingly critical (hence skeptical about skepticism and comical about irony but
yet not naively romantic), unapologetically moral (though bereft of
moralism) and, most importantly, improvisational in the service of
existential democracy. By any measure, prophetic criticism may be
too modern—hence blind to the pitfalls of Euro-American and New
World African modernities.

At Home

Enter Addis Ababa, a modern creation in a feudal society with a rich history of ancient civilization (Christian, Islamic and pagan) and the capital of the only African country that was never conquered or colonized in any significant or sustained manner by European imperial powers. Ethiopia is the land of New World African modern fantasies of "home": freedom, safety and self-determination. Ethiopia, the country of the Imperial Emperor Haile Selassie (from 1930 to 1974) and communist dictator Colonel Miriam Mengistu (from 1974 to 1991)—two of the most antidemocratic regimes in our century. Ethiopians are the only African people in the world who take their humanity for granted, with no inferiority complexes or anxieties about their intellectual or moral capacities. Yet theirs is one of the most economically impoverished countries in the world, and one that has never had a nationwide democratic election.

After nine generations of family roots in America I feel an urge to leave, to live in the house bequeathed to my wife and me by our mother. This urge rests on neither a romantic attachment to Africa nor a paternalistic commitment to uplift Ethiopians. Yet Africa does have a special appeal to me that Asia or Antarctica lack. And my project of prophetic criticism does commit me to promote the wise expansions of democratic practices in Ethiopia—as elsewhere. My thoughts of making Ethiopia my "home" are not based on brutal experiences of being black in America, or the relative paucity of enjoyable relations with Americans of all hues and colors. But, in all honesty, the extent to which race still so fundamentally matters in nearly every sphere of American life is—in the long run—depressing and debilitating. And my good fortune to have such fine friends across the racial divide is certainly not sufficient reason to be naively optimistic about America.

To put my cards on the table, the decline and decay in American life *appears*, at the moment, to be irreversible; yet it may not be. This slight possibility—the historic chance that a window of opportunity can be opened by our prophetic thought and action—is, in part, what keeping faith is all about. Ironically, the oldest surviving democracy in the world—with its precious yet precarious experiment in self-government and high standards of comfort and convenience—makes it more and more difficult to pursue a commitment to existential democracy. This is not only a question of whether prophetic criticism has a future in contemporary American culture. Rather it is a matter of whether one's exilic and experimental life as a New World African is worth living in the present-day United States.

I do not harbor vulgar anti-American feelings—I'm too much of a radical democrat to overlook how difficult it is to hammer out democratic practices over time and space. And I indeed acknowledge that Ethiopia may be on the verge of tribal-based civil war. But even the dim prospects of a life-acknowledging culture and a life-damaging society is, at times, more appealing than the dire ruins of a hedonistic culture and market-driven society. Needless to say, loving family and friends, the pleasures of American popular music and humor, the opportunities to pursue the life of the mind and the chance to help make America more democratic and free are major impediments to leaving the country. Yet the real possibility that dreams of substantive democracy and quality of life are becoming *less* palpable—especially for a disproportionate number of New World Africans—is difficult to bear. The idea that the deferred dream of black freedom may, out of pessimism, dry up like a raisin in the sun or, out of nihilism, simply explode is too much to entertain. The only options are to stay "at home" in exile in America and fight what may be a losing battle, or go to my "house" as an exile in Ethiopia and fight on a different front the same battle—a battle that holds up the bloodstained banner of the best of Euro-American and New World African modernities. I am sure that Ethiopia and Old World African modernity have much to teach me. Maybe I am simply too busy fighting in America to shift terrain as I approach forty.

Not since the 1920s have so many black folk been disappointed and disillusioned with America. I partake of this black zeitgeist; I share these sentiments. Yet I try to muster all that is within me, including my rich African and American traditions, to keep faith in the struggle for human dignity and existential democracy.

January 6, 1985 (in Ethiopia)
January 14, 1993 (in America)

Addis Ababa, Ethiopia

Faith means belief in something concerning which doubt is still theoretically possible; and as the test of belief is willingness to act, one may say that faith is the readiness to act in a cause the prosperous issue of which is not certified to us in advance. It is in fact the same moral quality which we call courage in practical affairs; and there will be a very widespread tendency in men of vigorous nature to enjoy a certain amount of uncertainty in their philosophic creed, just as risk lends a zest to worldly activity.

William James
"*The Sentiment of Rationality*" (1882)

Through all the sorrow of the Sorrow Songs there breathes a hope—a faith in the ultimate justice of things. The minor cadences of despair change often to triumph and calm confidence. Sometimes it is faith in life, sometimes a faith in death, sometimes assurance of boundless justice in some fair world beyond. But whichever it is, the meaning is always clear: that sometime, somewhere, men will judge men by their souls and not by their skins. Is such a hope justified? Do the Sorrow Songs sing true?

W.E.B. Du Bois
The Souls of Black Folk (1903)

Cultural Criticism and Race

1

The New Cultural Politics of Difference

In these last few years of the twentieth century, there is emerging a significant shift in the sensibilities and outlooks of critics and artists. In fact, I would go so far as to claim that a new kind of cultural worker is in the making, associated with a new politics of difference. These new forms of intellectual consciousness advance reconceptions of the vocation of critic and artist, attempting to undermine the prevailing disciplinary divisions of labor in the academy, museum, mass media and gallery networks, while preserving modes of critique within the ubiquitous commodification of culture in the global village. Distinctive features of the new cultural politics of difference are to trash the monolithic and homogeneous in the name of diversity, multiplicity and heterogeneity; to reject the abstract, general and universal in light of the concrete, specific and particular; and to historicize, contextualize and pluralize by highlighting the contingent, provisional, variable, tentative, shifting and changing. Needless to say, these gestures are not new in the history of criticism or art, yet what makes them novel—along with the cultural politics they produce—is how and what constitutes difference, the weight and gravity it is given in representation, and the way in which highlighting issues like exterminism, empire, class, race, gender, sexual orientation, age, nation, nature and region at this historical moment acknowledges some discontinuity and disruption from previous forms of cultural critique. To put it bluntly, the new cultural politics of difference consists of creative responses to the precise circumstances of our present moment—especially those of marginalized First World agents who shun degraded self-representations, articulating instead their sense of the flow of history in light of the contemporary terrors, anxieties and fears of highly commercialized North Atlantic capitalist cultures (with their escalating xenophobias against people of color, Jews, women, gays, lesbians and the elderly). The thawing, yet still rigid, Second World ex-communists cultures (with increasing nationalist revolts against the legacy of hegemonic party henchmen) and the diverse cultures of the majority of inhabitants on the globe smothered by international communication cartels and repressive postcolonial elites (sometimes in the name of communism, as was the case in Ethiopia) or starved by austere World Bank and IMF politics that subordinate them to the North (as in free-market capitalism in Chile) also locate vital areas of analysis in this new cultural terrain.

The new cultural politics of difference is neither simply oppositional in contesting the mainstream (or *male*stream) for inclusion, nor transgressive in the avant-gardist sense of shocking conventional bourgeois audiences. It embraces the distinct articulations of talented (and usually privileged) contributors to culture who desire to align themselves with demoralized, demobilized, depoliticized and disorganized people in order to empower and enable social action and, if possible, to enlist collective insurgency for the expansion of freedom, democracy and individuality. This perspective impels these cultural critics and artists to reveal, as an integral component of their production, the very operations of power within their immediate work contexts (academy, museum, gallery, mass media). This strategy, however, also puts them in an inescapable double bind—while linking their activities to the fundamental, structural overhaul of these institutions, they often remain financially dependent on them (so much for "independent" creation). For these critics of culture, theirs is a gesture that is simultaneously progressive and co-opted. Yet without social movement or political pressure from outside these institutions (extraparliamentary and extracurricular actions like the social movements of the recent past), transformation degenerates into mere accommodation or sheer stagnation, and the role of the "co-opted progressive"—no matter how fervent one's subversive rhetoric—is rendered more difficult. There can be no artistic breakthrough or social progress without some form of crisis in civilization—a crisis usually generated by organizations or collectivities that convince ordinary people to put their bodies and lives on the line. There is, of course, no guarantee that such pressure will yield the result one wants, but there is a guarantee that the status quo will remain or regress if no pressure is applied at all.

The new cultural politics of difference faces three basic challenges—intellectual, existential and political. The intellectual challenge—usually cast as methodological debate in these days in which academicist forms of expression have a monopoly on intellectual life—is how to think about representational practices in terms of history, culture and society. How does one understand, analyze and enact such practices today? An adequate answer to this question can be attempted only after one comes to terms with the insights and blindnesses of earlier attempts to grapple with the question in light of the evolving crisis in different histories, cultures and societies. I shall sketch a brief genealogy—a history that highlights the contingent origins and often ignoble outcomes—of exemplary critical responses to the question. This genealogy sets forth a historical framework that characterizes the rich yet deeply flawed Eurocentric traditions which the new cultural politics of difference builds upon yet goes beyond.

The Intellectual Challenge

An appropriate starting point is the ambiguous legacy of the Age of Europe. Between 1492 and 1945, European breakthroughs in oceanic transportation, agricultural production, state consolidation, bureaucratization, industrialization, urbanization and imperial dominion shaped the makings of the modern world. Precious ideals like the dignity of persons (individuality) or the popular accountability of institutions (democracy) were unleashed around the world. Powerful critiques of illegitimate authorities—of the Protestant Reformation against the Roman Catholic Church, the Enlightenment against state churches, liberal movements against absolutist states and feudal guild constraints, workers against managerial subordination, women against sexist practices, people of color and Jews against white and gentile supremacist decrees, gays and lesbians against homophobic sanctions—were fanned and fueled by these precious ideals refined within the crucible of the Age of Europe. Yet the discrepancy between sterling rhetoric and lived reality, glowing principles and actual practices, loomed large.

By the last European century—the last epoch in which European domination of most of the globe was uncontested and unchallenged in a substantive way—a new world seemed to be stirring. At the height of England's reign as the major imperial European power, its exemplary cultural critic, Matthew Arnold, painfully observed in his "Stanzas from the Grand Chartreuse" that he felt some sense of "wandering between two worlds, one dead / the other powerless to be born." Following his Burkean sensibilities of cautious reform and fear of anarchy, Arnold acknowledged that the old glue—religion—that had tenuously and often unsuccessfully held together the ailing European regimes could not do so in the mid-nineteenth century. Like Alexis de Tocqueville in France, Arnold saw that the democratic temper was the wave of the future. So he proposed a new conception of culture—a secular, humanistic one—that could play an integrative role in cementing and stabilizing an emerging bourgeois civil society and imperial state. His famous castigation of the immobilizing materialism of the declining aristocracy, the vulgar philistinism of the emerging middle classes and the latent explosiveness of the working-class majority was motivated by a desire to create new forms of cultural legitimacy, authority and order in a rapidly changing moment in nineteenth-century Europe.

For Arnold (in *Culture and Anarchy*, 1869), this new conception of culture

> seeks to do away with classes; to make the best that has been thought and known in the world current everywhere; to make all men live in an atmosphere of sweetness and light. . . .
>
> This is the *social idea* and the men of culture are the true apostles of equality. The great men of culture are those who have had a passion for diffusing, for making prevail, for carrying from one end of society to the other, the best knowledge, the best ideas of their time, who have laboured to divest knowledge of all that was harsh, uncouth, difficult, abstract, professional, exclusive; to humanize it, to make it efficient outside the clique of the cultivated and learned, yet still remaining the best knowledge and thought of the time, and a true source, therefore, of sweetness and light.

As an organic intellectual of an emergent middle class—as the inspector of schools in an expanding educational bureaucracy, Professor of Poetry at Oxford (the first non-cleric and the first to lecture in English rather than Latin) and an active participant in a thriving magazine network—Arnold defined and defended a new secular culture of critical discourse. For him, this discursive strategy would be lodged in the educational and periodical apparatuses of modern societies as they contained and incorporated the frightening threats of an arrogant aristocracy and especially of an "anarchic" working-class majority. His ideals of disinterested, dispassionate and objective inquiry would regulate this new secular cultural production, and his justifications for the use of state power to quell any threats to the survival and security of this culture were widely accepted. He aptly noted, "Through culture seems to lie our way, not only to perfection, but even to safety."

This sentence is revealing in two ways. First, it refers to "our way" without explicitly acknowledging who constitutes the "we." This move is symptomatic among many bourgeois, male, Eurocentric critics whose universalizing gestures exclude (by guarding a silence around) or explicitly degrade women and peoples of color. Second, the sentence links culture to safety—presumably the safety of the "we" against the barbaric threats of the "them," that is, those viewed as different in some debased manner. Needless to say, Arnold's negative attitudes toward British working-class people, women and especially Indians and Jamaicans in the Empire clarify why he conceives of culture as, in part, a weapon for bourgeois, male, European "safety."

For Arnold, the best of the Age of Europe—modeled on a mythological mélange of Periclean Athens, late Republican/early Imperial Rome and Elizabethan England—could be promoted only if there was an interlocking affiliation among the emerging middle classes, a homogenizing of cultural discourse in the educational and university networks, and a state advanced enough in its policing techniques to safeguard it. The candidates for participation and legitimation in this grand endeavor of cultural renewal and revision would be detached intellectuals willing to shed their parochialism, provincialism and class-bound identities for Arnold's middle-class-skewed project: ". . . Aliens, if we may so call them—persons who are mainly led, not by their class spirit, but by a general *humane* spirit, by the love of human perfection." Needless to say, this Arnoldian perspective still informs much of the academic practices and secular cultural attitudes today—dominant views about the canon, admission procedures and collective self-definitions of intellectuals. Yet Arnold's project was disrupted by the collapse of nineteenth-century Europe—World War I. This unprecedented war brought to the surface the crucial role and violent potential not of the masses Arnold feared but of the state he heralded. Upon the ashes of this wasteland of human carnage—some of it the civilian European population—T. S. Eliot emerged as the grand cultural spokesman.

Eliot's project of reconstituting and reconceiving European highbrow culture—and thereby regulating critical and artistic practices—after the internal collapse of imperial Europe can be viewed as a response to the probing question posed by Paul Valéry in "The Crisis of the Spirit" after World War I,

> This Europe, will it become *what it is in reality*, i.e., a little cape of the Asiatic continent? or will this Europe remain rather what it seems, i.e., the priceless part of the whole earth, the pearl of the globe, the brain of a vast body?

Eliot's image of Europe as a wasteland, a culture of fragments with no cementing center, predominated in postwar Europe. And though his early poetic practices were more radical, open and international than his Eurocentric criticism, Eliot posed a return to and revision of tradition as the only way of regaining European cultural order and political stability. For Eliot, contemporary history had become, as James Joyce's Stephen declared in *Ulysses* (1922), "a nightmare from which I am trying to awake"—"an immense panorama of futility and anarchy" as Eliot put it in his renowned review of Joyce's modernist masterpiece. In his influential essay "Tradition and the Individual Talent" (1919) Eliot stated:

> Yet if the only form of tradition, of handing down, consisted in following the ways of the immediate generation before us in a blind or timid adherence to its successes, "tradition" should positively be discouraged. We have seen many such simple currents soon lost in the sand; and novelty is better than repetition. Tradition is a matter of much wider significance. It cannot be inherited, and if you want it you must attain it by great labour.

Eliot's fecund notion of tradition is significant in that it promotes a historicist sensibility in artistic practice and cultural reflection. This historicist sensibility—regulated in Eliot's case by a reactionary politics—produced a powerful assault on existing literary canons (in which, for example, Romantic poets were displaced by the Metaphysical and Symbolist ones) and unrelenting attacks on modern Western civilization (such as the liberal ideas of democracy, equality and freedom). Like Arnold's notion of culture, Eliot's idea of tradition was part of his intellectual arsenal, to be used in the battles raging in European cultures and societies.

Eliot found this tradition in the Church of England, to which he converted in 1927. Here was a tradition that left room for his Catholic cast of mind. Calvinistic heritage, puritanical temperament and ebullient patriotism for the old American South (the place of his upbringing). Like Arnold, Eliot was obsessed with the idea of civilization and the horror of barbarism (echoes of Joseph Conrad's Kurtz in *Heart of Darkness*) or more pointedly the notion of the decline and decay of European civilization. With the advent of World War II, Eliot's obsession became a reality. Again unprecedented human carnage (fifty million dead)—including an undescribable genocidal attack on Jewish people—throughout Europe as well as around the globe, put the last nail in the coffin of the Age of Europe. After 1945, Europe consisted of a devastated and divided continent, crippled by a humiliating dependency on and deference to the USA and USSR.

The second historical coordinate of my genealogy is the emergence of the USA as *the* world power. The USA was unprepared for world power status. However, with the recovery of Stalin's Russia (after losing twenty million lives), the USA felt compelled to make its presence felt around the globe. Then with the Marshall Plan to strengthen Europe against Russian influence (and provide new markets for US products), the 1948 Russian takeover of Czechoslovakia, the 1948 Berlin blockade, the 1950 beginning of the Korean War and the 1952 establishment of NATO forces in Europe, it seemed clear that there was no escape from world power obligations.

The post–World War II era in the USA, or the first decades of what Henry Luce envisioned as "The American Century," was not only a period of incredible economic expansion but of active cultural ferment. In the classical Fordist formula, mass production required mass consumption. With unchallenged hegemony in the capitalist world, the USA took economic growth for granted. Next to exercising its crude, anticommunist, McCarthyist obsessions, buying commodities became the primary act of civic virtue for many American citizens at this time. The creation of a mass middle class—a prosperous working class with a bourgeois identity—was countered by the first major emergence of subcultures of American non-WASP intellectuals: the so-called New York intellectuals in criticism, the Abstract Expressionists in painting and the bebop artists in jazz music. This emergence signaled a vital challenge to an American, male, WASP elite loyal to an older and eroding European culture.

The first significant blow was dealt when assimilated Jewish Americans entered the higher echelons of the cultural apparatus (academy, museums, galleries, mass media). Lionel Trilling is an emblematic figure. This Jewish entrée into the anti-Semitic and patriarchal critical discourse of the exclusivistic institutions of American culture initiated the slow but sure undoing of the male WASP cultural hegemony and homogeneity. Lionel Trilling's project was to appropriate Matthew Arnold for his own political and cultural purposes—thereby unraveling the old male WASP consensus, while erecting a new post–World War II liberal academic consensus around cold-war, anticommunist renditions of the values of complexity, difficulty, variousness and modulation. In addition, the postwar boom laid the basis for intense professionalization and specialization in expanding institutions of higher education—especially in the natural sciences which were compelled to respond somehow to Russia's successful ventures in space. Humanistic scholars found themselves searching for new methodologies that could buttress self-images of rigor and scientific seriousness. For example, the close reading techniques of New Criticism (severed from their conservative, organicist, anti-industrialist ideological roots), the logical precision of reasoning in analytic philosophy, and the jargon of Parsonian structural-functionalism in sociology helped create such self-images. Yet towering cultural critics like C. Wright Mills, W. E. B. Du Bois, Richard Hofstadter, Margaret Mead and Dwight MacDonald bucked the tide. This suspicion of the academicization of knowledge is expressed in Trilling's well-known essay "On the Teaching of Modern Literature":

> can we not say that, when modern literature is brought into the classroom, the subject being taught is betrayed by the pedagogy of the subject? We have to ask ourselves whether in our day too much does not come within the purview of the academy. More and more, as the universities liberalize themselves, turn their beneficent imperialistic gaze upon what is called life itself, the feeling grows among our educated classes that little can be experienced unless it is validated by some established intellectual discipline. . . .

Trilling laments the fact that university instruction often quiets and domesticates radical and subversive works of art, turning them into objects "of merely habitual regard." This process of "the socialization of the anti-social, or the acculturation of the anti-cultural, or the legitimization of the subversive" leads Trilling to "question whether in our culture the study of literature is any longer a suitable means for developing and refining the intelligence." Trilling asks this question not in the spirit of denigrating and devaluing the academy but rather in the spirit of highlighting the possible failure of an Arnoldian conception of culture to contain what he perceives as the philistine and anarchic alternatives becoming more and more available to students of the sixties—namely, mass culture and radical politics.

This threat is partly associated with the third historical coordinate of my genealogy—the decolonization of the Third World. It is crucial to recognize the importance of this world-historical process if one wants to grasp the significance of the end of the Age of Europe and the emergence of the USA as a world power. With the first defeat of a Western nation by a non-Western nation—in Japan's victory over Russia (1905)—and with revolutions in Persia (1905), Turkey (1908), China (1912), and Mexico (1911–12), and much later the independence of India (1947) and China (1949) and the triumph of Ghana (1957), the actuality of a decolonized globe loomed large. Born of violent struggle, consciousness-raising and the reconstruction of identities, decolonization simultaneously brings with it new perspectives on that long-festering underside of the Age of Europe (of which colonial domination represents the *costs* of "progress," "order" and "culture"), as well as requiring new readings of the economic boom in the USA (wherein the black, brown, yellow, red, female, elderly, gay, lesbian, and white working class live the same *costs* as cheap labor at home in addition to US-dominated Latin American and Pacific Rim markets).

The impetuous ferocity and moral outrage that motors the decolonization process is best captured by Frantz Fanon in *The Wretched of the Earth* (1961).

> Decolonization, which sets out to change the order of the world, is obviously a program of complete disorder. . . . Decolonization is the meeting of two forces, opposed to each other by their very nature, which in fact owe their originality to that sort of substantification which results from and is nourished by the situation in the colonies. Their first encounter was marked by violence and their existence together—that is to say the exploitation of the native by the settler—was carried on by dint of a great array of bayonets and cannons. . . .
>
> In decolonization, there is therefore the need of a complete calling in question of the colonial situation. If we wish to describe it precisely, we might find it in the well-known words: "The last shall be first and the first last." Decolonization is the putting into practice of this sentence.
>
> The naked truth of decolonization evokes for us the searing bullets and bloodstained knives which emanate from it. For if the last shall be first, this will only come to pass after a murderous and decisive struggle between the two protagonists.

Fanon's strong words, though excessively Manichaean, still describe the feelings and thoughts between the occupying British Army and colonized Irish in Northern Ireland, the occupying Israeli Army and subjugated Palestinians on the West Bank and Gaza Strip, the South African Army and oppressed black South Africans in the townships, the Japanese police and Koreans living in Japan. His words also partly invoke the sense many black Americans have toward police departments in urban centers. In other words, Fanon is articulating century-long heartfelt human responses to being degraded and despised, hated and haunted, oppressed and exploited, marginalized and dehumanized at the hands of powerful, xenophobic, European, American, Russian and Japanese imperial countries.

During the late fifties, sixties and early seventies in the USA, these decolonized sensibilities fanned and fueled the Civil Rights and Black Power movements, as well as the student antiwar, feminist, gray, brown, gay and lesbian movements. In this period we witnessed the shattering of male, WASP, cultural homogeneity and the collapse of the short-lived liberal consensus. The inclusion of African Americans, Latino/a Americans, Asian Americans, Native Americans and American women into the culture of critical discourse yielded intense intellectual polemics and inescapable ideological polarization that focused principally on the exclusions, silences and blindnesses of male, WASP, cultural homogeneity and its concomitant Arnoldian notions of the canon.

In addition, these critiques promoted three crucial processes that affected intellectual life in the country. First is the appropriation of the theories of postwar Europe—especially the work of the Frankfurt school (Marcuse, Adorno, Horkheimer), French/Italian Marxisms (Sartre, Althusser, Lefebvre, Gramsci), structuralisms (Lévi-Strauss, Todorov) and poststructuralisms (Deleuze, Derrida, Foucault). These diverse and disparate theories—all preoccupied with keeping alive radical projects after the end of the Age of Europe— tend to fuse versions of transgressive European modernisms with Marxist or post-Marxist left politics and unanimously shun the term "postmodernism." Second, there is the recovery and revisioning of American history in light of the struggles of white male workers, women, African Americans, Native Americans, Latino/a Americans, gays and lesbians. Third is the impact of forms of popular culture, such as television, film, music videos and even sports, on highbrow literate culture. The black-based hip-hop culture of youth around the world is one grand example.

After 1973, with the crisis in the international world economy, America's slump in productivity, the challenge of OPEC nations to the North Atlantic monopoly of oil production, the increasing competition in hi-tech sectors of the economy from Japan and West Germany and the growing fragility of the international debt structure, the USA entered a period of waning self-confidence (compounded by Watergate) and a nearly contracting economy. As the standards of living for the middle classes declined, owing to runaway inflation, and the quality of living fell for most, due to escalating unemployment, underemployment and crime, religious and secular neoconservatism emerged with power and potency. This fusion of fervent neonationalism, traditional cultural values and "free market" policies served as the groundwork for the Reagan-Bush era.

The ambiguous legacies of the European Age, American preeminence and decolonization continue to haunt our postmodern moment as we come to terms with both the European, American, Japanese, Soviet and Third World *crimes against* and *contributions to* humanity. The plight of Africans in the New World can be instructive in this regard.

By 1914 European maritime empires had dominion over more than half of the land and a third of the peoples in the world—almost 72 million square kilometers of territory and more than 560 million people under colonial rule. Needless to say, this European control included brutal enslavement, institutional terrorism and cultural degradation of black diasporan people. The death of roughly seventy-five million Africans during the centuries-long transatlantic slave trade is but one reminder, among others, of the assault on black humanity. The black diasporan condition of New World servitude—in which they were viewed as mere commodities with production value, who had no proper legal status, social standing or public worth—can be characterized as, following Orlando Patterson, natal alienation. This state of perpetual and inheritable domination that diasporan Africans had at birth produced the *modern black diasporan problematic of invisibility and namelessness*. White-supremacist practices—enacted under the auspices of the prestigious cultural authorities of the churches, printed media and scientific academics—promoted black inferiority and constituted the European background against which black diasporan struggles for identity, dignity (self-confidence, self-respect, self-esteem) and material resources took place.

An inescapable aspect of this struggle was that the black diasporan peoples' quest for validation and recognition occurred on the ideological, social and cultural terrains of other nonblack peoples. White-supremacist assaults on black intelligence, ability, beauty and character required persistent black efforts to hold self-doubt, self-contempt and even self-hatred at bay. Selective appropriation, incorporation and rearticulation of European ideologies, cultures and institutions alongside an African heritage—a heritage more or less confined to linguistic innovation in rhetorical practices, stylizations of the body in forms of occupying an alien social space (hairstyles, ways of walking, standing, hand expressions, talking) and means of constituting and sustaining camaraderie and community (e.g. antiphonal, call-and-response styles, rhythmic repetition, risk-ridden syncopation in spectacular modes in musical and rhetorical expressions)—were some of the strategies employed.

The modern black diasporan problematic of invisibility and namelessness can be understood as the condition of *relative lack of black power to represent themselves to themselves and others as complex human beings, and thereby to contest the bombardment of negative, degrading stereotypes put forward by white-supremacist ideologies*. The initial black response to being caught in this whirlwind of Europeanization was to resist the misrepresentation and caricature of the terms set by uncontested nonblack norms and models, and to fight for self-representation and recognition. Every modern black person, especially cultural disseminators, encounters this problematic of invisibility and namelessness. The initial black diasporan response was a mode of resistance that was *moralistic in content* and *communal in character*. That is, the fight for representation and recognition highlighted moral judgments regarding black "positive" images over and against white-supremacist stereotypes. These images "re-presented" monolithic and homogeneous black communities, in a way that could displace past misrepresentations of these communities. Stuart Hall has talked about these responses as attempts to change "the relations of representation."

These courageous yet limited black efforts to combat racist cultural practices uncritically accepted nonblack conventions and standards in two ways. First, they proceeded in an *assimilationist manner* that set out to show that black people were really like white people—thereby eliding differences (in history, culture) between whites and blacks. Black specificity and particularity was thus banished in order to gain white acceptance and approval. Second, these black responses rested upon a *homogenizing impulse* that assumed that all black people were really alike—hence obliterating differences (class, gender, region, sexual orientation) between black peoples. I submit that there are elements of truth in both claims, yet the conclusions are unwarranted owing to the basic fact that nonblack paradigms set the terms of the replies.

The insight in the first claim is that blacks and whites are in some important sense alike—that is, in their positive capacities for human sympathy, moral sacrifice, service to others, intelligence and beauty, or negatively, in their capacity for cruelty. Yet the common humanity they share is jettisoned when the claim is cast in an assimilationist manner that subordinates black particularity to a false universalism, that is, nonblack rubrics or prototypes. Similarly, the insight in the second claim is that all blacks are in some significant sense "in the same boat"—that is, subject to white-supremacist abuse. Yet this common condition is stretched too far when viewed in a *homogenizing* way that overlooks how racist treatment vastly differs owing to class, gender, sexual orientation, nation, region, hue and age.

The moralistic and communal aspects of the initial black diasporan responses to social and psychic erasure were not simply cast into simplistic binary oppositions of positive-negative, good-bad images that privileged the first term in light of a white norm so that black efforts remained inscribed within the very logic that dehumanized them. They were further complicated by the fact that these responses were also advanced principally by anxiety-ridden, middle-class, black intellectuals (predominantly male and heterosexual), grappling with their sense of double-consciousness—namely their own crisis of identity, agency and audience—caught between a quest for white approval and acceptance and an endeavor to overcome the internalized association of blackness with inferiority. And I suggest that these complex anxieties of modern black diasporan intellectuals partly motivate the two major arguments that ground the assimilationist moralism and homogeneous communalism just outlined.

Kobena Mercer has talked about these two arguments as the *reflectionist* and the *social engineering* arguments. The reflectionist argument holds that the fight for black representation and recognition must reflect or mirror the real black community, not simply the negative and depressing representations of it. The social engineering argument claims that since any form of representation is constructed—that is, selective in light of broader aims—black representation (especially given the difficulty of blacks gaining access to positions of power to produce any black imagery) should offer positive images of themselves in order to inspire achievement among young black people, thereby countering racist stereotypes. The hidden assumption of both arguments is that we have unmediated access to what the "real black community" is and what "positive images" are. In short, these arguments presuppose the very phenomena to be interrogated, and thereby foreclose the very issues that should serve as the subject matter to be investigated.

Any notions of the "real black community" and "positive images" are value-laden, socially loaded and ideologically charged. To pursue this discussion is to call into question the possibility of such an uncontested consensus regarding them. Stuart Hall has rightly called this encounter "the end of innocence or the end of the innocent notion of the essential Black subject . . . the recognition that 'Black' is essentially a politically and culturally *constructed* category." This recognition—more and more pervasive among the postmodern black diasporan intelligentsia—is facilitated in part by the slow but sure dissolution of the European Age's maritime empires, and the unleashing of new political possibilities and cultural articulations among formerly colonialized peoples across the globe.

One crucial lesson of this decolonization process remains the manner in which most Third World, authoritarian, bureaucratic elites deploy essentialist rhetorics about "homogeneous national communities" and "positive images" in order to repress and regiment their diverse and heterogeneous populations. Yet in the diaspora, especially among First World countries, this critique has emerged not so much from the black male component of the left but rather from the black women's movement. The decisive push of postmodern black intellectuals toward a new cultural politics of difference has been made by the powerful critiques and constructive explorations of black diasporan women (for instance, Toni Morrison). The coffin used to bury the innocent notion of the essential black subject was nailed shut with the termination of the black male monopoly on the construction of the black subject. In this regard, the black diasporan womanist critique has had a greater impact than the critiques that highlight exclusively class, empire, age, sexual orientation or nature.

This decisive push toward the end of black innocence—though prefigured in various degrees in the best moments of W. E. B. Du

Bois, Anna Cooper, C. L. R. James, James Baldwin, Claudia Jones, the later Malcolm X, Frantz Fanon, Amiri Baraka and others— forces black diasporan cultural workers to encounter what Hall has called the "politics of representation." The main aim now is not simply access to representation in order to produce positive images of homogeneous communities—though broader access remains a practical and political problem. Nor is the primary goal here that of contesting stereotypes—though contestation remains a significant though limited venture. Following the model of the black diasporan traditions of music, athletics and rhetoric, black cultural workers must constitute and sustain discursive and institutional networks that deconstruct earlier modern black strategies for identity-formation, demystify power relations that incorporate class, patriarchal and homophobic biases, and construct more multivalent and multi-dimensional responses that articulate the complexity and diversity of black practices in the modern and postmodern world.

Furthermore, black cultural workers must investigate and inter-rogate the Other of blackness-whiteness. One cannot deconstruct the binary oppositional logic of images of blackness without extending it to the contrary condition of blackness-whiteness itself. However, a mere dismantling will not do—for the very notion of a deconstructive social theory is oxymoronic. Yet social theory is what is needed to examine and *explain* the historically specific ways in which "whiteness" is a politically constructed category parasitic on "blackness," and thereby to conceive of the profoundly hybrid character of what we mean by "race," "ethnicity" and "nationality." For instance, European immigrants arrived on American shores perceiving themselves as "Irish," "Sicilian," "Lithuanian" and so on. They had to learn that they were "white" principally by adopting an American discourse of positively valued whiteness and negatively charged blackness. This process by which people define themselves physically, socially, sexually and even politically in terms of whiteness or blackness has much bearing not only on constructed notions of race and ethnicity but also on how we understand the changing character of US nationalities.

And given the Americanization of the world, especially in the sphere of mass culture, such inquiries—encouraged by the new cultural politics of difference—raise critical issues of "hybridity," "exilic status" and "identity" on an international scale. Needless to say, these inquiries must traverse those of "male-female," "colonizer-colonized," "heterosexual-homosexual," and others, as well.

In light of this brief sketch of the emergence of our present crisis—and the turn toward history and difference in cultural work—four major historicist forms of theoretical activity provide resources for how we understand, analyze and enact our representational practices: Heideggerian *destruction* of the Western metaphysical tradition, Derridean *deconstruction* of the Western philosophical tradition, Rortian *demythologization* of the Western intellectual tradition and Marxist, Foucaultian, feminist, antiracist or antihomophobic *demystification* of Western cultural and artistic conventions.

Despite his abominable association with the Nazis, Martin Heidegger's project is useful in that it discloses the suppression of temporality and historicity in the dominant metaphysical systems of the West from Plato to Rudolf Carnap. This is noteworthy in that it forces one to understand philosophy's representational discourses as thoroughly historical phenomena. Hence, they should be viewed with skepticism as they are often flights from the specific, concrete, practical and particular. The major problem with Heidegger's project—as noted by his neo-Marxist student, Herbert Marcuse—is that he views history in terms of fate, heritage and destiny. He dramatizes the past and present as if it were a Greek tragedy with no tools of social analysis to relate cultural work to institutions and structures or antecedent forms and styles.

Jacques Derrida's version of deconstruction is one of the most influential schools of thought among young academic critics. It is salutary in that it focuses on the political power of rhetorical operations—of tropes and metaphors in binary oppositions like white/black, good/bad, male/female, machine/nature, ruler/ruled, reality/appearance—showing how these operations sustain hierar-

chal worldviews by devaluing the second terms as something subsumed under the first. Most of the controversy about Derrida's
project revolves around this austere epistemic doubt that both unsettles binary oppositions while it undermines any determinate meaning of a text, that is, book, art object, performance, building. Yet,
his views about skepticism are no more alarming than those of
David Hume, Ludwig Wittgenstein or Stanley Cavell. He simply
revels in it for transgressive purposes, whereas others provide us
with ways to dissolve, sidestep or cope with skepticism. None,
however, slide down the slippery, crypto-Nietzschean slope of sophomoric relativism as alleged by old-style humanists, be they Plato-
nists, Kantians or Arnoldians.

The major shortcoming of Derrida's deconstructive project is
that it puts a premium on a sophisticated ironic consciousness that
tends to preclude and foreclose analyses that guide action with
purpose. And given Derrida's own status as an Algerian-born, Jewish leftist marginalized by a hostile French academic establishment
(quite different from his reception by the youth in the American
academic establishment), the sense of political impotence and hesita-
tion regarding the efficacy of moral action is understandable—but
not justifiable. His works and those of his followers too often become rather monotonous, Johnny-one-note rhetorical readings that
disassemble texts with little attention to the effects and consequences
these dismantlings have in relation to the operations of military,
economic and social powers.

Richard Rorty's neopragmatic project of demythologization is
insightful in that it provides descriptive mappings of the transient
metaphors—especially the ocular and specular ones—that regulate
some of the fundamental dynamics in the construction of self-de-
scriptions dominant in highbrow European and American philosophy. His perspective is instructive because it discloses the crucial
role of narrative as the background for rational exchange and critical
conversation. To put it crudely, Rorty shows why we should speak
not of History, but histories, not of Reason, but historically consti-

tuted forms of rationality, not of Criticism or Art, but of socially constructed notions of criticism and art—all linked but not reducible to political purposes, material interests and cultural prejudices.

Rorty's project nonetheless leaves one wanting, owing to its distrust of social analytical explanation. Similar to the dazzling new historicism of Stephen Greenblatt, Louis Montrose and Catherine Gallagher—inspired by the subtle symbolic-cum-textual anthropology of Clifford Geertz and the powerful discursive materialism of Michel Foucault—Rorty's work gives us mappings and descriptions with no explanatory accounts for change and conflict. In this way, it gives us an aestheticized version of historicism in which the provisional and variable are celebrated at the expense of highlighting who gains, loses or bears what costs.

Demystification is the most illuminating mode of theoretical inquiry for those who promote the new cultural politics of difference. Social structural analyses of empire, exterminism, class, race, gender, nature, age, sexual orientation, nation and region are the springboards—though not landing grounds—for the most desirable forms of critical practice that take history (and herstory) seriously. Demystification tries to keep track of the complex dynamics of institutional and other related power structures in order to disclose options and alternatives for transformative praxis; it also attempts to grasp the way in which representational strategies are creative responses to novel circumstances and conditions. In this way, the central role of human agency (always enacted under circumstances not of one's choosing)—be it in the critic, artist or constituency and audience—is accented.

I call demystificatory criticism "prophetic criticism"—the approach appropriate for the new cultural politics of difference—because while it begins with social structural analyses it also makes explicit its moral and political aims. It is partisan, partial, engaged and crisis-centered, yet always keeps open a skeptical eye to avoid dogmatic traps, premature closures, formulaic formulations or rigid conclusions. In addition to social structural analyses, moral and political judgments, and sheer critical consciousness, there indeed is evaluation. Yet the aim of this evaluation is neither to pit art objects against one another like racehorses nor to create eternal canons that dull, discourage or even dwarf contemporary achievements. We listen to Ludwig van Beethoven, Charlie Parker, Luciano Pavarotti, Laurie Anderson, Sarah Vaughn, Stevie Wonder or Kathleen Battle, read William Shakespeare, Anton Chekhov, Ralph Ellison, Doris Lessing, Thomas Pynchon, Toni Morrison or Gabriel García Márquez, see works of Pablo Picasso, Ingmar Bergman, Le Corbusier, Martin Puryear, Barbara Kruger, Spike Lee, Frank Gehry or Howardena Pindell—not in order to undergird bureaucratic assents or enliven cocktail party conversations, but rather to be summoned by the styles they deploy for their profound insight, pleasures and challenges. Yet all evaluation—including a delight in Eliot's poetry despite his reactionary politics, or a love of Zora Neale Hurston's novels despite her Republican party affiliations—is inseparable from, though not identical or reducible to, social structural analyses, moral and political judgments and the workings of a curious critical consciousness.

The deadly traps of demystification—and any form of prophetic criticism—are those of reductionism, be it of the sociological, psychological or historical sort. By reductionism I mean either one factor analyses (that is, crude Marxisms, feminisms, racialisms, etc.) that yield a one-dimensional functionalism, or a hyper-subtle analytical perspective that loses touch with the specificity of an artwork's form and the context of its reception. Few cultural workers of whatever stripe can walk the tightrope between the Scylla of reductionism and the Charybdis of aestheticism—yet demystificatory (or prophetic) critics must.

The Existential Challenge

The existential challenge to the new cultural politics of difference can be stated simply: how does one acquire the resources to survive and the cultural capital to thrive as a critic or artist? By cultural capital (Pierre Bourdieu's term), I mean not only the high-quality skills required to engage in critical practices but, more important, the self-confidence, discipline and perseverance necessary for success without an undue reliance on the mainstream for approval and acceptance. This challenge holds for all prophetic critics, yet it is especially difficult for those of color. The widespread, modern, European denial of the intelligence, ability, beauty and character of people of color puts a tremendous burden on critics and artists of color to "prove" themselves in light of norms and models set by white elites whose own heritage devalued and dehumanized them. In short, in the court of criticism and art—or any matters regarding the life of the mind—people of color are guilty, that is, not expected to meet standards of intellectual achievement, until "proven" innocent, that is, acceptable to "us."

This is more a structural dilemma than a matter of personal attitudes. The profoundly racist and sexist heritage of the European Age has bequeathed to us a set of deeply ingrained perceptions about people of color, including, of course, the self-perceptions that people of color bring. It is not surprising that most intellectuals of color in the past exerted much of their energies and efforts to gain acceptance from and approval by "white normative gazes." The new cultural politics of difference advises critics and artists of color to put aside this mode of mental bondage, thereby freeing themselves to both interrogate the ways in which they are bound by certain conventions and to learn from and build on these very norms and models. One hallmark of wisdom in the context of any struggle is to avoid knee-jerk rejection and uncritical acceptance.

Self-confidence, discipline and perseverance are not ends in themselves. Rather they are the necessary stuff of which enabling criticism and self-criticism are made. Notwithstanding inescapable jealousies, insecurities and anxieties, one telling characteristic of critics and artists of color linked to the new prophetic criticism should be their capacity for and promotion of relentless criticism and self-criticism—be it the normative paradigms of their white colleagues that tend to leave out considerations of empire, race, gender and sexual orientation, or the damaging dogmas about the homogeneous character of communities of color.

There are four basic options for people of color interested in representation—if they are to survive and thrive as serious practitioners of their craft. First, there is the Booker T. Temptation, namely the individual preoccupation with the mainstream and its legitimizing power. Most critics and artists of color try to bite this bait. It is nearly unavoidable, yet few succeed in a substantive manner. It is no accident that the most creative and profound among them—especially those with staying power beyond mere flashes in the pan to satisfy faddish tokenism—are usually marginal to the mainstream. Even the pervasive professionalization of cultural practitioners of color in the past few decades has not produced towering figures who reside within the established white patronage system that bestows the rewards and prestige for chosen contributions to American society.

It certainly helps to have some trustworthy allies within this system, yet most of those who enter and remain tend to lose much of their creativity, diffuse their prophetic energy and dilute their critiques. Still, it is unrealistic for creative people of color to think they can sidestep the white patronage system. And though there are indeed some white allies conscious of the tremendous need to rethink politics, it's naive to think that being comfortably nested within this very same system—even if one can be a patron to others—does not affect one's work, one's outlook and, most important, one's soul.

The second option is the Talented Tenth Seduction, namely, a move toward arrogant group insularity. This alternative has a limited function—to preserve one's sanity and sense of self as one copes with the mainstream. Yet it is, at best, a transitional and transient activity. If it becomes a permanent option it is self-defeating, in that it usually reinforces the very inferiority complexes promoted by the subtly racist mainstream. Hence it tends to revel in a parochialism and encourage a narrow racialist and chauvinistic outlook.

The third strategy is the Go It Alone Option. This is an extreme rejectionist perspective that shuns the mainstream and group insularity. Almost every critic and artist of color contemplates or enacts this option at some time in their pilgrimage. It is healthy in that it reflects the presence of independent, critical and skeptical sensibilities toward perceived constraints on one's creativity. Yet it is, in the end, difficult if not impossible to sustain if one is to grow, develop and mature intellectually, as some semblance of dialogue with a community is necessary for almost any creative practice.

The most desirable option for people of color who promote the new cultural politics of difference is to be a Critical Organic Catalyst. By this I mean a person who stays attuned to the best of what the mainstream has to offer—its paradigms, viewpoints and methods—yet maintains a grounding in affirming and enabling subcultures of criticism. Prophetic critics and artists of color should be exemplars of what it means to be intellectual freedom fighters, that is, cultural workers who simultaneously position themselves within (or alongside) the mainstream while clearly aligned with groups who vow to keep alive potent traditions of critique and resistance. In this regard, one can take clues from the great musicians or preachers of color who are open to the best of what other traditions offer yet are rooted in nourishing subcultures that build on the grand achievements of a vital heritage. Openness to others—including the mainstream—does not entail wholesale cooptation, and group autonomy is not group insularity. Louis Armstrong, W. E. B. Du Bois, Ella Baker, Jose Carlos Mariatequi, M. M. Thomas, Wynton Marsalis, Martin Luther King, Jr., and Ronald Takaki have understood this well.

The new cultural politics of difference can thrive only if there are communities, groups, organizations, institutions, subcultures and networks of people of color who cultivate critical sensibilities and personal accountability—without inhibiting individual expressions, curiosities and idiosyncrasies. This is especially needed given the escalating racial hostility, violence and polarization in the USA. Yet this critical coming together must not be a narrow closing ranks. Rather it is a strengthening and nurturing endeavor that can forge more solid alliances and coalitions. In this way, prophetic criticism—with its stress on historical specificity and artistic complexity—directly addresses the intellectual challenge. The cultural capital of people of color—with its emphasis on self-confidence, discipline, perseverance and subcultures of criticism—also tries to meet the existential requirement. Both are mutually reinforcing. Both are motivated by a deep commitment to individuality and democracy—the moral and political ideals that guide the creative response to the political challenge.

The Political Challenge

Adequate rejoinders to intellectual and existential challenges equip the practitioners of the new cultural politics of difference to meet the political ones. This challenge principally consists of forging solid and reliable alliances of people of color and white progressives guided by a moral and political vision of greater democracy and individual freedom in communities, states and transnational enterprises, for instance, corporations, and information and communications conglomerates.

Jesse Jackson's Rainbow Coalition is a gallant yet flawed effort in this regard—gallant due to the tremendous energy, vision and courage of its leader and followers, yet flawed because of its failure to take seriously critical and democratic sensibilities within its own operations. In fact, Jackson's attempt to gain power at the national level is a symptom of the weakness of US progressive politics, and a sign that the capacity to generate extraparliamentary social motion or movements has waned. Yet given the present organizational weakness and intellectual timidity of left politics in the USA, the major option is that of multiracial grass-roots citizens' participation in credible projects in which people see that their efforts can make a difference. The salutary revolutionary developments in Eastern Europe are encouraging and inspiring in this regard. Ordinary people organized can change societies.

The most significant theme of the new cultural politics of difference is the agency, capacity and ability of human beings who have been culturally degraded, politically oppressed and economically exploited by bourgeois liberal and communist illiberal status quos. This theme neither romanticizes nor idealizes marginalized peoples. Rather it accentuates their humanity and tries to attenuate the institutional constraints on their life-chances for surviving and thriving. In this way, the new cultural politics of difference shuns narrow particularisms, parochialisms and separatisms, just as it rejects false universalisms and homogeneous totalisms. Instead, the new cultural politics of difference affirms the perennial quest for the precious ideals of individuality and democracy by digging deep in the depths of human particularities and social specificities in order to construct new kinds of connections, affinities and communities across empire, nation, region, race, gender, age and sexual orientation.

The major impediments of the radical libertarian and democratic projects of the new cultural politics are threefold: the pervasive processes of objectification, rationalization and commodification throughout the world. The first process—best highlighted in Georg Simmel's *The Philosophy of Money* (1900)—consists of transforming human beings into manipulable objects. It promotes the notion that people's actions have no impact on the world, that we are but spectators not participants in making and remaking ourselves and the larger society. The second process—initially examined in the seminal works of Max Weber—expands bureaucratic hierarchies that impose impersonal rules and regulations in order to increase efficiency, be they defined in terms of better service or better surveillance. This process leads to disenchantment with past mythologies of deadening, flat, banal ways of life. The third and most important process—best examined in the works of Karl Marx,

Georg Lukács and Walter Benjamin—augments market forces in the form of oligopolies and monopolies that centralize resources and powers and promote cultures of consumption that view people as mere spectatorial consumers and passive citizens.

These processes cannot be eliminated, but their pernicious effects can be substantially alleviated. The audacious attempt to lessen their impact—to preserve people's agency, increase the scope of their freedom and expand the operations of democracy—is the fundamental aim of the new cultural politics of difference. This is why the crucial questions become: What is the moral content of one's cultural identity? And what are the political consequences of this moral content and cultural identity?

In the recent past, the dominant cultural identities have been circumscribed by immoral patriarchal, imperial, jingoistic and xenophobic constraints. The political consequences have been principally a public sphere regulated by and for well-to-do, white males in the name of freedom and democracy. The new cultural criticism exposes and explodes the exclusions, blindnesses and silences of this past, calling from it radical libertarian and democratic projects that will create a better present and future. The new cultural politics of difference is neither an ahistorical Jacobin program that discards tradition and ushers in new self-righteous authoritarianisms, nor a guilt-ridden, leveling, anti-imperialist liberalism that celebrates token pluralism for smooth inclusion. Rather, it acknowledges the uphill struggle of fundamentally transforming highly objectified, rationalized and commodified societies and cultures in the name of individuality and democracy. This means locating the structural causes of unnecessary forms of social misery (without reducing all such human suffering to historical causes), depicting the plight and predicaments of demoralized and depoliticized citizens caught in market-driven cycles of therapeutic release—drugs, alcoholism, consumerism—and projecting alternative visions, analyses and actions that proceed from particularities and arrive at moral and political connectedness. This connectedness does not signal a homogeneous unity or monolithic totality but rather a contingent, fragile coalition building in an effort to pursue common radical libertarian and democratic goals that overlap.

In a world in which most of the resources, wealth and power are centered in huge corporations and supportive political elites, the new cultural politics of difference may appear to be solely visionary, utopian and fanciful. The recent cutbacks of social service programs, business takebacks at the negotiation tables of workers and management, speedups at the workplace and buildups of military budgets reinforce this perception. And surely the growing disintegration and decomposition of civil society—of shattered families, neighborhoods and schools—adds to this perception. Can a civilization that evolves more and more around market activity, more and more around the buying and selling of commodities, expand the scope of freedom and democracy? Can we simply bear witness to its slow decay and doom—a painful denouement prefigured already in many poor black and brown communities and rapidly embracing all of us? These haunting questions remain unanswered yet the challenge they pose must not remain unmet. The new cultural politics of difference tries to confront these enormous and urgent challenges. It will require all the imagination, intelligence, courage, sacrifice, care and laughter we can muster.

The time has come for critics and artists of the new cultural politics of difference to cast their nets widely, flex their muscles broadly and thereby refuse to limit their visions, analyses and praxis to their particular terrains. The aim is to dare to recast, redefine and revise the very notions of "modernity," "mainstream," "margins," "difference," "otherness." We have now reached a new stage in the perennial struggle for freedom and dignity. And while much of the First World intelligentsia adopts retrospective and conservative outlooks that defend the crisis-ridden present, we promote a prospective and prophetic vision with a sense of possibility and potential, especially for those who bear the social costs of the present. We look to the past for strength, not solace; we look at the present and see people perishing, not profits mounting; we look toward the future and vow to make it different and better.

To put it boldly, the new kind of critic and artist associated with the new cultural politics of difference consists of an energetic breed of New World *bricoleurs* with improvisational and flexible sensibilities that sidestep mere opportunism and mindless eclecticism; persons from all countries, cultures, genders, sexual orientations, ages and regions with protean identities who avoid ethnic chauvinism and faceless universalism; intellectual and political freedom fighters with partisan passion, international perspectives and, thank God, a sense of humor that combats the ever-present absurdity that forever threatens our democratic and libertarian projects and dampens the fire that fuels our will to struggle. Yet we will struggle and stay, as those brothers and sisters on the block say, "out there"—with intellectual rigor, existential dignity, moral vision, political courage and soulful style.

with the fascinating and ingenious ways in which these canonizers reevaluated and readjusted the old canon. As a cultural critic, I would like to see more attention paid to the prevailing historical interpretations of the cultural crisis which prompts, guides and regulates the canonizing efforts. In this sense, attempts to revise or reconstitute literary canons rest upon prior—though often tacit—interpretive acts of rendering a canonical historical reading of the crisis that in part authorizes literary canons. So the first battle over literary canon formation has to do with one's historical interpretation of the crisis achieving canonical status.

For instance, the power of T. S. Eliot's canonizing efforts had as much to do with his canonical reading of the crisis of European civilization after the unprecedented carnage and dislocations of World War I as with his literary evaluations of the Metaphysicals and Dryden over Spenser and Milton or his nearly wholesale disapproval of Romantic and Victorian poetry. As the first moment of my own self-inventory as an African American cultural critic, I focus not on the kinds of texts to choose for an enlargement of the old canon or the making of a new one but rather on a historical reading of the present-day crisis of American civilization, an aspiring canonical historical reading that shapes the way in which literary canon formation itself ought to proceed and the kind of cultural archives that should constitute this formation. This reading is informed by a particular sense of history in which conflict, struggle and contestation are prominent. It accents the complex interplay of rhetorical practices (and their effects, for example, rational persuasion and intellectual pleasure) and the operations of power and authority (and their effects, for example, subordination and resistance).

My historical reading of the present cultural crisis begins with a distinctive feature of the twentieth century: the decolonization of the Third World associated with the historical agency of those oppressed and exploited, devalued and degraded by European civilization. This interpretive point of entry is in no way exhaustive—it does not treat other significant aspects of our time—yet neither is it merely arbitrary. Rather it is a world-historical process that has fundamentally changed not only our conceptions of ourselves and those constituted as "Others" (non-Europeans, women, gays, lesbians) but, more important, our understanding of how we have constructed and do construct conceptions of ourselves and others as selves, subjects and peoples. In short, the decolonization of the Third World has unleashed attitudes, values, sensibilities and perspectives with which we have yet fully to come to terms.

More specifically, the decolonization process signaled the end of the European age—an age that extends from 1492 to 1945. The eclipse of European domination and the dwarfing of European populations enabled the intellectual activities of demystifying European cultural hegemony and of deconstructing European philosophical edifices. In other words, as the prolonged period of European self-confidence came to an end with the emergence of the United States as the major world power after World War II, the reverberations and ramifications of the decline of European civilization could be felt in the upper reaches of the WASP elite institutions of higher learning—including its humanistic disciplines. The emergence of the first major subcultures of American non-WASP intellectuals as exemplified by the so-called New York intellectuals, the Abstract Expressionists and the bebop jazz artists constituted a major challenge to an American, male, WASP cultural elite loyal to an older and eroding European culture.

The first significant blow—a salutary one, I might add—was dealt when assimilated Jewish Americans entered the high echelons of the academy—especially Ivy league institutions. Lionel Trilling at Columbia, Oscar Handlin at Harvard and John Blum at Yale initiated the slow but sure undoing of male, WASP cultural homogeneity—that is, the snobbish gentility, tribal civility and institutional loyalty that circumscribed the relative consensus which rests upon the Arnoldian conception of culture and its concomitant canon. The genius of Lionel Trilling was to appropriate this conception for his own political and cultural purposes—thereby unraveling the old male WASP consensus yet erecting a new liberal academic consensus around the cold-war anticommunist rendition of the values of complexity, difficulty and modulation. In addition, the professionalization and specialization of teaching in the humanities that resulted from the postwar American economic boom promoted the close reading techniques of the New Critics—severed from their conservative and organicist anticapitalist (or anti-industrialist) ideology. Like Trilling's revisionist Arnoldian criticism, the New Critics' academic preoccupation with paradox, irony and ambiguity both helped to canonize modernist literature and provided new readers of literary studies with a formal rigor and intellectual vigor which buttressed beleaguered humanist self-images in an expanding, technocentric culture. The new programs of American studies provided one of the few discursive spaces—especially for second-generation immigrants with progressive sentiments—wherein critiques of the emerging liberal consensus could be put forward, and even this space was limited by the ebullient postwar American nationalism which partly fueled the new interdisciplinary endeavor and by the subsequent repressive atmosphere of McCarthyism, which discouraged explicit social criticism.

The sixties constitute the watershed period in my schematic sketch of our present cultural crisis. During that decade we witnessed the shattering of male, WASP, cultural homogeneity and the collapse of the short-lived liberal consensus. More pointedly, the inclusion of African Americans, Hispanic Americans, Asian Americans, Native Americans and American women in the academy repoliticized literary studies in a way that went against the grain of the old, male, WASP, cultural hegemony and the new, revisionist, liberal consensus. This repoliticizing of the humanities yielded disorienting intellectual polemics and inescapable ideological polarization. These polemics and this polarization focused primarily on the limits, blindnesses, and exclusions of the prevailing forms of gentility, civility, and loyalty as well as the accompanying notions of culture and canonicity.

The radical and thorough questioning of male, Euro-American, cultural elites by Americans of color, American women, and New Left white males highlighted three crucial processes in the life of the country. First, the reception of the traveling theories from continental Europe—especially the work of the Frankfurt School and French Marxisms, structuralisms and poststructuralisms. A distinctive feature of these theories was the degree to which they grappled with the devastation, decline and decay of European civilization since the defeat of fascism and the fall of the British and French empires in Asia and Africa. The American reception of these theories undoubtedly domesticated them for academic consumption. But the theories also internationalized American humanistic discourses so that they extended beyond the North Atlantic connection. For the first time, significant Latin American, African and Asian writers figured visibly in academic literary studies.

The second noteworthy process accelerated by the struggles of the sixties was the recovery and revisioning of American history in light of those on its underside. Marxist histories, new social histories, women's histories, histories of peoples of color, gay and lesbian histories, all made new demands of scholars in literary studies. Issues concerning texts in history and history in texts loomed large. The third process I shall note is the onslaught of forms of popular culture such as film and television on highbrow literate culture. American technology—under the aegis of capital—transformed the cultural sphere and everyday life of people and thereby questioned the very place, presence and power of the printed word.

The establishmentarian response in the humanities was to accommodate the new social forces. In order to avoid divisive infighting within departments and to overcome the incommensurability of discourses among colleagues, ideologies of pluralism emerged to mediate clashing methods and perspectives in structurally fragmented departments. These ideologies served both to contain and often conceal irresoluble conflict and to ensure slots for ambitious and upwardly mobile young professors who were anxiety-ridden about their professional-managerial class status and fascinated with their bold, transgressive rhetoric, given their relative political impotence and inactivity. Needless to say, conservative spokespersons both inside and especially outside the academy lamented what they perceived as an "assault on the life of the mind" and made nostalgic calls for a return to older forms of consensus. Contemporary reflections on ideologies of canon formation take their place within this context of cultural heterogeneity, political struggle and academic dissensus—a context which itself is a particular historical reading of our prevailing critical struggle for canonical status in the midst of the battle over literary canon formation.

Not surprisingly, attempts to justify and legitimate canon formation in African American literary criticism are made in the name of pluralism. In our present historical context (with its highly limited options), these efforts are worthy of critical support. Yet I remain suspicious of them for two basic reasons. First, they tend to direct the energies of African American critics toward scrutinizing and defending primarily African American literary texts for a new or emerging canon and away from demystifying the already existing canon. The mere addition of African American texts to the present canon without any explicit and persuasive account of how this addition leads us to see the canon anew reveals the worst of academic pluralist ideology. Serious African American literary canon formation cannot take place without a wholesale reconsideration of the canon already in place. This is so not because "existing monuments form an ideal order among themselves which is modified by the introduction of the new (the really new) work of art among them"—as T. S. Eliot posited in his influential essay "Tradition and the Individual Talent." Rather the interdependence of the canonical and noncanonical as well as the interplay of the old canonical texts and the new canonical ones again require us to examine the crucial role of our historical readings of the current crisis that acknowledges this interdependence and promotes this interplay. Mere preoccupation with African American literary texts—already marginalized and ghettoized in literary studies—which leads toward a marginal and ghetto status in an enlarged canon or independent canon, forecloses this broader examination of the present crisis and thereby precludes action to transform it.

This foreclosure is neither fortuitous nor accidental. Rather it is symptomatic of the class interests of African American literary critics: they become the academic superintendents of a segment of an expanded canon or a separate canon. Such supervisory power over African American literary culture—including its significant consulting activities and sometimes patronage relations to powerful, white, academic critics and publishers—not only ensures slots for black literary scholars in highly competitive English departments. More important, these slots are themselves held up as evidence for the success of prevailing ideologies of pluralism. Such talk of success masks the ever-growing power of universities over American literary culture and, more specifically, the increasing authority of black literary professional managers over African American literary practices and products. This authority cannot but have a major impact on the kinds of literary texts produced—especially as African American literary programs increasingly produce the people who write the texts. It is fortunate that Richard Wright, Ann Petry and Ralph Ellison did not labor under such authority. In fact, I would go as far as to postulate that the glacier shift from an African American literature of racial confrontation during the four decades of the forties to the seventies to one of cultural introspection in our time is linked in some complex and mediated way to the existential needs and accommodating values of the black and white literary professional-managerial classes who assess and promote most of this literature.

Lest I be misunderstood I am not suggesting that literary studies would be better off without African American literary critics or with fewer of them. Nor am I arguing that canon formation among African American critics ought not to take place. Rather I am making three fundamental claims. First, that African American canon formation regulated by an ideology of pluralism is more an emblem of the prevailing crisis in contemporary humanistic studies than a creative response to it. Second, that this activity—despite its limited positive effects such as rendering visible African American literary texts of high quality—principally reproduces and reinforces prevailing forms of cultural authority in our professionalized supervision of literary products. Third, that black inclusion in these forms of cultural authority—with black literary critics overseeing a black canon—primarily serves the class interests of African American literary academic critics.

A brief glance at the history of African American literary criticism—including its present state—bears out these claims. Like most black literate intellectual activity in the Western world and especially in the United States, African American literary criticism has tended to take a defensive posture. That is, it has viewed itself as evidence of the humanity and intellectual capacity of black people that are often questioned by the dominant culture. This posture is understandably shot through with self-doubts and inferiority anxieties. And it often has resulted in bloated and exorbitant claims about black literary achievement. In stark contrast to black artistic practices in homiletics and music, in which blacks' self-confidence abounds owing to the vitality of rich and varied indigenous traditions, black literary artists and critics have proclaimed a Harlem Renaissance that never took place, novelistic breakthroughs that amounted to poignant yet narrow mediums of social protest (for example, *Native Son*) and literary movements that consist of talented though disparate women writers with little more than their gender and color in common. Such defensive posturing overlooks and downplays the grand contributions of the major twentieth-century African American literary artists—Jean Toomer, Ralph Ellison, James Baldwin (more his essays than his fiction), Toni Morrison and Ishmael Reed. Such diminishment takes place because these authors arbitrarily get lumped with a group of black writers or associated with a particular theme in African American intellectual history, which obscures their literary profundity and accents their less important aspects.

For instance, Toomer's ingenious modernist formal innovations and his chilling encounter with black southern culture in *Cane* are masked by associating him with the assertion of pride by the "new Negro" in the twenties. Ellison's existentialist blues novelistic practices, with their deep sources in African American music, folklore, Western literary humanism, and American pluralist ideology, are concealed by subsuming him under a "post-Wright school of black writing." Baldwin's masterful and memorable essays that mix Jamesian prose with black sermonic rhythms are similarly treated. Toni Morrison's magic realist portrayal of forms of African American cultural disruption and transformation links her more closely to contemporary Latin American literary treatments of the arrested agency of colonized peoples than with American feminist preoccupations with self-fulfillment and sisterhood. Last, Ishmael Reed's bizarre and brilliant postmodernist stories fall well outside black literary lineages and genealogies. In short, it is difficult to imagine an African American canon formation that does not domesticate and dilute the literary power and historical significance of these major figures.

Recent developments in African American literary criticism that focus on the figurative language of the texts are indeed improvements over the flat content analyses, vague black aesthetic efforts and political didacticism of earlier critics of African American literature. Yet this new black formalism—under whose auspices African American literary canon formation will more than likely take place—overreacts to the limits of the older approaches and thereby captures only select rhetorical features of texts while dehistoricizing their form and content. It ignores the way in which issues of power, political struggle and cultural identity are inscribed within the formal structures of texts and thereby misses the implicit historical readings of the crisis that circumscribes the texts and to which the texts inescapably and subtly respond.

This new formalism goes even farther astray when it attempts, in the words of critic Henry Louis Gates, Jr., to "turn to the Black tradition itself to develop theories of criticism indigenous to our literature." It goes farther astray because it proceeds on the dubious notion that theories of criticism must be developed from literature itself—be it vernacular, oral or highbrow literature. To put it crudely, this notion rests upon a fetishism of literature—a religious belief in the magical powers of a glorified set of particular cultural archives somehow autonomous and disconnected from other social practices. Must film criticism develop only from film itself? Must jazz criticism emerge only from jazz itself? One set of distinctive cultural archives must never be reducible or intelligible in terms of another set of cultural archives—including criticism itself. Yet it is impossible to grasp the complexity and multidimensionality of a specific set of artistic practices without relating it to other broader cultural and political practices at a given historical moment. In this sense, the move African American literary critics have made from a preoccupation with Northrop Frye's myth structuralism (with its assumption of the autonomy of the literary universe) and Paul de Man's rigorous deconstructive criticism (with its guiding notion of the self-reflexive and self-contradictory rhetorics of literary texts) to the signifying activity of dynamic black vernacular literature is but a displacement of one kind of formalism for another; it is but a shift from Euro-American elitist formalism to African American populist formalism, and it continues to resist viewing political conflict and cultural contestation within the forms themselves.

The appropriate role and function of opposition cultural critics regarding current forms of canon formation are threefold. First, we must no longer be literary critics who presume that our cultivated gaze on literary objects—the reified objects of our compartmentalized and professionalized disciplines—yields solely or principally judgments about the literary properties of these objects. There is indeed an inescapable evaluative dimension to any valid cultural criticism. Yet the literary objects upon which we focus are themselves cultural responses to specific crises in particular historical moments. Because these crises and moments must themselves be mediated through textual constructs, the literary objects we examine are never merely literary, and attempts to see them as such constitute a dehistoricizing and depoliticizing of literary texts that should be scrutinized for their ideological content, role and function. In this sense, canon formations that invoke the sole criterion of form—be it of the elitist or populist variety—are suspect.

Second, as cultural critics attuned to political conflict and struggle inscribed within the rhetorical enactments of texts, we should relate such conflict and struggle to larger institutional and structural battles occurring in and across societies, cultures and economies. This means that knowledge of sophisticated versions of historiography and refined perspectives of social theory are indispensable for a serious cultural critic. In other words—like the cultural critics of old—we must simply know much more than a professional literary critical training provides. The key here is not mere interdisciplinary work that traverses existing boundaries of disciplines but rather the more demanding efforts of pursuing dedisciplinizing modes of knowing that call into question the very boundaries of the disciplines themselves.

Finally, cultural critics should promote types of canon formation that serve as strategic weapons in the contemporary battle over how best to respond to the current crisis in one's society and culture. This view does not entail a crude, unidimensional, instrumental approach to literature; it simply acknowledges that so-called noninstrumental approaches are themselves always already implicated in the raging battle in one's society and culture. The fundamental question is not how one's canon can transcend this battle but rather how old or new canons, enlarged or conflicting canons, guide particular historical interpretations of this battle and enable individual and collective action within it. I simply hope that as canon formation proceeds among African American cultural critics and others we can try to avoid as much as possible the pitfalls I have sketched.

and architectural practices. The major fear is that of falling into the trap of economic determinism—of reducing the grandeur of precious architecture to the grub of pecuniary avidity. And surely the forms, techniques, and styles of architecture are not reducible to the needs and interests of public or private patrons. But this deadly reductionist trap should not discourage architectural critics from pursuing more refined investigations into how economic and political power help shape how buildings are made—and not simply how they come to be. Needless to say, Manfredo Tafuri's *Architecture and Utopia: Design and Capitalist Development* (1973) is a move in this direction, yet even this work stays a bit too far removed from the ground where detailed historical work should focus.

A plausible objection to this line of reasoning is that architectural critics do not have the historical and analytical training to do such analyses. So it is better to leave this work to be done by cultural historians and even economists. This objection leads us to the crucial issue of the political legitimacy of architectural critics—namely, why are they trained as they are, how are they reproduced, and what set of assumptions about history, economics, culture and art inform the curriculum and faculties that educate them? Gone are the days of Montgomery Schuyler, George Shepperd Chappell and the great Lewis Mumford. The professionalization of architectural criticism—which has its own traps of insular jargon, codes and etiquette for the initiated—requires genealogies of the changing frameworks and paradigms that become dominant at particular historical moments and of how these frameworks and paradigms yield insights and blindnesses for those who work within them. These genealogies should highlight not simply the dynamic changes of influential critical perspectives in the academy but also how these perspectives shape and are shaped by the actual building of edifices and how these perspectives relate to other significant cultural practices, for instance, painting in Le Corbusier's early work and populism in Venturi's thought. What Aaron Betsky calls "the trivialization of the architectural profession" and James Wines dubs its "failure of vision"[3] must be unpacked by means of structural and institutional analyses of what goes into molding architects and their critics.

In this way, the issue of the political legitimacy of architecture is posed neither in a nostalgic, moralistic manner that translates the will of an epoch into space, nor in a sophomoric, nihilistic mode that promotes an easy and lucrative despair. Rather the challenge is to try to understand architectural practices as power-laden cultural practices that are deeply affected by larger historical forces, for instance, markets, the state, the academy, but also as practices that have their own specificity and social effects—even if they are not the kind of effects one approves of. This is why the kind of Miesian nostalgia of Roger Kimball will not suffice.[4]

The political legitimacy of architecture is linked to an even deeper issue: the intellectual crisis in architectural criticism. The half-century predominance of the international styles in architecture left critics with little room to maneuver. Robert Venturi's groundbreaking *Complexity and Contradiction* (1966)—with its empirical, relativistic and anti-Platonic approach—created new space for critics. Yet its treatment of the semantic dimension of architecture remained wedded to the Olympian Platonism of the great modernists; that is, his truncated perspective covered only the conventional styles and "extrinsic" factors such as poor design. As Alan Colquhoun perceptively notes,

> the book does not exclude the possibility that the general principles of the modern movement were sound and might still form the basis of a complex and subtle architecture. . . .[5]

Yet Venturi indeed opened Pandora's box. Architectural criticism has been a Towel of Babel ever since.

The intellectual crisis in architectural criticism is primarily rooted in the modernist promotion of what Lewis Mumford called "the myth of the machine." This myth is not simply an isolated aesthetic ideology but rather a pervasive sociocultural phenomenon that promotes expert scientific knowledge and elaborate bureaucratic structures that facilitate five Ps—power, productivity for profit, political control and publicity.[6] Architecture is distinct from the other arts in that it associated its own modernist avant-garde movements—its formalism and newness—with the myth of the machine. For Colquhoun,

> Modern architecture conflated absolute formalism with the actual productive forces of society. There was in Modern architecture an overlap between nineteenth-century instrumentalism and modernist formalism which did not occur in any of the other arts.[7]

This is why modernism in architecture enthusiastically embraced technology in an excessive utopian manner, whereas modernism in literature put a premium on myth (over against science and technology) in a dystopian way. Le Corbusier—with his complex bundle of tensions between architecture as machine production and architecture as intuitive expression—proclaimed in his epoch-making manifesto, *Towards a New Architecture* (1923): "The Modern age is spread before them [engineers & others], sparkling and radiant."[8] Yet James Joyce's Stephen in *Ulysses* (1922) sees history as a nightmare from which he is trying to awake and T. S. Eliot perceives, in his review of Joyce's text, modern history as an "immense panorama of futility and anarchy." My point here is not simply that the early Le Corbusier and fellow Modernists in architecture were naive and duped, but more importantly, that the distinctive development of architecture produced such an idealizing of technology and industry. The subsequent collapse of this utopianism into a sheer productivism with a Platonic formalism that sustains an architectural monumentality (as in the genius of Ludwig Mies van der Rohe, transplanted from Germany to Chicago) set the framework of our present intellectual crisis in architectural criticism.[9] Needless to say, the call for irony and ambiguity that focuses on the symbolic content (not space or structure) in the populism of Robert Venturi, the forms of historical eclecticism in the postmodernism of Charles Jencks, or the plea for communication in the public art of James Wines's de-architecture provide inadequate responses to this crisis.[10] This is primarily because all three provocative responses fail to grasp on a deep level the content and character of the larger cultural crisis of our time.

The recent appropriations of the ironic skepticism of Jacques Derrida (as in the provocative writings of Peter Eisenman) and the genealogical materialism of Michel Foucault (as with the criticism of Anthony Vidler and Michael Hayes) can be viewed as the awakening of architectural criticism to the depths of our cultural crisis. Although deconstructivist architecture is, as Mark Wrigley rightly observes, more an extension of and deviation from Russian constructivism than a blanket architectural application of Derrida's thought,[11] it does force architectural critics to put forward their own conception of the current cultural crisis—even if it seems to amount to mere sloganeering about "the end of Western metaphysics" or the omnipresence of "the disciplinary order." In short, the French invasion of architectural criticism—twenty years after a similar affair in literary criticism—has injected new energy and excitement into a discipline suffering a cultural lag. Yet this invasion has led many architectural critics to the most deadly of traps: *the loss of identity as architectural critics.*

The assimilation of architectural criticism into literary criticism or the immersion of architectural objects into larger cultural practices has led, in many cases, to a loss of the specificity of architectural practices and objects. Such a loss results in the loss of the *architectural* dimension of what architectural critics do. The major virtue of the French invasion is that new possibilities, heretofore foreclosed, are unleashed; the vice is that architectural critics lose their identity and focus primarily on academicist perspectives on the larger crisis of our culture—a focus that requires a deeper knowledge of history, economics, sociology and so on than most architectural critics have or care to pursue. My point here is not that this task should be abandoned by architectural critics. Rather I am claiming that what architectural critics do know—the specificity of the diverse traditions of architectural practices (from the nitty-gritty matters of calculations to artistic styles, perspectives, visions and links to structures of power)—should inform how we understand the present cultural crisis.

None of us have the definitive understanding of the complex cultural crisis that confronts us, though some views are better than others. My own view is that an appropriate starting point is a reexamination of what the modernists valorized: the myth of the machine. Hence, the work of Lewis Mumford is indispensable. Yet, since faith in progress by means of expanding productive forces— be it the liberal or Marxist version—is a secular illusion, the myth of the machine must be questioned in new ways. This questioning must go far beyond a playful explosion of modernist formalism which heralds ornamentation and decoration of past heroic efforts. It also must be more than a defense of the autonomy of architectural discourse in the guise of its textualization—an outdated, avant-gardist gesture in a culture that now thrives and survives on such fashionable and faddish gestures.

Rather, the demystifying of the machine can proceed—thanks, in part, to the insights of poststructuralist analyses—by examining the second term in the binary opposition of machine-nature, civilized-primitive, ruler-ruled, Apollonian-Dionysian, male-female, white-black, in relation to architectural practices. This examination should neither be a mechanical deconstructive operation that stays on the discursive surfaces at the expense of an analysis of structural and institutional dynamics of power, nor should it result in a mere turning of the tables that trashes the first terms in the binary oppositions. Rather what is required is a sophisticated, architectural-historical inquiry into how these notions operate in the complex formulations of diverse and developing discourses and practices of actual architects and critics. Such an inquiry presupposes precisely what contemporary architectural criticism shuns: *a distinctive architectural historiography that sheds light on the emergence and develop-*

ment of the current cultural crisis as it shapes and is shaped by architectural practices. As Mark Jarzombek rightly states,

> architects have read too many history books and have not done enough on-location history of their own. It used to be, from the Renaissance on, that architects told the historians what was important about a building of the past and what was not. Now it is historians who tell architects. That architects so willingly give up their birthright marks, perhaps, the dawning of a new age in architectural history. The Pre-modern Post-modern used the past to create a historiographic understanding of the present. Once the ancient ruins had all been studied and the archaeologists took over, the modernists were free to turn the same historiographic principles used by earlier generations against history itself. The post-modern historicists now use history to kill historiography. There may not be much left to talk about when the next generation of architects comes along.[12]

These remarks hold from the Adorno-informed pessimism of Tafuri through the presentist populism of Venturi to the "classical" post-modernism of Jencks.

The major challenge of a new architectural historiography is that its conception of the "past" and "present" be attuned to the complex role of difference—nature, primitive, ruled, Dionysian, female, black and so on. In this sense, the recent talk about the end of architecture, the exhaustion of the architectural tradition, the loss of architecture as a social force and so on, is a parochial and nostalgic talk about a particular consensus—and its circumstances—that indeed no longer exists. This consensus rests upon certain governing myths (machine), narratives (Eurocentric ones), design strategies (urban building efforts) and styles (phallocentric monuments) that no longer aesthetically convince or effectively function for us. This "us" is a diverse and heterogeneous one—not just architects and their critics.

The case of the great Le Corbusier may serve as an illustration. His serious grappling with the binary oppositions above reaches a saturation point in his critique of the classical theory of architectural design (Vitruvius) in the form of the Modulor. This new form of measure derived not just from the proportions of the human figure but, more specifically, from women's bodies—especially fat, "primitive," "uncivilized," non-European, Dionysian-driven, black, brown and red women's bodies. It is no secret that Le Corbusier's paintings and pencil sketches in the early thirties began to focus on the shapes of women's bodies, highlighting the curves of buttocks and shoulder arches. This preoccupation is often viewed as a slow shift from a machine aesthetic to a nature aesthetic. Like Picasso's use of "primitive" art to revitalize the art of the new epoch, Corbusier turns toward female and Third World sources for demystifying—not simply displacing—the myth of the machine he had earlier heralded. Corbusier's move toward these sources was not a simple rejection of the myth of the machine. As Charles Jencks notes,

> Le Corbusier found in Negro music, in the hot jazz of Louis Armstrong, "implacable exactitude," "mathematics, equilibrium on a tightrope" and all the masculine virtues of the machine.[13]

And in regard to Josephine Baker's performance on board the "Julius Caesar" on a trip to South America in 1929, Le Corbusier writes,

> In a stupid variety show, Josephine Baker sang "Baby" with such an intense and dramatic sensibility that I was moved to tears. There is in this American Negro music a lyrical "contemporary" mass so invincible that I could see the foundation of a new sentiment of music capable of being the expression of the new epoch and also capable of classifying its European origins as stone age— just as has happened with the new architecture.[14]

Although Baker is, for Le Corbusier, "a small child pure, simple and limpid," more than mere European male paternalism is at work here. Rather he also is in search of new forms of space, proportion, structure and order in light of the products, bodies and sensibilities of those subsumed under the second terms of the aforementioned binary oppositions—natural, primitive, ruled, Dionysian, female and peoples of color.

I look for primitive men not for their barbarity but for their wisdom.[15]

The columns of a building should be like the strong curvaceous thighs of a woman.[16]

I like the skin of women.[17]

Le Corbusier's Ronchamp chapel in eastern France, the Unité at Marseille and his Carpenter Center at Harvard all bear this so-called brutalist stamp. Like Mumford's subtle nostalgia for the medieval "Garden Village," Corbusier's search for non-European and female sources was intimately linked to his conception of architectural practices as forms of and means for collective life—a life he associated first and foremost with hierarchical religious communities such as the monastic order of the Carthusians.

The efforts of Le Corbusier's "middle" period can be neither imitated nor emulated. Yet his gallant yet flawed attempt to come to terms with difference—with those constituted as Other—must inform any new architectural historiography in our postcolonial world and postmodern culture of megamachines, multinational corporations, nation-states and fragmented communities. Where then do we go from here?

The future of architectural criticism rests on the development of a refined and revisionist architectural historiography that creatively fuses social histories of architectural practices and social histories of technology in light of sophisticated interpretations of the present cultural crisis. This historiography must be informed by the current theoretical debates in the larger discourse of cultural criticism. Yet the benefits of these debates are in the enabling methodological insights that facilitate history-writing and cultural analyses of specific past and present architectural practices, not ontological and epistemological conclusions that promote mere avant-gardist posturing. Theory is not historiography, though no historiography escapes theory. Yet the present obsession with theory must now yield to theory-laden historiography if architectural criticism is to have any chance of grasping the impasse that now engulfs us. There are no guarantees for any resolutions, but there are certain routes that weaken our efforts to move beyond this fascinating, and possibly fecund, moment in architectural criticism.[18]

4

Horace Pippin's Challenge to Art Criticism

The art of Horace Pippin poses grave challenges to how we appreciate and assess artworks in late twentieth-century America. A serious examination of Pippin's place in art history leads us into the thicket of difficult issues that now beset art critics. What does it mean to talk about high art and popular culture? Do these rubrics help us to evaluate and understand visual artifacts? Is folk art an illuminating or oxymoronic category? Can art be more than personal, racial or national therapy in American culture? Has the commercialization of art rendered it a mere commodity in our market-driven culture? Can the reception of the work of a black artist transcend mere documentary, social pleading or exotic appeal?

These complex questions often yield Manichaean responses—self-appointed defenders of high culture who beat their breasts in the name of craftsmanship and quality, and self-styled avant-gardists who call for critique and relevance. The former tend to use the monumental touchstones of the recent past—especially those of high modernism—to judge the present. The latter reject monumentalist views of art history even as they sometimes become highly paid celebrities in the art world. Pippin's work shows this debate to be a sterile exchange that overlooks much of the best art in the American grain: high-quality craftsmanship of art objects that disclose the humanity of people whose plight points to flaws in American society. Pippin's paintings are neither monumentalist in the modernist sense nor political in a postmodernist way. Rather they are expressions

of a rich Emersonian tradition in American art that puts a premium
on the grandeur in the commonplace, ordinary and quotidian lives
of people. This tradition promotes neither a glib celebration of
everyday experiences nor a naive ignorance of the tragic aspects of
our condition. Rather, Pippin's Emersonian sensibility affirms what
John Dewey dubbed "experience in its integrity."[1] Pippin's so-called
folk art boldly exclaims with Emerson,

> I ask not for the great, the remote, the romantic; what is doing
> in Italy or Arabia; what is Greek art, or Provencal minstrelsy; I
> embrace the common, I explore and sit at the feet of the familiar,
> the low. Give me insight into day and you may have the antique
> and future worlds.[2]

This artistic affirmation of everyday experiences of ordinary people
is anti-elitist but not anti-intellectual—that is, it shuns a narrow
mentality that downplays the joys and sufferings of the degraded
and despised, yet it heralds high standards for how these joys and
sufferings are represented in art. Pippin's paintings—as a grand
instance of the Emersonian tradition in American art—attempt to
democratize (not denigrate) the aesthetic by discerning and dis-
playing tragedy and comedy in the ordinary experiences of common
folk. In this way, his work echoes the Emersonian sensibility of
John Dewey:

> In order to *understand* the aesthetic in its ultimate and approved
> forms, one must begin with it in the raw; in the events and scenes
> that hold the attentive eye and ear of man, arousing his interest
> and affording him enjoyment as he looks and listens. . . . The
> sources of art in human experience will be learned by him who
> sees how the tense grace of the ball-player infects the onlooking
> crowd; who notes the delight of the housewife in tending her
> plants, and the intent interest of her goodman in tending the patch
> of green in front of the house; the zest of the spectator in poking
> the wood burning on the hearth and in watching the darting
> flames and crumbling coals.[3]

We see such precious moments in Pippin's *Harmonizing* (1944) with black men *joyfully* singing on the block—or *Domino Players* (1943) with black women *enjoying* a domino game. We also realize that Pippin's link to Abraham Lincoln is not so much a link to the President as emancipator of black people, nor the President as hypocrite, but rather to Abe as the folk hero who is believed to have said that God must have loved common folk since he made so many of them. *Abe Lincoln, The Good Samaritan* (1943) fuses this Emersonian sensibility of Lincoln with a Christian theme of concern for the disadvantaged ("let Christianity speak ever for the poor and the low"[4]).

Yet Pippin's Emersonian practice—which sidesteps the sterile "quality versus diversity" debate—lends itself to establishmentarian abuse. A genuine artistic concern with the common easily appears as an aspiration for authenticity—especially for an art establishment that puts a premium on the "primitive" and hungers for the exotic. The relative attention and support of the self-taught Pippin at the expense of academically trained black artists reflects this establishmentarianism abuse. This situation is captured by Richard J. Powell in his pioneering book *Homecoming: The Art and Life of William H. Johnson,* when he discusses the response of Alain Locke and a local critic to Johnson's new "primitive" works in the summer of 1940 at the Exhibition of the Art of the American Negro (1851–1940) for the American Negro Exposition in Chicago:

> For both the reviewer in Chicago and Alain Locke, Johnson's flirtation with images and forms that suggested naiveté was symptomatic of the art world's then-current fascination with self-trained "daubers," "scribblers," and "whittlers," whose creative lives had been spent (for the most part) outside of the art world proper. One of the most celebrated of these folk artists, black American painter Horace Pippin, worked in a somewhat similar manner to Johnson, with oil paints applied in a thick, impasto consistency, and visual narratives punctuated by strong, solid areas of pure color. Schooled and dedicated artists like Johnson

must have felt a little envious of these self-taught painters such as Pippin who, in only a few years, had several museum and gallery exhibitions to their credit.

As Johnson's past comments about primitivism and folk culture demonstrate, he acknowledged the innate power and spirituality that emanated from the art of common people and had decided to allow that part of his own folk heritage to assert itself in his work. Although no less eager to have his own work seen and appreciated, Johnson no doubt accepted the broad appeal of those folk artists then deservedly enjoying the art world's spotlight.[5]

This institutional dilemma regarding the dominant white reception of Pippin's work raises crucial issues about the trials and tribulations of being a black artist in America. In Pippin's case, being a self-taught black artist in America in the Emersonian tradition complicates the matter. On the one hand, a professional envy among highly trained black (and white) artists is understandable, given the limited slots of visibility—and given the history of racist exclusion of black artists in the art world. On the other hand, the absence of professional training does not mean that there is no quality in Pippin's art. Even Alain Locke, the elitist dean of African American art in mid-century America, described Pippin as "a real and rare genius, combining folk quality with artistic maturity so uniquely as almost to defy classification."[6] Yet the relation of the politics of artistic visibility to the quality of visible artworks requires critical scrutiny. As James Clifford rightly notes,

> the fact that rather abruptly, in the space of a few decades, a large class of non-Western artifacts came to be redefined as art is a taxonomic shift that requires critical historical discussion, not celebration.[7]

Clifford does not have Pippin's work in mind here—especially since Pippin's art was recognized as such, as seen in the inclusion of four of his works in a Museum of Modern Art exhibit called Masters of Popular Painting in 1938.[8] But Pippin's works can easily be tarred with the brush of "primitivism," even "exoticism," highlighting his lack of schooling and his subject matter rather than the quality of his art. In her discussion of the Primitivism show at the Museum of Modern Art in 1984, Michele Wallace shows how these issues surrounding the reception of Pippin's work remain alive in our time:

> Black criticism was blocked from the discussions of Modernism, which are defined as exclusively white by an intricate and insidious cooperation of art galleries, museums and academic art history, and also blocked from any discussion of "primitivism," which has been colonized beyond recognition in the space of the international and now global museum. At this juncture one is compelled to ask, "Is multiculturalism, as it is being institutionally defined, occupying the same space as 'primitivism' in relationship to Postmodernism?" For me, a response to such a question would need to include a careful scrutiny of the history of black popular culture and race relations, and account for the sexualization of both, thus defining the perimeters of a new knowledge which I can only name, at this point, as the problem of the visual in Afro-American culture.[9]

Is a black artist like Pippin caught in a Catch-22 dilemma—unjustly excluded owing to his blackness *qua* "inferior" (artist) or suspiciously included due to his blackness *qua* "primitive" (artist)? Is this especially so for those black artists in the Emersonian tradition, such as Sterling Brown in poetry or Bessie Smith in music? These questions get at the heart of what it is to be a black artist in America.

To be a black artist in America is to be caught in what I have called elsewhere "the modern black diasporan problematic of invisibility and namelessness."[10] This problematic requires that black people search for validation and recognition in a culture in which white-supremacist assaults on black intelligence, ability, beauty and character circumscribe such a search. Pippin's example is instructive in that, unlike the other two celebrated mid-century black artists in this country—Richmond Barthé and Jacob Lawrence—Pippin lived and functioned outside the cosmopolitan art world. Like the early blues and jazz artists in American music, Pippin's art remained rooted in black folk culture, yet also appealed to the culture industry of his day. He indeed gained significant validation and recognition from the white art establishment—but at what personal and artistic cost? Do all American artists in our market culture bear similar costs?

Unlike William H. Johnson and Beauford Delaney, Pippin did not go mad. But his wife did spend her last months in a mental institution after a breakdown. Pippin did drink heavily—yet we do not know whether this was related directly to his art career. So in regard to the personal costs, our answer remains open-ended. The artistic cost paid by Pippin is best summed up in this brief characterization of his career by a leading art historian in 1956:

> Horace Pippin (1888–1946), an unschooled Negro of West Chester, Pennsylvania, unfitted for labor by a war wound, turned to painting. "Pictures just come to my mind," he explained, "and I tell my head to go ahead," an explanation of his innocent art which needs no further comment. His discovery and exploitation as a painter in 1937 did not change his art, although it was too much for him as a human being.[11]

This view of Pippin as an "innocent autodidact" chimes well with the image of the black artist lacking sophistication and subtlety. We cannot deny the poignant simplicity of Pippin's art—yet simplicity is neither simplistic nor sophomoric. Rather Pippin's burden of being a black artist in America required that he do battle with either primitivist designations or inferiority claims about his art. This struggle is best seen in the words of one of Pippin's black artistic contemporaries, William H. Johnson, quoted by the distinguished abstract sculptor of African descent, Martin Puryear:

> I myself feel like a primitive man—like one who is at the same time both a primitive and a cultured painter.[12]

This sense of feeling like a primitive and modern person-artist is one form of the black mode of being in a white-supremacist world—

a world in which W. E. B. Du Bois claimed that the black person and artist is

> born with a veil, and gifted with second-sight in this American world,—a world which yields him no true self-consciousness, but only lets him see himself through the revelation of the other world. It is a peculiar sensation, this double-consciousness, this sense always looking at one's self through the eyes of others, of measuring one's soul by the tape of a world that looks on in amused contempt and pity. One ever feels his twoness,—an American, a Negro; two souls, two thoughts, two unreconciled strivings; two warring ideals in one dark body, whose dogged strength alone keeps it from being torn asunder.
>
> The history of the American Negro is the history of this strife—this longing to attain self-conscious manhood, to merge his double self into a better and truer self. In this merging he wishes neither 'of the older selves to be lost. He would not Africanize America, for America has too much to teach the world and Africa. He would not bleach his Negro soul in a flood of white Americanism, for he knows that Negro blood has a message for the world. He simply wishes to make it possible for a man to be both a Negro and an American, without being cursed and spit upon by his fellows, without having the doors of Opportunity closed roughly in his face.[13]

This classic characterization of being black in xenophobic America means that black artists are always suspect for not measuring up to rigorous standards or made to feel exotic in a white world that often associates blackness with bodily energy, visceral vitality and sexual vibrancy. Pippin's art is a powerful expression of black spiritual strivings to attain self-conscious humanhood—to believe truly one is fully human and to believe truly that whites can accept one's black humanity. This utopian endeavor indeed is crippled by black self-hatred and white contempt, yet the underlying fire that sustains it is not extinguished by them. Rather this fire is fueled by the dogged fortitude of ordinary black folk who decide that if they cannot be truly free, they can, at least, be fully themselves. Pippin's art portrays black people as "fully themselves"—that is, as they are outside of the white normative gaze that requires elaborate masks and intricate posturing for black survival and sanity. This does not mean that behind the masks one finds the "real faces" of black folk or that beneath the posturing one sees the "true gestures" of black bodies. Instead, Pippin's art suggests that black people within the white normative gaze wear certain kind of masks and enact particular kinds of postures, and outside the white normative gaze wear other kind of masks and enact different sort of postures. In short, black people tend to behave differently when they are "outside the white world"—though how they behave within black spaces is shaped by their battles with self-hatred and white contempt.

As I noted earlier, Pippin's art reminds one of Sterling Brown's poetry or Bessie Smith's music, in that all three artists reject the two dominant models of black art in the *white* world at the time: black art as expressive of the "new Negro" and black art as protest. Instead they build on the major paradigm of black art in the *black* world: black art as healing, soothing yet humorously unsettling illuminations of what it means to be human in black skin in America.

Pippin's work appears a decade or so after the celebrated Harlem Renaissance. This fascinating moment in black culture remains a highly contested one in regard to what it was and what it means. A renaissance is a rebirth by means of recovering a classical heritage heretofore overlooked or ignored. Do the works of the major artists of the Harlem Renaissance—Countee Cullen, Claude McKay, Nella Larsen, Jessie Fauset, Rudolf Fisher, Wallace Thurman, early Aaron Douglas and others—engage in such a recovery? I think not. Instead of serious and substantive attempts to recover the culturally hybrid heritage of black folk, we witnessed the cantankerous reportage of a black, middle-class identity crisis. The Harlem Renaissance was not so much a genuine renaissance, but rather a yearning for a renaissance aborted by its major artists owing to a conscious distance from the very cultural creativity they desired. In this sense, the Harlem Renaissance was a self-complimentary construct concocted by rising, black, middle-class, artistic figures to gain attention for their own anxieties at the expense of their individual and social identities, and to acquire authority to impose their conceptions of legitimate forms of black cultural productions on black America.

The dominant theme of romanticizing the "primitivism" of poor black folk and showing how such "primitivism" fundamentally affects the plights and predicaments of refined and educated, black, middle-class individuals (Claude McKay's best-seller *Home to Harlem* is paradigmatic here) looms large in the Harlem Renaissance. This theme fits in well with the crisis in European and American civilization after World War I. The war was the end of a epoch— an epoch regulated by nineteenth-century illusions of inevitable progress and perennial stability for emerging industrial societies. With the shattering of European self-confidence—as history is viewed no longer as a train for smooth amelioration but rather as Joyce's "nightmare" or Eliot's "immense panorama of futility and anarchy"—appetites for "primitivism" were whetted. With the rise of non-Western nations—Japan's victory over Russia (1905), revolutions in Persia (1905), Turkey (1907), Mexico (1911), China (1912)—ferocious nationalisms appealed to machismo-driven myths of virility and vitality as Woodrow Wilson's Fourteen Points squared off against Lenin's doctrine of national self-determination. The economic boom in the USA, facilitated by economic expansionism abroad (especially the takeover of Latin American markets from Britain after the war) and protectionism at home, ushered in mass communications (radio, phonograph and talking film) and mass culture for the middle classes—a mass culture already saturated with black cultural products. The great talents of George Gershwin, Jerome Kern, Benny Goodman and Paul Whiteman rest in large part on the undeniable genius of Louis Armstrong, Duke Ellington, Bessie Smith and Ma Rainey. Lastly, the great migration of black people from the Jim and Jane Crow South to the industrial urban centers of the North produced not only social dislocation, cultural disorientation and personal disillusionment; it also contributed to the makings of a massive political movement (Marcus Garvey's Universal Negro Improvement Association) and the refinement of the great black cultural renaissance actually taking place far removed from most of the Harlem Renaissance artists and critics— the evolution of jazz in New Orleans, St. Louis, Memphis and Chicago.

Like its European counterpart in France (the Negritude movement led by Léopold Senghor), the Harlem Renaissance conceived of black art as the refined expressions of the new Negro. In the exemplary text of the Harlem Renaissance, *The New Negro* (1925)—"its bible," as rightly noted by Arnold Rampersad[14]— black art is conceived to be the imposition of form on the rich substance of black folk culture. Influenced by the high modernisms of Europe, and suspicious of art forms already operative in black folk culture (e.g. blues, dance, sermon, sports—none of which are examined in *The New Negro*) Locke states

> there is ample evidence of a New Negro in the latest phases of social change and progress, but still more in the internal world of the Negro mind and spirit. Here in the very heart of the folk-spirit are the essential forces, and folk interpretation is truly vital and representative only in terms of these. (Foreword)

These "essential forces" of the folk, primitive, raw, coarse, and unrefined, require the skills of cultivated and educated artists to disclose black life to the world. In the only essay on jazz in *The New Negro,* by J. A. Rogers, this Lockean aesthetic attitude is amplified:

> Yet in spite of its present vices and vulgarizations, its sex informalities, its morally anarchic spirit, jazz has a popular mission to perform. Joy after all, has a physical basis. . . . Moreover, jazz with its mocking disregard for formality is a leveller and makes for democracy. The jazz spirit, being primitive, demands more frankness and sincerity. . . . And so this new spirit of joy and spontaneity may itself play the role of reformer. Where at present it vulgarizes, with more wholesome growth in the future, it may on the contrary truly democratize. At all events, jazz is rejuvenation, a

recharging of the batteries of civilization with primitive new vigor. It has come to stay, and they are wise, who instead of protesting against it, try to lift and divert it into nobler channels. ("Jazz at Home," pp. 223–24)

For Rogers, jazz is not a distinct art form with its own integrity and cultivated artists. Instead it is a primitive energy in search of political funnels that will expand American democracy. In fact, he claims that jazz is popular because, after the horrors of the war, "in its fresh joyousness men found a temporary forgetfulness, infinitely less harmful than drugs or alcohol" (pp. 222–23). Locke would not go this far in his therapeutic view of folk culture and his modernist conception of art—yet Locke and Rogers agree that popular culture is not a place where art resides but rather provides raw material for sophisticated artists (with university pedigrees and usually white patrons) to create expressions of the "New Negro."

Pippin's Emersonian sensibility rejects this highly influential view of black art—a view that shaped the crucial activities of the Harmon Foundation.[15] And although Locke recognized Pippin's genius in 1947, it is doubtful whether he would have in 1925.[16] Like Sterling Brown or Bessie Smith, Pippin is less concerned about expressing the sense of being a "New Negro" and more focussed on artistic rendering of the extraordinariness of ordinary black folk then and now. The "New Negro" still seems too preoccupied with how black folk appear to the white normative gaze, too obsessed with showing white people how sophisticated they are, how worthy of white validation and recognition. For Pippin, such validation and recognition is fine, yet only if it does not lead him to violate the integrity of his art or blind him to the rich experiences of ordinary black folk white trying to peddle "the black experience" to white America.

The next dominant conception of black art as protest emerged after the collapse of the Harlem Renaissance, principally owing to the depression. The great black literary artwork of protest was Richard Wright's *Native Son* (1940). This conception of black art displaced the sophisticated and cultivated New Negro with the outraged and angry Mad Negro. Gone were the attempts to distance oneself from the uncouth, "primitive" black masses. In place of the sentimental journeys behind the veil to see how black folk live and are, we got the pervasive physical and psychic violence of black life turned outward to white America.

The irony of the view of black art as protest—as description of the inhumane circumstances of much of black life and as heartfelt resistance to these circumstances—is that it is still preoccupied with the white normative gaze, and it reduces black people to mere reactors to white power. Pippin's *Mr. Prejudice* (1942) contains protest elements, yet it refuses to view the multilayered character of black life as a reaction to the sick dictates of xenophobic America. Pippin's Emersonian orientation refuses to cast art as a primary agent for social change or a central medium for protest—even when he shares the values of those seeking such change or promoting such protest. This kind of redemptive culturalism—the notion that culture can yield political redemption—flies in the face of Pippin's view of black art as those ritualistic activities that heal and soothe, generate laughter and unsettle dogmas with such style and form that they constitute black ways of being human. To pursue such a conception of black art in a white world obsessed with black incapacities and atavistic proclivities means to run the risk of falling into the traps of "primitivism."

Nearly fifty years after his death, Pippin's art still reminds us of how far we have *not* come in creating new languages and frameworks that do justice to his work, account for his narrow receptions and stay attuned to the risks he took and the costs he paid. The Horace Pippin exhibition (January 1994) courageously and meticulously mounted by the Pennsylvania Academy of Fine Arts once again puts American art criticism on trial—not for its verdict on Horace Pippin but for how our understandings of Pippin's art force us to reconceive and reform the art world as it now exists.

5

The Dilemma of the Black Intellectual

The peculiarities of the American social structure, and the position of the intellectual class within it, make the functional role of the negro intellectual a special one. The negro intellectual must deal intimately with the white power structure and cultural apparatus, and the inner realities of the black world at one and the same time. But in order to function successfully in this role, he has to be acutely aware of the nature of the American social dynamic and how it monitors the ingredients of class stratifications in American society. . . . Therefore the functional role of the negro intellectual demands that he *cannot* be absolutely separated from either the black or white world.

Harold Cruse
The Crisis of the Negro Intellectual (1967)

The contemporary black intellectual faces a grim predicament. Caught between an insolent American society and an insouciant black community, the African American who takes seriously the life of the mind inhabits an isolated and insulated world. This condition has little to do with the motives and intentions of black intellectuals; rather it is an objective situation created by circumstances not of their own choosing. In this meditative essay, I will explore this dilemma of the black intellectual and suggest various ways of understanding and transforming it.

On Becoming a Black Intellectual

The choice of becoming a black intellectual is an act of self-imposed marginality; it assures a peripheral status in and to the black community. The quest for literacy indeed is a fundamental theme in African American history and a basic impulse in the black community. But for blacks, as with most Americans, the uses for literacy are usually perceived to be for more substantive pecuniary benefits than those of the writer, artist, teacher or professor. The reasons some black people choose to become serious intellectuals are diverse. But in most cases these reasons can be traced back to a common root: a conversionlike experience with a highly influential teacher or peer that convinced one to dedicate one's life to the activities of reading, writing and conversing for the purposes of individual pleasure, personal worth and political enhancement of black (and often other oppressed) people.

The way in which one becomes a black intellectual is highly problematic. This is so because the traditional roads others travel to become intellectuals in American society have only recently been opened to black people—and remain quite difficult. The main avenues are the academy or the literate subcultures of art, culture and politics. Prior to the acceptance of black undergraduate students to elite white universities and colleges in the late sixties, select black educational institutions served as the initial stimulus for potential black intellectuals. And in all honesty, there were relatively more and better black intellectuals then than now. After a decent grounding in a black college, where self-worth and self-confidence were affirmed, bright black students then matriculated to leading white institutions to be trained by liberal, sympathetic scholars, often of renowned stature. Stellar figures such as W. E. B. Du Bois, E. Franklin Frazier and John Hope Franklin were products of this system. For those black intellectuals-to-be who missed college opportunities for financial or personal reasons, there were literate subcultures—especially in the large urban centers—of writers, painters, musicians and politicos for unconventional educational enhancement. Major personages such as Richard Wright, Ralph Ellison and James Baldwin were products of this process.

Ironically, the present-day academy and contemporary literate subcultures present more obstacles for young blacks than those in decades past. This is so for three basic reasons. First, the attitudes of white scholars in the academy are quite different from those in the past. It is much more difficult for black students, especially graduate students, to be taken seriously as *potential scholars and intellectuals* owing to the managerial ethos of our universities and colleges (in which less time is spent with students) and to the vulgar (racist) perceptions fueled by affirmative action programs which pollute many black student–white professor relations.

Second, literate subcultures are less open to blacks now than they were three or four decades ago, not because white avant-garde journals or leftist groups are more racist today, but rather because heated political and cultural issues, such as the legacy of the Black Power movement, the Israeli-Palestinian conflict, the invisibility of Africa in American political discourse, have created rigid lines of demarcation and distance between black and white intellectuals. Needless to say, black presence in leading liberal journals like the *New York Review of Books* and the *New York Times Book Review* is negligible—nearly nonexistent. And more leftist periodicals such as *Dissent, Socialist Review, the Nation* and *Telos,* or avant-garde scholarly ones like *Diacritics, Salmagundi, Partisan Review* and *Raritan* do not do much better. Only *Monthly Review,* the *Massachusetts Review, Boundary 2* and *Social Text* make persistent efforts to cover black subject matter and have regular black contributors. The point here is not mere finger-pointing at negligent journals (though it would not hurt matters), but rather an attempt to highlight the racially separatist publishing patterns and practices of American intellectual life which are characteristic of the chasm between black and white intellectuals.

Third, the general politicization of American intellectual life (in the academy and outside), along with the rightward ideological drift, constitutes a hostile climate for the making of black intellectuals. To some extent, this has always been so, but the ideological capitulation of a significant segment of former left-liberals to the new-style conservatism and old-style imperialism has left black students and black professors with few allies in the academy and in influential periodicals. This hostile climate requires that black intellectuals fall back upon their own resources—institutions, journals and periodicals—which, in turn, reinforce the de facto racially separatist practices of American intellectual life.

The tragedy of black intellectual activity is that the black institutional support for such activity is in shambles. The quantity and quality of black intellectual exchange is at its worst since the Civil War. There is no major black academic journal; no major black intellectual magazine; no major black periodical of highbrow journalism; not even a major black newspaper of national scope. In short, the black infrastructure for intellectual discourse and dialogue is nearly nonexistent. This tragedy is, in part, the price for integration—which has yielded mere marginal black groups within the professional disciplines of a fragmented academic community. But this tragedy also has to do with the refusal of black intellectuals to establish and sustain their own institutional mechanisms of criticism and self-criticism, organized in such a way that people of whatever color would be able to contribute to them. This refusal over the past decade is significant in that it has lessened the appetite for, and the capacity to withstand, razor-sharp criticism among many black intellectuals whose formative years were passed in a kind of intellectual vacuum. So besides the external hostile climate, the tradition of serious black intellectual activity is also threatened from within.

The creation of an intelligentsia is a monumental task. Yet black churches and colleges, along with white support, served as resources for the first black intellectuals with formal training. The formation of high-quality habits of criticism and international networks of serious intellectual exchange among a relatively isolated and insulated intelligentsia is a gargantuan endeavor. Yet black intellectuals have little choice: either continued intellectual lethargy on the edges of the academy and literate subcultures unnoticed by the black community, or insurgent creative activity on the margins of the mainstream ensconced within bludgeoning new infrastructures.

Black Intellectuals and the Black Community

The paucity of black infrastructures for intellectual activity results, in part, from the inability of black intellectuals to gain respect and support from the black community—and especially the black middle class. In addition to the general anti-intellectual tenor of American society, there is a deep distrust and suspicion of black intellectuals within the black community. This distrust and suspicion stem not simply from the usual arrogant and haughty disposition of intellectuals toward ordinary folk, but, more importantly, from the widespread refusal of black intellectuals to remain, in some visible way, organically linked with African American cultural life. The relatively high rates of exogamous marriage, the abandonment of black institutions and the preoccupation with Euro-American intellectual products are often perceived by the black community as intentional efforts to escape the negative stigma of blackness or are viewed as symptoms of self-hatred. And the minimal immediate impact of black intellectual activity on the black community and American society reinforces common perceptions of the impotence, even uselessness, of black intellectuals. In good American fashion, the black community lauds those black intellectuals who excel as *political activists* and *cultural artists;* the life of the mind is viewed as neither possessing intrinsic virtues nor harboring emancipatory possibilities—solely short-term political gain and social status.

This truncated perception of intellectual activity is widely held by black intellectuals themselves. Given the constraints upon black upward social mobility and the pressures for status and affluence among middle-class peers, many black intellectuals principally seek material gain and cultural prestige. Since these intellectuals are members of an anxiety-ridden and status-hungry black middle class, their proclivities are understandable and, to some extent, justifiable. For most intellectuals are in search of recognition, status, power and often wealth. Yet for black intellectuals this search requires immersing oneself in and addressing oneself to the very culture and society which degrade and devalue the black community from whence one comes. And, to put it crudely, most black intellectuals tend to fall within the two camps created by this predicament: "successful" ones, distant from (and usually condescending toward) the black community, and "unsuccessful" ones, disdainful of the white intellectual world. But both camps remain marginal to the black community—dangling between two worlds with little or no black infrastructural bases. Therefore, the "successful" black intellectual capitulates, often uncritically, to the prevailing paradigms and research programs of the white bourgeois academy, and the "unsuccessful" black intellectual remains encapsulated within the parochial discourses of African American intellectual life. The alternatives of meretricious pseudo-cosmopolitanism and tendentious, cathartic provincialism loom large in the lives of black intellectuals. And the black community views both alternatives with distrust and disdain—and with good reason. Neither alternative has had a positive impact on the black community. The major black intellectuals from W. E. B. Du Bois and St. Clair Drake to Ralph Ellison and Toni Morrison have shunned both alternatives.

This situation has resulted in the major obstacle confronting black intellectuals: the inability to transmit and sustain the requisite institutional mechanisms for the persistence of a discernible intellectual tradition. The racism of American society, the relative lack of black community support, and hence the dangling status of black intellectuals have prevented the creation of a rich heritage of intellectual exchange, intercourse and dialogue. There indeed have been grand black intellectual achievements, but such achievements do not substitute for tradition.

I would suggest that there are two *organic* intellectual traditions in African American life: *the black Christian tradition of preaching* and *the black musical tradition of performance*. Both traditions, though undoubtedly linked to the life of the mind, are oral, improvisational and histrionic. Both traditions are rooted in black life and possess precisely what the literate forms of black intellectual activity lack: institutional matrices over time and space within which there are accepted rules of procedure, criteria for judgment, canons for assessing performance, models of past achievement and present emulation and an acknowledged succession and accumulation of superb accomplishments. The richness, diversity and vitality of the traditions of black preaching and black music stand in strong contrast to the paucity, even poverty, of black literate intellectual production. There simply have been no black literate intellectuals who have mastered their craft commensurate with the achievements of Louis Armstrong, Charlie Parker or Rev. Manuel Scott—just as there are no black literate intellectuals today comparable to Miles Davis, Sarah Vaughn or Rev. Gardner Taylor. This is so not because there have been or are no first-rate black literate intellectuals, but rather because without strong institutional channels to sustain traditions, great achievement is impossible. And, to be honest, black America has yet to produce a great literate intellectual with the exception of Toni Morrison. There indeed have been superb ones— Du Bois, Frazier, Ellison, Baldwin, Hurston—and many good ones. But none can compare to the heights achieved by black preachers and musicians.

What is most troubling about black literate intellectual activity is that as it slowly evolved out of the black Christian tradition and interacted more intimately with secular Euro-American styles and forms, it seemed as if by the latter part of the twentieth century maturation would set in. Yet, as we approach the last few years of this century, black literate intellectual activity has declined in both quantity and quality. As I noted earlier, this is so primarily because of relatively greater black integration into postindustrial capitalist America with its bureaucratized elite universities, dull middlebrow colleges and decaying high schools, which have little concern for or confidence in black students as potential intellectuals. Needless to say, the predicament of the black intellectual is inseparable from that of the black community—especially the black middle-class community—in American society. And only a fundamental transformation of American society can possibly change the situation of the black community and the black intellectual. And though my own Christian skepticism regarding human totalistic schemes for change chastens my deep socialist sentiments regarding radically democratic and libertarian socioeconomic and cultural arrangements, I shall forego these larger issues and focus on more specific ways to enhance the quantity and quality of black literate intellectual activity in the USA. This focus shall take the form of sketching four models for black intellectual activity, with the intent to promote the crystallization of infrastructures for such activity.

The Bourgeois Model: Black Intellectual as Humanist

For black intellectuals, the bourgeois model of intellectual activity is problematic. On the one hand, the racist heritage—aspects of the exclusionary and repressive effects of white academic institutions and humanistic scholarship—puts black intellectuals on the defensive: there is always the need to assert and defend the humanity of black people, including their ability and capacity to reason logically, think coherently and write lucidly. The weight of this inescapable burden for black students in the white academy has often determined the content and character of black intellectual activity. In fact, black intellectual life remains largely preoccupied with such defensiveness, with "successful" black intellectuals often proud of their white approval and "unsuccessful" ones usually scornful of their white rejection. This concern is especially acute among the first generation of black intellectuals accepted as teachers and scholars within elite white universities and colleges, largely a post-1968 phenomenon. Only with the publication of the intimate memoirs of these black intellectuals and their students will we have the gripping stories of how this defensiveness cut at much of the heart of their intellectual activity and creativity within white academic contexts. Yet, however personally painful such battles have been, they had to be fought, given the racist milieu of American intellectual and academic life. These battles will continue, but with far fewer negative consequences for the younger generation because of the struggles by the older black trailblazers.

On the other hand, the state of siege raging in the black community requires that black intellectuals accent the practical dimension of their work. And the prestige and status, as well as the skills and techniques provided by the white bourgeois academy, render it attractive for the task at hand. The accentuation of the practical dimension holds for most black intellectuals regardless of ideological persuasion—even more than for the stereotypical, pragmatic, American intellectual. This is so not simply because of the power-seeking lifestyles and status-oriented dispositions of many black intellectuals, but also because of their relatively small number, which forces them to play multiple roles vis-à-vis the black community and, in addition, intensifies their need for self-vindication—the attempt to justify to themselves that, given such unique opportunities and privileges, they are spending their time as they ought—which often results in activistic and pragmatic interests.

The linchpin of the bourgeois model is academic legitimation and placement. Without the proper certificate, degree and position, the bourgeois model loses its raison d'être. The influence and attractiveness of the bourgeois model permeate the American academic system; yet the effectiveness of the bourgeois model is credible for black intellectuals only if they possess sufficient legitimacy and placement. Such legitimacy and placement will give one access to select networks and contacts which may facilitate black impact on public policies. This seems to have been the aim of the first generation of blacks trained in elite white institutions (though not permitted to teach there), given their predominant interests in the social sciences.

The basic problem with the bourgeois model is that it is existentially and intellectually stultifying for black intellectuals. It is existentially debilitating because it not only generates anxieties of defensiveness on the part of black intellectuals; it also thrives on them. The need for hierarchical ranking and the deep-seated racism shot through bourgeois humanistic scholarship cannot provide black intellectuals with either the proper ethos or conceptual framework to overcome a defensive posture. And charges of intellectual inferiority can never be met upon the opponent's terrain—to try to do so only intensifies one's anxieties. Rather the terrain itself must be viewed as part and parcel of an antiquated form of life unworthy of setting the terms of contemporary discourse.

The bourgeois model sets intellectual limits, in that one is prone to adopt uncritically prevailing paradigms predominant in the bourgeois academy because of the pressures of practical tasks and deferential emulation. Every intellectual passes through some kind of apprenticeship stage in which s/he learns the language and style of the authorities, but when s/he is already viewed as marginally talented s/he may be either excessively encouraged or misleadingly discouraged to examine critically paradigms deemed marginal by the authorities. This hostile environment results in the suppression of one's critical analyses and in the limited use of one's skills in a manner considered legitimate and practical.

Despite its limitations, the bourgeois model is inescapable for most black intellectuals. This is so because most of the important and illuminating discourses in the country take place in white bourgeois academic institutions and because the more significant intellectuals teach in such places. Many of the elite white universities and colleges remain high-powered schools of education, learning and training principally due to large resources and civil traditions that provide the leisure time and atmosphere necessary for sustained and serious intellectual endeavor. So aside from the few serious autodidactic black intellectuals (who often have impressive scope but lack grounding and depth), black intellectuals must pass through the white bourgeois academy (or its black imitators).

Black academic legitimation and placement can provide a foothold in American intellectual life so that black infrastructures for intellectual anxiety can be created. At present, there is a small yet significant black presence within the white bourgeois academic organizations, and it is able to produce newsletters and small periodicals. The next step is to institutionalize more broadly black intellectual presence, as the Society of Black Philosophers of New York has done, by publishing journals anchored in a discipline (crucial for the careers of prospective professors) yet relevant to other disciplines. It should be noted that such a black infrastructure for intellectual activity should attract persons of whatever hue or color. Black literary critics and especially black psychologists are far ahead of other black intellectuals in this regard, with journals such as the *Black American Literature Forum,* the *College Language Association* and the *Journal of Black Psychology.*

Black academic legitimation and placement also can result in black control over a portion of, or significant participation within, the larger white infrastructures for intellectual activity. This has not yet occurred on a broad scale. More black representation is needed on the editorial boards of significant journals so that a larger black intellectual presence is permitted. This process is much slower and has less visibility, yet, given the hegemony of the bourgeois model, it must be pursued by those so inclined.

The bourgeois model is, in some fundamental and ultimate sense, more part of the problem than the solution in regard to black intellectuals. Yet, since we live our lives daily and penultimately within this system, those of us highly critical of the bourgeois model must try to subvert it, in part, from within the white bourgeois academy. For black intellectuals—in alliance with nonblack progressive intellectuals—this means creating and augmenting infrastructures for black intellectual activity.

The Marxist Model: Black Intellectual as Revolutionary

Among many black intellectuals, there is a knee-jerk reaction to the severe limitations of the bourgeois model (and capitalist society)—namely, to adopt the Marxist model. This adoption satisfies certain basic needs of the black intelligentsia: the need for social relevance, political engagement and organizational involvement. The Marxist model also provides entry into the least xenophobic white intellectual subculture available to black intellectuals.

The Marxist model privileges the activity of black intellectuals and promotes their prophetic role. As Harold Cruse has noted, such privileging is highly circumscribed and rarely accents the theoretical dimension of black intellectual activity. In short, the Marxist privileging of black intellectuals often reeks of condescension that confines black prophetic roles to spokespersons and organizers; only rarely are they allowed to function as creative thinkers who warrant serious critical attention. It is no accident that the relatively large numbers of black intellectuals attracted to Marxism over the past sixty years have yet to produce a major black Marxist theoretician with the exception of C. L. R. James. Only W. E. B. Du Bois's *Black Reconstruction* (1935), Oliver Cox's *Caste, Class and Race* (1948) and, to some degree, Harold Cruse's *The Crisis of the Negro Intellectual* (1967) are even candidates for such a designation. This is so not because of the absence of black intellectual talent in the Marxist camp but rather because of the absence of the kind of tradition and community (including intense critical exchange) that would allow such talent to flower.

In stark contrast to the bourgeois model, the Marxist model neither generates black intellectual defensiveness nor provides an adequate analytical apparatus for short-term public policies. Rather the Marxist model yields black intellectual self-satisfaction which often inhibits growth; it also highlights social structural constraints with little practical direction regarding conjunctural opportunities. This self-satisfaction results in either dogmatic submission to and upward mobility within sectarian party or preparty formations or marginal placement in the bourgeois academy equipped with cantankerous Marxist rhetoric and sometimes insightful analysis utterly divorced from the integral dynamics, concrete realities and progressive possibilities of the black community. The preoccupation with social structural constraints tends to produce either preposterous chiliastic projections or paralyzing pessimistic pronouncements. Such projections and pronouncements have as much to do with the self-image of black Marxist intellectuals as with the prognosis for black liberation.

It is often claimed "that Marxism is the false consciousness of the radicalized, bourgeois intelligentsia." For black intellectuals, the Marxist model functions in a more complex manner than this glib formulation permits. On the one hand, the Marxist model is liberating for black intellectuals in that it promotes critical consciousness and attitudes toward the dominant bourgeois paradigms and research programs. Marxism provides attractive roles for black intellectuals—usually highly visible leadership roles—and infuses new meaning and urgency into their work. On the other hand, the Marxist model is debilitating for black intellectuals because the cathartic needs it satisfies tend to stifle the further development of black critical consciousness and attitudes.

The Marxist model, despite its shortcomings, is more part of the solution than part of the problem for black intellectuals. This is so because Marxism is the brook of fire—the purgatory—of our postmodern times. Black intellectuals must pass through it, come to terms with it, and creatively respond to it if black intellectual activity is to reach any recognizable level of sophistication and refinement.

The Foucaultian Model: Black Intellectual as Postmodern Skeptic

As Western intellectual life moves more deeply into crisis and as black intellectuals become more fully integrated into intellectual life—or into "the culture of careful and critical discourse" (as the late Alvin Gouldner called it)—a new model appears on the horizon. This model, based primarily upon the influential work of the late Michel Foucault, unequivocably rejects the bourgeois model and eschews the Marxist model. It constitutes one of the most exciting intellectual challenges of our day: the Foucaultian project of historical nominalism. This detailed investigation into the complex relations of knowledge and power, discourses and politics, cognition and social control compels intellectuals to rethink and redefine their self-image and function in our contemporary situation.

The Foucaultian model and project are attractive to black intellectuals primarily because they speak to the black postmodern predicament, defined by the rampant xenophobia of bourgeois humanism predominant in the whole academy, the waning attraction to orthodox reductionist and scientific versions of Marxism, and the need for reconceptualization regarding the specificity and complexity of African American oppression. Foucault's deep antibourgeois sentiments, explicit post-Marxist convictions and profound preoccupations with those viewed as radically "Other" by dominant discourses and traditions are quite seductive for politicized black intellectuals wary of antiquated panaceas for black liberation.

Foucault's specific analyses of the "political economy of truth"—the study of the discursive ways in which and institutional means by which "regimes of truth" are constituted by societies over space and time—result in a new conception of the intellectual. This conception no longer rests upon the smooth transmittance of "the best that has been thought and said," as in the bourgeois humanist model, nor on the engaged utopian energies of the Marxist model. Rather the postmodern situation requires "the specific intellectual" who shuns the labels of scientificity, civility and prophecy and instead delves into the specificity of the political, economic and cultural matrices within which regimes of truth are produced, distributed, circulated and consumed. No longer should intellectuals deceive themselves by believing—as do humanist and Marxist intellectuals—that they are struggling "on behalf" of the truth; rather the problem is the struggle over the very status of truth and the vast institutional mechanisms which account for this status. The favored code words of "science," "taste," "tact," "ideology," "progress" and "liberation" of bourgeois humanism and Marxism are no longer applicable to the self-image of postmodern intellectuals. Instead, the new key terms become those of "regime of truth," "power/knowledge" and "discursive practices."

Foucault's notion of the specific intellectual rests upon his demystification of conservative, liberal and Marxist rhetorics which restore, resituate and reconstruct intellectuals' self-identities so that they remain captive to and supportive of institutional forms of domination and control. These rhetorics authorize and legitimate, in different ways, the privileged status of intellectuals, which not only reproduces ideological divisions between intellectual and manual labor but also reinforces disciplinary mechanisms of subjection and subjugation. This self-authorizing is best exemplified in the claims made by intellectuals that they "safeguard" the achievement of highbrow culture or "represent" the "universal interests" of particular classes and groups. In African American intellectual history, similar self-authorizing claims such as "the talented tenth," "prophets in the wilderness," "articulators of a black aesthetic," "creators of a black renaissance" and "vanguard of a revolutionary movement" are widespread.

The Foucaultian model promotes a leftist form of postmodern skepticism; that is, it encourages an intense and incessant interrogation of power-laden discourses in the service of neither restoration, reformation nor revolution, but rather of revolt. And the kind of revolt enacted by intellectuals consists of the disrupting and dismantling of prevailing "regimes of truth"—including their repressive effects—of present-day societies. This model suits the critical, skeptical, and historical concerns of progressive black intellectuals and provides a sophisticated excuse for ideological and social distance from insurgent black movements for liberation. By conceiving intellectual work as oppositional political praxis, it satisfies the leftist self-image of black intellectuals, and, by making a fetish of critical consciousness, it encapsulates black intellectual activity within the comfortable bourgeois academy of postmodern America.

The Insurgency Model: Black Intellectual as Critical Organic Catalyst

Black intellectuals can learn much from each of the three previous models, yet should not uncritically adopt any one of them. This is so because the bourgeois, Marxist and Foucaultian models indeed relate to, but do not adequately speak to, the uniqueness of the black intellectual predicament. This uniqueness remains relatively unexplored, and will remain so until black intellectuals articulate a new "regime of truth" linked to, yet not confined by, indigenous institutional practices permeated by the kinetic orality and emotional physicality, the rhythmic syncopation, the protean improvisation and the religious, rhetorical and antiphonal repetition of African American life. Such articulation depends, in part, upon elaborate black infrastructures which put a premium on creative and cultivated black thought; it also entails intimate knowledge of prevailing Euro-American "regimes of truth" which must be demystified, deconstructed and decomposed in ways which enhance and enrich future black intellectual life. The new "regime of truth" to be pioneered by black thinkers is neither a hermetic discourse (or set of discourses), which safeguards mediocre black intellectual production, nor the latest fashion of black writing, which is often motivated by the desire to parade for the white bourgeois intellectual establishment. Rather it is inseparable from the emergence of new cultural forms which prefigure (and point toward) a post-Western civilization. At present, such talk may seem mere dream and fantasy. So we shall confine ourselves to the first step: black insurgency and the role of the black intellectual.

The major priority of black intellectuals should be the creation or reactivation of institutional networks that promote high-quality critical habits primarily for the purpose of black insurgency. An intelligentsia without institutionalized critical consciousness is blind, and critical consciousness severed from collective insurgency is empty. The central task of postmodern black intellectuals is to stimulate, hasten and enable alternative perceptions and practices by dislodging prevailing discourses and powers. This can be done only by intense intellectual work and engaged insurgent praxis.

The insurgency model for black intellectual activity builds upon, yet goes beyond, the previous three models. From the bourgeois model, it recuperates the emphasis on human will and heroic effort. Yet the insurgency model refuses to conceive of this will and effort in individualistic and elitist terms. Instead of the solitary hero, embattled exile and isolated genius—the intellectual as star, celebrity, commodity—this model privileges collective intellectual work that contributes to communal resistance and struggle. In other words, it creatively accents the voluntarism and heroism of the bourgeois model, but it rejects the latter's naiveté about the role of society and history. From the Marxist model it recovers the stress on structural constraints, class formations and radical democratic values. Yet the insurgency model does not view these constraints, formations and values in economistic and deterministic terms. Instead of the a priori privileging of the industrial working class and the metaphysical positing of a relatively harmonious socialist society, there is the wholesale assault on varieties of social hierarchy and the radical democratic (and libertarian) mediation, not elimination, of social heterogeneity. In short, the insurgency model ingeniously incorporates the structural, class and democratic concerns of the Marxist model, yet it acknowledges the latter's naiveté about culture.

Lastly, from the Foucaultian model, the insurgency model recaptures the preoccupation with worldly skepticism, the historical constitution of "regimes of truth," and the multifarious operations of "power/knowledge." Yet the insurgency model does not confine this skepticism, this truth-constituting and detailed genealogical inquiry to micronetworks of power. Instead of the ubiquity of power (which simplifies and flattens multidimensional social conflict) and the paralyzing overreaction to past utopianisms, there is the possibility of effective resistance and meaningful societal transformation. The insurgency model carefully highlights the profound Nietzschean suspicion and the illuminating oppositional descriptions of the Foucaultian model, though it recognizes the latter's naiveté about social conflict, struggle and insurgency—a naiveté primarily caused by the rejection of any form of utopianism and any positing of a telos.

Black intellectual work and black collective insurgency must be rooted in the specificity of African American life and history; but they also are inextricably linked to the American, European and African elements which shape and mold them. Such work and insurgency are explicitly particularist though not exclusivist—hence they are international in outlook and practice. Like their historical forerunners, black preachers and black musical artists (with all their strengths and weaknesses), black intellectuals must realize that the creation of "new" and alternative practices results from the heroic efforts of collective intellectual work and communal resistance which shape and are shaped by present structural constraints, workings of power and modes of cultural fusion. The distinctive African American cultural forms such as the black sermonic and prayer styles, gospel, blues and jazz should inspire, but not constrain, future black intellectual production; that is, the process by which they came to be should provide valuable insights, but they should serve as models neither to imitate nor emulate. Needless to say, these forms thrive on incessant critical innovation and concomitant insurgency.

The Future of the Black Intellectual

The predicament of the black intellectual need not be grim and dismal. Despite the pervasive racism of American society and anti-intellectualism of the black community, critical space and insurgent activity can be expanded. This expansion will occur more readily when black intellectuals take a more candid look at themselves, the historical and social forces that shape them, and the limited though significant resources of the community from whence they come. A critical "self-inventory" that scrutinizes the social positions, class locations and cultural socializations of black intellectuals is imperative. Such scrutiny should be motivated by neither self-pity nor self-satisfaction. Rather this "self-inventory" should embody the sense of critique and resistance applicable to the black community, American society and Western civilization as a whole. James Baldwin has noted that the black intellectual is "a kind of bastard of the West." The future of the black intellectual lies neither in a deferential disposition toward the Western parent nor a nostalgic search for the African one. Rather it resides in a critical negation, wise preservation and insurgent transformation of this black lineage which protects the earth and projects a better world.

Philosophy and
Political Engagement

6

Theory, Pragmatisms and Politics

Pragmatism has emerged within contemporary literary criticism in relation to two fundamental issues: the role of theory and the vocation of the humanistic intellectual. The most influential pragmatic literary critics such as Stanley Fish and Frank Lentricchia are masterful mappers; that is, they clearly situate and sort out various positions in the current debate and give some idea of what is at stake. Masterful mappers in the pragmatic grain such as Richard Rorty's illuminating narratives about modern philosophy are demythologizers. To demythologize is to render contingent and provisional what is widely considered to be necessary and permanent. Yet to demythologize is not to demystify. To demystify—the primary mode of critical theory—is to lay bare the complex ways in which meaning is produced and mobilized for the maintenance of relations of domination.[1]

Demythologization is a *mapping* activity that reconstructs and redescribes forms of signification for the purpose of situating them in the dynamic flow of social practices. Demystification is a *theoretical* activity that attempts to give explanations that account for the role and function of specific social practices. Both activities presuppose and promote profound historical consciousness—that is, awareness of the fragile and fragmented character of social practices—but demythologization leaves open the crucial issues of the role of theory and the vocation of the humanistic intellectual. In sharp contrast, demystification gives theory a prominent role and the intellectual a political task. Needless to say, sophisticated demystifiers neither consider theory as an attempt "to stand outside practice in order to govern practice from without"[2] nor view the political task of intellectuals to be the mere articulation of a theoretical enterprise. The former assumes a rather naive conception of theory, and the latter presupposes that theory is inherently oppositional and emancipatory. Rather, appropriate forms of demystification subsume the pragmatic lessons of demythologization, preserve a crucial role for theory as a social practice, and highlight how modes of interpretation "serve to sustain social relations which are asymmetrical with regard to the organization of power."[3]

In a renowned essay, Arthur O. Lovejoy examined the difficulty of defining the often used yet slippery rubric "romanticism."[4] In a less well-known paper, Lovejoy put forward thirteen different varieties of "pragmatism."[5] I suggest that we map the versions of pragmatism on the current scene in reference to three major axes: namely, the levels of philosophy, theory and politics. The philosophical level highlights various perspectives regarding epistemological foundations and ontological commitments; the theoretical level, attitudes toward the possibility for or role of theory; and the political level, the vocation of the humanistic intellectual.

All pragmatists are epistemic antifoundationalists, though not all epistemic antifoundationalists are pragmatists. To be an epistemic antifoundationalist is simply to agree with the now familiar claims that "all interpretation is value laden," "there are no unmediated facts," "there is no such thing as a neutral observation language," and so on. One may unpack these assertions in various ways, with the help of Hegel, Nietzsche, Derrida, Quine, Davidson, Goodman, Wittgenstein or Rorty, but it means that one gives up on the notion that epistemic justification terminates in something other than social practice.

Yet not all pragmatists are ontological antirealists. To be a realist is principally to be worried about the bottomless pit of relativism. Therefore philosophical restraints and regulations are set in place to ward off an "anything goes" ontological position. Conservative pragmatists such as Charles Sanders Peirce and Hilary Putnam (in his present incarnation) put forward limiting processes and procedures to ensure that some notion of scientific objectivity (grounded in social practices) is preserved. For Peirce, this means conceiving truth as whatever results in the long run are reached by the unending community of inquirers who deploy a reliable method based on deduction, induction and, to some degree, inference to the best explanation. Putnam builds on Peirce by affirming the need for constraints yet allowing for the proliferation of methods of inquiry and styles of reasoning. Therefore Putnam promotes two limiting processes: the long-term results of a dominant style of reasoning among inquirers who pull from accumulated modes of thinking, and the long-term results of the facts produced by this dominant style of reasoning yielded by evolving kinds of thinking.[6] In this sense, conservative pragmatists like Peirce and Putnam are "regulative realists" in that "reality" is what inquirers agree on owing to rational canons that regulate and restrain inquirers.

Moderate pragmatists such as John Dewey and William James are not worried about relativism. They are minimalist realists in order to shun the position of idealism but remain more concerned with the plurality of versions of "reality." Like Peirce and Putnam, they put a premium on restraints and regulations yet do so not with the intention of privileging scientific objectivity but rather with the aim of noting how different forms of rational deliberation achieve their respective goals. In this way, the notion of scientific objectivity is not rejected; it simply becomes a self-complimenting term for a particular community who excel at explaining and predicting experience. The notions of inquiry and experimentation remain crucial but only insofar as they promote self-critical and self-correcting enterprises in the varieties of human activities, be they in sciences, arts or everyday life.

Avant-garde pragmatists such as Richard Rorty not only jettison anxieties about relativism but also adopt a thoroughgoing antirealism. Rorty's concern here is not to ensure that restraints and regulations are in place, as they always already are, but to explode these restraints and regulations for the edifying purpose of creating new vocabularies of self-description and self-creation. For Rorty, these transgressions—Kuhnian paradigm shifts—consist of new and novel moves in the ongoing conversation of intellectuals.

For most literary critics, these philosophical differences within the pragmatist camp are mere intramural affairs with little relevance. This is so because once one adopts the epistemic antifoundationalist position, the issue of ontological realism or antirealism primarily concerns whether the language of physicists actually refers or not; that is, the terrain is confined to the philosophy of science. Yet this philosophical debate does pertain indirectly to literary critics in that the status, role and function of restraints and regulations relate to the fundamental issues of objectivity and relativism in literary hermeneutics.

The obsessive concern with theory in literary criticism has much to do with the status, role and function of restraints and regulations in literary interpretation after a rather widespread agreement on epistemic antifoundationalism. The unsettling impact on literary studies of Derrida, de Man, Foucault, Said, Jameson, Showalter, Baker and others is not that relativism reigns, as old-style humanists tend to put it, but rather that disagreement reigns as to what the appropriate restraints and regulations for ascertaining the meanings of texts ought to be after epistemic antifoundationalism is accepted. To put it another way, the debate over the consequences of theory emerged not as a means of settling upon the right restraints and regulations outside of practice in a foundationalist manner, as Steven Knapp and Walter Benn Michaels misleadingly view it, but rather as a way of rendering explicit the discursive space or conversational activity now made legitimate owing to widespread acceptance of epistemic antifoundationalism. This hegemony of epistemic anti-foundationalism in the literary academy has pushed critics in the direction of historicism and skepticism.

At the level of theory, there are moderate pragmatists such as

Knapp and Michaels who are against theory because they see the theoretical enterprise as a cover for new forms of epistemic foundationalism—as attempts to "occupy a position outside practice."[7] Unfortunately, they view theory as *grand theory* and consider practice as close reading in search of agential-inscribed intentions, and thereby truncate the debate on the consequences of theory.

On the other hand, there are proponents of grand theory such as Fredric Jameson who associate pragmatism with this antitheory stance, who deny that grand theorists must locate theory outside social practice and who insist that historicist forms of demystification are preferable to limited historicist forms of demythologization. For Jameson, only grand theory of a certain sort can provide the adequate explanatory model for detecting the role and function of literary meanings in relation to larger developments and happenings in society and history.

Between these two positions lurk ultratheorists like Frank Lentricchia, Paul Bové and Jonathan Arac who acknowledge the indispensability of theory, especially the insights of Marxists and feminists, yet who also shun the option of grand theory. Following exemplary ultratheorists—Michel Foucault and Edward Said—who move skillfully between theory and politics, Lentricchia, Bové and Arac stand at the crossroads of history and rhetoric, at the intersection of the operations of institutional powers and the operations of linguistic figures and tropes.

All pragmatists are against grand theory, but not all pragmatists need be against theory. Lentricchia, who describes himself loosely as a "dialectical rhetorician" drawing from pragmatism,[8] must be challenged when he asserts that

> to be a pragmatist is in a sense to have no theory—and having a position requires having a theory. The liberating, critical move of pragmatism against the "antecedent" is compromised by its inability—built into the position of pragmatism as such—to say clearly what it wants for the future. Though not practice for its

own sake, pragmatism cannot say what practice should be aimed at without ceasing to be pragmatism, without violating its reverence for experimental method.[9]

This critique, echoing that of Randolph Bourne more than half a century ago, holds only for certain crude versions of pragmatism which have not adequately confronted the ideological and political issue concerning the vocation of humanistic intellectuals.

This issue of vocation is a political and ideological one even though it surfaces in our time as a discourse about professionalism.

The term "vocation" is rather unpopular these days in academic circles principally owing to the predominance of words like "profession" and "career." Yet I suggest that recent historical investigations into the rise of professionalism and sociological inquiries into the content and character of careerism require that we rethink, revise and retain a notion of vocation. Such a notion must not presuppose that we have an unmediated access to truth nor assume that we must preserve a pristine tradition free of ideological contamination. Rather we live at a particular historical moment in which a serious interrogation regarding "vocations" of intellectuals and academicians in American society can contribute to *a more enabling and empowering sense of the moral and political dimensions of our functioning in the present-day academy.* To take seriously one's vocation as an intellectual is to justify in moral and political terms why one pursues a rather privileged life of the mind in a world that seems to require forms of more direct and urgent action.

Allan Bloom's bestseller, *The Closing of the American Mind*— a nostalgic and, for some, seductive depiction of the decline and decay of the highbrow, classical, humanist tradition—and Russell Jacoby's provocative book, *The Last Intellectuals*—a premature requiem for left public intellectuals—are both emblematic symptoms of the crisis in vocation of contemporary intellectuals. The professionalization, specialization and bureaucratization of academic knowledge-forms has become a kind of deus ex machina in discussions about the crises of purpose among the humanistic intelligentsia. Yet even these noteworthy developments, along with others such as the intensified commodification of intellectuals themselves and the reification of intellectual conversation, fail to capture crucial features of the lived experience of many intellectuals in the academy. If we take Bloom, Jacoby and others at their word, the lives of many academic intellectuals are characterized by *demoralization, marginalization* and *irrelevance.*

Demoralization results from a variety of reasons, but the primary ones consist of what Roberto Unger has called the "Downbeat Alexandrian Cynicism" of the American academy, in which the obsession with status often overshadows the preoccupation with substance, and the naked operations of power are usually masked behind a thin veil of civility. Needless to say, demoralization takes forms among the tenured facility different from those among the untenured ones, with the former often fearful of becoming mere deadwood and the latter usually mindful of being too creative (adventurous). It is important to keep in mind that most serious intellectuals today become academics by default; that is, they simply cannot pursue the life of the mind anywhere but in the academy and maintain upper-middle-class life-styles that provide leisure time. Self-invested, hedonistic indulgence in precious moments of reading, lecturing, writing and conversing indeed occurs alongside the demoralization of many academic intellectuals. Yet few intellectuals would justify their activity on sheer hedonistic grounds. Most would candidly acknowledge the pleasure of their intellectual work yet cast the justification of this work on a higher moral and political ground. And it is precisely this ground that seems to be slipping away.

For example, the increasing marginalization of humanistic studies in the academy, primarily due to the popularity of business schools and computer studies, is depriving many intellectuals of their "higher" moral and political reasons for remaining in the academy, for they can no longer claim that they train the best and the brightest undergraduates in order to preserve the best that has been thought and known in the world, or hold to what Richard Rorty has called the "Cynical Prudential Strategy" of academic humanists which says to American society: "You let us have your gifted children for our universities, where we will estrange them from you and keep the best ones for ourselves. In return, we will send the second-best back to keep you supplied with technology, entertainment and soothing presidential lies."[10]

In the past few decades, it is clear that most of the "best ones" have not gone into the humanities or politics but rather into the private sphere of quick money-making, be it in business, legal or medical enterprises. This has resulted not simply in a relative brain drain in humanistic studies but also in a sense that humanistic intellectuals are missing out on where the "real action" is. This situation is compounded by ideological dynamics; that is, those students most attracted to humanistic studies tend to be those of a slightly more left-liberal bent, in part due to a revulsion against a boring life of money-making and rat-racing. As a result, many students and faculty (especially younger faculty) find themselves rather averse to a pecuniary-oriented life-style on moral and ideological grounds yet compelled to spell out to themselves and others the *political relevance* of their academic life-styles; and yet the sense persists that what they are doing is, in large part, irrelevant. I shall put forward my response to this situation in the form of an examination of the three major vocational models of intellectual work. I will highlight the blindness and insights, strengths and weaknesses of these models. Then I shall suggest that a more acceptable model may be on the horizon.

Before specifying what these models are, I think it instructive to mention briefly the most influential and celebrated literary theorist of our time, the late Paul de Man. In fact, his little book *The Resistance to Theory* (1986) is an appropriate starting place for considering the complex relation of the vocational and the theoretical. Furthermore, to render invisible his enormous presence and challenge in our discussion, especially given the recent revelations of his youthful anti-Semitic writings, is to impoverish the discussion. It is always sad to discover that one of the most engaging minds of one's time succumbed years ago to one of the most pernicious prejudices of our century. Yet it only reminds us that even the finest of intellects must breathe the polluted air of any zeitgeist. And few escape some degree of moral asphyxiation. To use this profound moral lapse to downplay de Man's later insights is sophomoric, just as to overlook it in the name of these insights is idolatrous.

I am interested here in de Man's sense of vocation as an intellectual. I would go as far as to suggest that what separated de Man as a literary theorist from his contemporaries—besides his prodigious talent, intense discipline and cautious scholarship—was his dogged single-mindedness regarding his conception of himself as an intellectual. To put it boldly, de Man seemed never to waver in viewing himself as a philological scholar, as one dedicated and devoted to a critical discourse that examines the rhetorical devices of language. For de Man, the vocation of the literary intellectual was to stay attuned to the multifarious operations of tropes in language, especially literary language, which are in no way reducible to religious, moral, political or ideological quests for wholeness and harmony. His aim was to push to the limits, by means of high-powered rigor and precision, the inherent inability to control meaning even as we inescapably quest for it. His kind of philological scholarship revealed the various ways in which "simultaneous asymmetry" is shot through the semantic operations of language.

De Man's viewpoint is not a simple relativism in which epistemic restraints and regulations are nonexistent, but is rather a tortuous rendering of how such restraints and regulations ineluctably fail to contain transgressions. His perspective is not a form of idealism in that it is grounded in the material practices of language using decentered subjects, that is, human bodies who try to generate meanings by way of speech and texts. It is rather a version of linguistic materialism which focuses narrowly on select conditions under which meaning is both produced and undone.

For de Man, theory is an integral part of one's vocation as an intellectual. He paradoxically argued that theory is inescapable yet unable to sustain itself as theory owing to its self-undermining character—a character that yields more theory only to be resisted by means of more theory. This theoretical resistance to theory could not but be shot through with ideology, a focus de Man was deepening before his death.

De Man's formulations may be persuasive or unpersuasive. My aim here is neither to explicate them nor defend them, but rather to note how a clear sense of one's vocation shapes a project—one that seizes the imagination of a generation of critics. The loss of Paul de Man, his authorizing and legitimizing intellectual presence, intensified the crisis of vocation among humanistic intellectuals. Some simply abandoned his challenge. Others tried to follow but found the going too tough. Many slavishly jumped from one bandwagon to the other, often dictated by market forces and personal inertia with little sense of how positions enrich or impoverish the sense of what we are about, who we are, and why we do what we do. It strikes me that much of the attraction to Foucault and Said is due to the fact that they grapple with vocational questions as part and parcel of their critical practice. In addition, much of the hoopla about the new pragmatism and new historicism—even as we leave most of the formidable challenges of de Man unmet—has to do with the hunger for vocational purpose in the profession.

In the current and rather confused discussion about vocation and intellectual work, three major models loom large. First, there is the *oppositional professional intellectual* model, which claims that we must do political work where we are in the academy. This model encompasses liberals who call for cultivating critical sensibilities; Marxists such as Jim Merod, who promote a revolutionary trade union of oppositional critics; and leftists such as Paul Bové, who envision an unceasing attack on the reigning "regimes of truth" with no humanist illusions about "truth" or "revolution." Second, there is the *professional political intellectual* model, which encourages academicians to intervene in the public conversation of the nation regarding some of the most controversial issues as citizens who bring their professional status and expertise to bear in a political manner. The outstanding exemplar of this model is Edward Said, although people such as Catherine MacKinnon and William Julius Wilson also come to mind. The last model is that of the *oppositional intellectual groupings within the academy,* which seek to create, sustain and expand intellectual subcultures inside the university networks, usually with little success at gaining visibility and potency in the larger culture and society. The pertinent figures here would be Fredric Jameson, Elaine Showalter and Houston Baker, namely leading Marxist, feminist, and African American critics who remain thoroughly inscribed in the academy and have successfully colonized legitimate space for their oppositional agendas. Analogues can be found in the critical legal studies movement in law schools and the liberation theology subgroups in seminaries.[11]

Each of these models is regulated by a dominant theoretical orientation. The guiding spirit behind the first model is that of the late Michel Foucault. It is, I conjecture, the most attractive model for young aspiring oppositional humanistic intellectuals, although it may fade quickly in the coming years. To put it crudely, Foucault admonishes intellectuals to scrutinize the specific local contexts in which they work and highlight the complex operations of power which produce and perpetuate the kind of styles and standards, curriculum and committees, the proliferation of jargon and the relative absence of comic high spirits in the academy. Foucault holds that different societies preserve and reproduce themselves in part by encouraging intellectuals to be unmindful of how they are socialized and acculturated into prevailing "regimes of truth"; that is, intellectuals often remain uncritical of the very culture of critical discourse they inhabit and thereby fail to inquire into why they usually remain within the parameters of what is considered "legitimate," "tactful," "civil" discourse. Furthermore, Foucault suggests that this failure leads intellectuals often to overlook the ways in which these mainstream (or malestream) discourses construct identities and constitute forms of subjectivity that devalue and degrade, harm and harass those who are viewed as other, alien, marginal and abnormal owing to these discourses.

The basic insight of this model is that it rightly understands the academy to be an important terrain for political and ideological contestation; and because it grasps the degree to which knowledges are forms of power in societies, this model correctly views battles over the kind of knowledge produced in the academy as forms of political practice. The major shortcoming of this model is that it feeds on an excessive pessimism regarding the capacity of oppositional intellectuals to break out of the local academic context and make links with nonacademic groups and organizations. This viewpoint is echoed in Jim Merod's noteworthy text *The Political Responsibility of the Critic:*

> Right now and for the imaginable future we have no intellectual, professional, or political base for alliances between radical theorists and dispossessed people. . . . It seems, therefore, that the concrete political means to build an intellectual coalition of professional and nonprofessional groups are not available.[12]

Yet the overriding theoretical perspective of the second model, that of Edward Said, calls this excessive pessimism into question. Motivated by the historical voluntarism of Vico, the antidogmatic sense of engagement of R. P. Blackmur and the subversive worldliness of Antonio Gramsci, Said stands now as the towering figure among left humanistic intellectuals. Said creatively appropriates Gramsci's notions of hegemony and elaboration in light of his own ideas of filiation and affiliation. For Said, intellectuals are always already implicated in incessant battles in their own local academic contexts. Yet these contexts themselves are part of a larger process of mobilizing and manufacturing a dynamic "consent" of subaltern peoples to their subordination by means of the exercise of moral, cultural and political leadership. Following Gramsci, Said acknowledges that neither force nor coercion is principally responsible for the widespread depoliticization and effective subordination of the populace. Instead, the particular ways of life and ways of struggle, values and sensibilities, moods and manners, structures of seeings and structures of feelings promoted by schools, churches, radio, television and films primarily account for the level of political and moral consciousness in our country. And intellectuals of various sorts—teachers, preachers, journalists, artists, professors—play a partisan role in this never-ceasing struggle.

This model is instructive in that it leads academic intellectuals outside the academy and into the more popular magazines and mass media; and for Said, it has led to the White House (meeting with George Schultz) due to the unprecedented heroic resistance of Palestinians on the West Bank and Gaza Strip against the inhumane treatments and pernicious policies of the conservative Israeli government. Such public interventions by academic intellectuals (especially that of left intellectuals) broaden the political possibilities for present-day intellectual work. The recent example of Yale's Paul Kennedy (*The Rise and Fall of the Great Powers: Economic Change and Military Conflict from 1500 to 2000*) is worth noting in this regard.

The major shortcomings of this model are first, that the public intervention of select intellectual celebrities gives even more authority and legitimacy to their academic professions, owing to the status of the expert; and second, that the scope of the public intervention is usually rather narrow, that is, confined to one issue with little chance of making connections to other issues. In this way, the very way in which one is a political intellectual promotes academic respectability, careerist individualism and a highly confined terrain of political maneuvering.

The last model—of oppositional intellectual groupings within the academy constituting vital subcultures for space and resources—accents the crucial issues of *community* and *camaraderie* in left intellectual work. Unlike conservative intellectuals who have access to well-funded think tanks, foundations and institutes, progressive academics must gather within the liberal universities and colleges and thereby adjust their agendas to the powers that be for survival and sustenance. The grand contribution of the Fredric Jamesons, Elaine Showalters and Henry Louis Gates, Jrs., has been to bombard the academy with texts, students and programs that ride the tide of intellectual interest in—and political struggle influenced by—Marxism, feminism, and African American studies. This model surely signifies the academization of Marxism, feminism and black studies, with the concomitant problems this entails. Yet it also constitutes noteworthy efforts of left community-building among academics in relatively anti-Marxist, patriarchal and racist environments, in regard to the academy and the larger American culture and society.

Yet the major challenges of this model, namely the spilling over of Marxist, feminist and black studies into working-class, women's and black communities, remain unmet; and without significant social motion, momentum and ultimately movements, this situation will remain relatively the same. The crucial questions facing progressive humanistic intellectuals are how to help generate the conditions and circumstances of such social motion, momentum and movements that move society in more democratic and free directions. How to bring more power and pressure to bear on the status quos so as to enhance the life chances of the jobless and homeless, landless and luckless, empower degraded and devalued working people, and increase the quality of life for all?

I suggest that these challenging queries can be answered through a conception of the intellectual as a critical organic catalyst. This conception requires that the intellectual function inside the academy, principally in order to survive and stay attuned to the most sophisticated reflections about the past, present and future destinies of the relevant cultures, economies and states of our time. This conception also entails that the intellectual be grounded outside the academy: in progressive political organizations and cultural institutions of the most likely agents of social change in America, for example, those of black and brown people, organized workers, women, lesbians and gays. This model pushes academic intellectuals beyond contestation within the academy—be it the important struggles over standards and curriculum or institutionalizing oppositional subcultures—and links this contestation with political activity in grass-roots organizations, pre-party formations, or progressive associations intent on bringing together potential agents of social change. In this sense, to be an engaged progressive intellectual is to be a critical organic catalyst whose vocation is to fuse the best of the life of the mind from within the academy with the best of the organized forces for greater democracy and freedom from outside the academy. This model is neither a panacea for the crisis of vocation of humanistic intellectuals nor a solution to the relation of academics to grass-roots organizing. Rather it is a candid admission that this may be simply the best one can do in the present situation, a situation that can change in the near future depending in part on what some intellectuals do.

This primacy of the vocational has much to do with pragmatism, in that pragmatism began and prospered due in part to a new conception of the vocation of the humanistic intellectual in America at the turn of the century. Although initiated by that reclusive genius Charles Sanders Peirce, pragmatism served as a beacon for intellectuals under the leadership of William James and John Dewey. Similar to the attraction to Marxism among serious European thinkers at the time (and Third World intellectuals in our time), pragmatism gave many American intellectuals a sense of political purpose and moral orientation. At its worst, it became a mere ideological cloak for corporate liberalism and managerial social engineering which served the long-term interests of American capital; at its best, it survived as a form of cultural critique and social reform at the service of expanding the scope of democratic process and broadening the arena of individual self-development here and abroad. The story of the rise and fall of American pragmatism is a fascinating one—one that I try to tell elsewhere.[13] Yet the resurgence of pragmatism in our time will be even more impoverished and impotent if the vocational questions are jettisoned.

My own kind of pragmatism—what I call prophetic pragmatism—is closely akin to the philosophy of praxis put forward by Antonio Gramsci. The major difference is that my attitude toward Marxism as a grand theory is heuristic rather than dogmatic. Furthermore, my focus on the theoretical development in emerging forms of oppositional thought—feminist theory, antiracist theory, gay and lesbian theory—leads me to posit or look for not an overarching synthesis but rather an articulated assemblage of analytical outlooks, to further more morally principled and politically effective forms of action to ameliorate the plight of the wretched of the earth.

On the philosophical level, this means adopting the moderate pragmatic views of John Dewey. Epistemic antifoundationalism and minimalist ontological realism (in its pluralist version) proceed from taking seriously the impact of modern historical and rhetorical consciousness on truth and knowledge. "Anything goes" relativism and disenabling forms of skepticism fall by the wayside, serving only as noteworthy reminders to avoid dogmatic traps and to accept intellectual humility rather than as substantive philosophical positions.

On the level of theory, to be against theory per se is to be against inquiry into heuristic posits regarding the institutional and individual causes of alterable forms of human misery and human suffering, just as uncritical allegiance to grand theories can blind one from seeing and examining kinds of human oppression. Therefore I adopt strategic attitudes toward the use and deployment of theory, a position more charitable toward grand theory than are the ultra-theorists and more suspicious of grand theory than are the grand theorists themselves.

Lastly, at the level of politics and ideology, I envision the intellectual as a critical organic catalyst, one who brings the most subtle and sophisticated analytical tools to bear to explain and illuminate how structures of domination and effects of individual choices in language and in nondiscursive institutions operate. The social location of this activity is the space wherein everyday affairs of ordinary people intersect with possible political mobilization and existential empowerment, for example, in churches, schools, trade unions and movements. The moral aim and political goal of such intellectual activity are the creation of greater individual freedom in culture and broader democracy in the economy and society. In this sense, the consequences of my own intervention into the debate over the consequences of theory are understood as being explicitly though not exclusively political.

7

Pragmatism and the Sense of the Tragic

The recent revival of pragmatism provides a timely intellectual background for the most urgent problematic of our postmodern moment: the complex cluster of questions and queries regarding the meaning and value of democracy. No other modern philosophical tradition has grappled with the various dimensions of this problematic more than that of American pragmatism. Thomas Jefferson, Ralph Waldo Emerson and Abraham Lincoln—the grand spiritual godfathers of pragmatism—laid the foundations for the meaning and value of democracy in America and in the modern world. These foundations consisted roughly of the irreducibility of individuality within participatory communities, heroic action of ordinary folk in a world of radical contingency, and a deep sense of evil that fuels struggles for justice.

Jeffersonian notions of the irreducibility of individuality within participatory communities attempt to sidestep rapacious individualisms and authoritarian communitarianisms by situating unique selves within active networks of power-sharing that protect liberties, promote prosperity and highlight accountability. In this sense, Jefferson's ideals combine much of the best of liberalism, populism and civic republicanism. Emersonian formulations of heroic action of ordinary folk in a world of radical contingency try to jettison static dogmatisms and impersonal determinisms by accenting the powers of unique selves to make and remake themselves with no original models to imitate or emulate. Emersonian ideals bring together salutary aspects of Romanticism, libertarianism and Protestantism. Lincoln's profound wrestling with a deep sense of evil that fuels struggle for justice endeavors to hold at bay facile optimisms and paralyzing pessimisms by positing unique selves that fight other finite opponents rather than demonic foes. Lincoln's ideals hold together valuable insights of evangelical Christianity, American constitutionalism and Scottish commonsensical realism. Yet not one American *philosophical* thinker has put forward a conception of the meaning and significance of democracy in light of these foundations laid by Jefferson, Emerson and Lincoln.

If there is one plausible candidate, it would have to be John Dewey. Like Maurice Maeterlinck and Walt Whitman ("In Lincoln's lifetime Whitman was the only writer to describe him with love."),[1] Dewey understood that if one takes democracy as an object of philosophical investigation, then one must grapple with the contributions of Jefferson and Emerson. But, I suggest, Dewey failed to seriously meet the challenge posed by Lincoln—namely, defining the relation of democratic ways of thought and life to a profound sense of evil. Within the development of post-Deweyan pragmatism, only Sidney Hook's suggestive essay "Pragmatism and the Tragic Sense of Life" responds to Lincoln's challenge in a serious manner.[2] Yet it remains far from the depths of other tragic democratic thinkers like Herman Melville, F.O. Matthiessen and Reinhold Niebuhr.

There is only one great American philosopher (Alfred North Whitehead's origins exclude him) who seriously grappled with the challenge posed by Lincoln—namely, Josiah Royce. In fact, I would go as far as to claim that Royce's systematic post-Kantian idealism is primarily a long and winding set of profound meditations on the relation of a deep sense of evil to human agency. Therefore a contemporary encounter between Dewey and Royce is neither an antiquarian reconstruction of exchanges in philosophical journals nor a synoptic synthesis of instrumentalism and idealism. Rather it is a response to the most pressing problematic of our day, which creatively fuses the contributions of Jefferson, Emerson and Lincoln in our quest for the meaning and value of democracy. Since Royce viewed his project as a kind of "absolute pragmatism" (principally owing to valuable lessons learned from his close friend William James), the Dewey-Royce encounter is an affair within the pragmatist tradition. Hence, the major philosophic progeny of Jefferson, Emerson and Lincoln carry the banner of American pragmatism.

The three principal philosophic slogans of this banner are voluntarism, fallibilism and experimentalism. Both Dewey and Royce are philosophers of human will, human power and human action. Structured and unstructured social practices sit at the center of their distinct philosophic visions. In short, they agree with the best characterization of pragmatism ever formulated—that of C. I. Lewis:

> Pragmatism could be characterized as the doctrine that all problems are at bottom problems of conduct, that all judgments are, implicitly, judgments of value, and that, as there can be ultimately no valid distinction of theoretical and practical, so there can be no final separation of questions of truth of any kind from questions of the justifiable ends of action.[3]

Dewey's stress on the primacy of human will and practice is shot through all of his major works. So his seminal conception of experience—over against that of British empiricists and Kantian transcendentialists—will suffice. It is found in one of the classic essays of modern philosophy, his "The Need for a Recovery of Philosophy" (1917):

> Experience is primarily a process of undergoing: a process of standing something; of suffering and passion, of affection, in the literal sense of these words. The organism has to endure, to undergo, the consequence of its own actions.

> Experience, in other words, is a matter of *simultaneous* doings and sufferings. Our undergoings are experiments in varying the course of events; our active tryings are trials and tests of ourselves. . . .[4]

Royce also puts a premium on human will and embraces this stress of James and Dewey.

> No truth is a saving truth—yes, no truth is a truth at all unless it guides and directs life. Therein I heartily agree with current pragmatism and with James himself. . . .
>
> I agree that every opinion expresses an attitude of the will, a preparedness for action, a determination to guide a plan of action in accordance with an idea. . . . There is no such thing as a purely intellectual form of assertion which has no element of action about it. An opinion is a deed. It is a deed intended to guide other deeds. It proposes to have what the pragmatists call "workings." That is, it undertakes to guide the life of the one who asserts the opinion. In that sense, all truth is practical.[5]

The voluntaristic impulse in Dewey and Royce leads to two basic notions. First, that truth is a species of the good. Second, that the conception of the good is defined in relation to temporal consequences. The first notion that truth is a species of the good means that our beliefs about the way the world is have ethical significance. This is what James means when he writes "our opinions about the nature of things belong to our moral life. . . ."[6] Or what Dewey highlights when he notes:

> . . . philosophy is a form of desire, of effort at action—a love, namely, of wisdom; but with the thorough proviso, not attached to the Platonic use of the word, that wisdom, whatever it is, is not a mode of science or knowledge. A philosophy which was conscious of its own business and province would then perceive that it is an intellectualized wish, an aspiration subjected to rational discrimination and tests, a social hope reduced to a working program of action, a prophecy of the future, but one disciplined by serious thought and knowledge.[7]

Royce chimes in on the same theme in this way:

> Opinions about the universe are counsels as to how to adjust your deeds to the purposes and requirements which a survey of the

whole of the life whereto your life belongs shows to be the genuinely rational purposes and requirements.[8]

The second notion, that the conception of the good is defined in relation to temporal consequences, means that the future has ethical significance. In fact, the key to pragmatism, the distinctive feature that sets it apart from other philosophical traditions—and maybe its unique American character—is its emphasis on the ethical significance of the future. In a rare moment of reflection on the beginnings and traits of pragmatism in "The Development of American Pragmatism" (1922), Dewey states that

> pragmatism, thus, presents itself as an extension of historical empiricism, but with this fundamental difference, that it does not insist upon antecedent phenomena but upon consequent phenomena; not upon the precedents but upon the possibilities of action. And this change in point of view is almost revolutionary in its consequences. An empiricism which is content with repeating facts already past has no place for possibility and for liberty. . . .
>
> Pragmatism thus has a metaphysical implication. The doctrine of the value of consequences leads us to take the future into consideration. And this taking into consideration of the future takes us to the conception of a universe whose evolution is not finished, of a universe which is still, in James' term "in the making," "in the process of becoming," of a universe up to a certain point still plastic.[9]

For pragmatists, the future has ethical significance because human will—human thought and action—can make a difference in relation to human aims and purposes. There is moral substance in the fact that human will can make the future different and, possibly, better relative to human ends and aims. As a young man of twenty-four (March 10, 1879), just beginning his assistantship in English Literature at the University of California, Berkeley, Royce outlined his system of philosophy:

> Faust's contract with Mephisto is, in Goethe's view, no extraordinary act, no great crime, but simply the necessary fundament of

an active life that strives for the Ideal. Here is the whole view as I just now conceive it to have been. . . .

. . . The essence of life is found in the individual moments of accomplishment, and in those alone. . . . The individual moment is the Real; but it is so only in so far forth as it denies itself, strives to pass out over itself, to plunge on into a future. . . .

The individual moments of our lives must be full of action, the fuller the better; but they must also be, for the very same reason, full of unrest. No content of the moment, however great, must lead us to wish to remain stationary in this moment. This content in the present moment is denial of activity; it is death.[10]

More than a year later, Royce writes in his diary (July 21, 1880):

Reflected further on the present state of the systematic development of philosophy I am undertaking. The opening and foundation thereof is surely the theory of the world of reality as a projection from the present moment. (*Fugitive Essays*, p. 35)

Royce's student, editor and most able contemporary expositor, Jacob Loewenberg, comments on these fragments from the early diaries in this way:

The present—be it a present moment, a present idea, a present thought, a present self—derives its meaning from a constructive process of self-extension. And the whole technique of Royce's thinking is dominated, as we have seen, by this process. (pp. 30–31)

This preoccupation with the prospective perspective—rooted in post-Kantian idealism and given distinctive pragmatic twists by Royce and Dewey—leads Dewey to quip

What should experience be but a future implicated in a present![11]

Echoes of Jefferson's notion of periodic revolutions and Emerson's view of power as onward transitions and upward crossings loom large here. The pragmatic emphasis on the future as the terrain for humans-making-a-difference (including a *better* difference) results in a full-blown fallibilism and experimentalism. All facts are fallible and all experience is experimental. This is the common ground of pragmatism upon which both Dewey and Royce stand. Unique selves acting in and through participatory communities give ethical significance to an open, risk-ridden future. The slogans of voluntarism, fallibilism and experimentalism posit self-criticism and self-correction as a central component of human enterprises. The "majesty of community" and "the true spirituality of genuine doubting" combine to ensure that nothing blocks the Peircean road to inquiry.

Yet Dewey and Royce part company in response to Lincoln's challenge. The deep sense of evil affects Royce more than it does Dewey. Ironically, Royce clings to his post-Kantian idealism—even after his appropriation of Peirce's theory of interpretive communities—owing to his philosophic grappling with suffering and sorrow. Jamesian injunctions about the strenuous mood against evil do not suffice for Royce. Nor do Deweyan leaps of faith in critical intelligence. Royce holds on to his Christianlike dramatic portrait of reality—with its hope for and assurance of ultimate triumph—precisely because his sense of evil and the tragic is so deep.

What separates Royce from other American pragmatists and most American philosophers—though Arthur Danto comes to mind—is his prolonged and poignant engagement with the thought of Arthur Schopenhauer. Royce's response to Lincoln's challenge takes the form of a lifelong struggle with Schopenhauer's pessimism. The first course Royce ever taught (by choice) as a graduate fellow at Johns Hopkins University at twenty-two years of age in 1877 (January to March) was on Schopenhauer. His classic text *The Spirit of Modern Philosophy* (1892) contains thirty-three pages on Kant, twenty-eight pages on Fichte, thirty-seven pages on Hegel and thirty-six pages on Schopenhauer. I know of no other American history of modern philosophy in which Schopenhauer is treated so extensively and respectfully. For Royce, Schopenhauer is "noteworthy," "significant," "a great thinker," "a philosopher of considerable dignity," equipped with "an erudition vast rather than technical," and "enjoyed manifold labors rather than professional completeness."[12] Royce states that "Schopenhauer's principal work, 'Die Welt als Wille und Vorstellung' is in form the most artistic philosophical treatise in existence, if one excepts the best of Plato's 'Dialogues.' " Furthermore, Schopenhauer is the crucial transitional figure "from the romantic idealism to the modern realism."[13] In every major text of Royce—including his *Lectures on Modern Idealism,* published posthumously—Schopenhauer makes a significant appearance. In sharp contrast, Schopenhauer—along with Lincoln's challenge of a deep sense of evil and the tragic—makes no appearances in Dewey's vast corpus. This is why I find Royce profound and poignant though ultimately unpersuasive while I find Dewey sane and fascinating though, in the end, unsatisfactory. Like Melville, Matthiessen and Niebuhr, I believe that a deep sense of evil and the tragic must infuse any meaning and value of democracy. The culture of democratic societies requires not only the civic virtues of participation, tolerance, openness, mutual respect and mobility, but also dramatic struggles with the two major culprits—disease and death—that defeat and cut off the joys of democratic citizenship. Such citizenship must not be so preoccupied—or obsessed—with possibility that it conceals or represses the ultimate facts of the human predicament.

I will not here plunge into Royce's rich reflections on evil—ranging from his famous essays "The Problem of Job" (1897) and "The Practical Significance of Pessimism" (1879) to his treatments in his major works. Instead I shall only sketch his notion of "irrevocable deeds" as a source of his conception of the Absolute in his most straightforward book, *Sources of Religious Insight* (1912). Royce introduces this notion in the midst of his complimentary discussion of pragmatism.

> But now one of the central facts about life is that every deed once done is *ipso facto* irrevocable. That is, at any moment you perform a given deed or you do not. If you perform it, it is done and cannot be undone. This difference between what is done and what is undone is, in the real and empirical world, *a perfectly absolute*

difference. The opportunity for a given individual deed returns not; for the moment when that individual deed can be done never recurs. Here is a case where the rational constitution of the whole universe gets into definite relation to our momentary experience. *And if any one wants to be in touch with the "absolute"—with that reality which the pragmatists fancy to be peculiarly remote and abstract—let him simply do any individual deed whatever and then try to undo that deed. Let the experiment teach him what one means by calling reality absolute. Let the truths which that experience teaches any rational being show him also what is meant by absolute truth.*[14]

Royce's point here is not simply to draw attention to the limits the past imposes on the future. Rather it is to show just how concrete and practical notions of an absolute can be. His aim is to unhinge such notions from their association with unpractical and inaccessible abstractions. Furthermore, he wants to better enable unique selves to act in the present and give ethical significance to the future by providing standards that transcend the present. Royce recognizes that there must be some notions of standards with regulative and critical force—though always partial and fragmentary—which sustain our strenuous mood in the perennial fight against the "capricious irrationality of the world," and the "blind irrationality of fortune."[15]

Royce defends his version of the absolute because he "looks to the truth for aid."[16] On the one hand, he accents the interplay of what he calls "the *no longer* and *not yet* of past and future, so that fulfillment never at one present instant is to be found."[17] Like Hegel's unhappy consciousness, dissatisfaction reigns and "temporal peace is a contradiction in terms." Yet he is "ready to accept the dear sorrow of possessing ideals and of taking my share of the divine task."[18] In this way,

absolute reality (namely, the sort of reality that belongs to irrevocable deeds), absolute truth (namely, the sort of truth that belongs to those opinions which, for a given purpose, counsel individual deeds, when the deeds in fact meet the purpose for which they were intended)—these two are not remote affairs invented by philosophers for the sake of "barren intellectualism." *Such absolute reality and absolute truth are the most concrete and practical and familiar of matters.* The pragmatist who denies that there is any absolute truth accessible has never rightly considered the very most characteristic feature of the reasonable will, namely, that it is always counselling irrevocable deeds, and therefore is always giving counsel that is for its own determinate purpose irrevocably right or wrong precisely in so far as it is definite counsel.[19]

On the other hand, I suspect that something deeper is going on. Royce believes more is at stake than warding off willful subjectivism and epistemic relativism. Reality and truth must, in some sense, be absolute not only because skepticism lurks about, but also—and more important, because it is the last and only hope for giving meaning to the strenuous mood, for justifying the worthwhileness of our struggle to endure. In one of the great moments in Royce's corpus—a moment not to be found in Dewey—Royce questions his idealist response to the problem of evil. After pushing pessimism to the brink, he holds on for dear life.

For I do not feel that I have yet quite expressed the full force of the deepest argument for pessimism, or the full seriousness of the eternal problem of evil. . . .

Pessimism, in the true sense, isn't the doctrine of the merely peevish man, but of the man who to borrow a word of Hegel's, "has once feared not for this moment or for that in his life, but who has feared with all his nature; so that he has trembled through and through, and all that was most fixed in him has become shaken." There are experiences in life that do just this for us. And when the fountains of the great deep are once thus broken up, and the floods have come, it isn't over this or that lost spot of our green earth that we sorrow; it is because of all that endless waste of tossing waves which now rolls cubits deep above the top of what were our highest mountains. . . .

No, the worst tragedy of the world is the tragedy of brute chance to which everything spiritual seems to be subject amongst us—the tragedy of the diabolical irrationality of so many among the foes of whatever is significant. An open enemy you can face. The temptation to do evil is indeed a necessity for spirituality. But one's own foolishness, one's ignorance, the cruel accidents of disease, the fatal misunderstandings that part friends and lovers, the chance mistakes that wreck nations:—these things we lament most bitterly, not because they are painful, but because they are farcical, distracting,—not foe-men worthy of the sword of the spirit, nor yet mere pangs of our finitude that we can easily learn to face courageously, as one can be indifferent to physical pain. No, these things do not make life merely painful to us; they make it hideously petty.[20]

At this point, Royce seems to virtually throw up his hands and throw in the towel. Fresh memories of his nervous breakdown— only three years earlier—and his recovery in Australia—loom large. He concludes, "From our finite point of view there is no remotely discoverable justification for this caprice." Yet he refuses to give in to Schopenhauer and holds we must "dare to hope for an answer":

. . . *were* our insight into the truth of Logos based upon any sort of empirical assurance, it would surely fail us here. But now, as it is, if we have the true insight of deeper idealism, we can turn from our chaos to him . . . the suffering God . . . who actually and in our flesh bears the sins of the world, and whose natural body is pierced by the capricious wounds that hateful fools inflict upon him—it is this thought, I say, that traditional Christianity has in its deep symbolism first taught the world, but that, in its fullness, only an idealistic interpretation can really and rationally express. . . .

What in time is hopelessly lost, is attained for him in his eternity. . . .

We have found in a world of doubt but one assurance—but one, and yet how rich! All else is hypothesis.[21]

I have quoted at length to convey Royce's implicit response to Lincoln's challenge, answering Schopenhauer. The point here is not whether his response is persuasive or convincing; rather the point is to highlight the depths of Royce's efforts to sustain the strenuous mood in the face of the deep sense of evil. Never in the tradition of American pragmatism has Lincoln's challenge been taken so seriously. Yet the democratic legacy of Jefferson, Emerson and Lincoln in our ghastly century demands nothing less. The encounter between Dewey and Royce may help us preserve the ethical significance of *our* future.

8

The Historicist Turn in Philosophy of Religion

From the disintegration of Hegelianism derives the beginning of a new cultural process, different in character from its predecessors, a process in which practical movement and theoretical thought are united (or are trying to unite through a struggle that is both theoretical and practical). . . . Out of the critique of Hegelianism arose modern idealism and the philosophy of praxis. Hegelian immanentism becomes historicism, but it is absolute historicism only with the philosophy of praxis. . . . One should not be surprised if this beginning arises from the convergence of various elements, apparently heterogeneous. . . . Instead it is worth noting that such an overthrow could not but have connections with religion.

Antonio Gramsci,
Prison Notebooks

In the past few decades philosophy of religion has suffered decline as a discipline. Consider the towering figures in the field: the synoptic vision of Edgar Sheffield Brightman, the tough-minded empiricism of Henry Nelson Wieman and the magisterial metaphysics of Alfred North Whitehead are now distant memories for present-day participants in this discipline. Here I shall sketch a brief account of this decline and, more important, suggest a new conception of philosophy of religion which warrants serious attention. This new conception promotes a historicist turn in philosophy of religion which remains within yet deepens the American grain—empirical, pluralist, pragmatic and activist.[1]

The Golden Age of Philosophy of Religion

The Enlightenment critiques of religious thought—such as David Hume's *Dialogue Concerning Natural Religion* and Immanuel Kant's chapter on "The Ideal of Pure Reason" in his *Critique of Pure Reason*—set the terms for the modern philosophical debate concerning the status of religious beliefs. These terms accepted the subjectivist turn which puts philosophical reflection first and foremost within the arena of immediate awareness or self-consciousness. Undergirded by the rising authority of science—with its probabilistic reasoning and fallibilistic conclusions—post-Humean and post-Kantian philosophers of religion were forced either to give up or to redefine the scientific character of religious beliefs and thereby to conceptually redescribe such beliefs in moral, affective, aesthetic or existential terms. In other words, one became a neo-Kantian, Schleiermachean, Hegelian or Kierkegaardian. Whether such descriptions yielded epistemic status to religious beliefs became the question for modern philosophy of religion.

Yet this question was not the central issue for the masters of European philosophy in the late nineteenth century. Karl Marx, John Stuart Mill and Friedrich Nietzsche were obsessed primarily with the nature of modern science and the character of modern society and culture. Modern theologians were preoccupied with the epistemic status of religious beliefs, but this preoccupation signified their marginality in European intellectual life.

In stark contrast to their European counterparts, religious concerns loomed large in the first significant American philosophical response to modernity. The first generation of American pragmatists, especially Charles Peirce and William James, attempted not only to demythologize modern science but also to update religion. For American pragmatists, religious beliefs were not simply practical postulates for moral behavior, pietistic modes of self-consciousness, pictorial representations of absolute knowledge or anxiety-ridden, self-involving choices. Religious beliefs were on the same spectrum as any other beliefs—always linked to experience. The pragmatism of Peirce and James incredibly seized the imagination of a whole generation of American philosophers, including idealist philosophers like Josiah Royce, William Ernest Hocking and Edgar Sheffield Brightman—thereby initiating the Golden Age of philosophy of religion in modern Euro-American thought.

Nowhere in the modern world did philosophers take religion more seriously than in the United States between 1900 and 1940. No other national philosophical tradition compares with the set of American texts such as William James's book *The Varieties of Religious Experience* (1902), John Elof Boodin's *Truth and Reality* (1911), William Ernest Hocking's work *The Meaning of God in Human Experience* (1912), Josiah Royce's text *The Problem of Christianity* (1913), Douglas Clyde MacIntosh's *Theology as an Empirical Science* (1919), Henry Nelson Wieman's *Religious Experience and Scientific Method* (1926), Alfred North Whitehead's *Process and Reality* (1929), Shailer Mathews's book *The Growth of the Idea of God* (1931), John Dewey's work *A Common Faith* (1934) and Edgar Sheffield Brightman's text *A Philosophy of Religion* (1940).

There are complex sociological and historical reasons which account for this phenomenon. My basic point is simply that for the first four decades of this century most of the major American philosophers were philosophers of religion and that the Golden Age of philosophy of religion in the modern West was primarily an American affair.

This American predominance in philosophy of religion produced profound philosophical breakthroughs. First, major American philosophers, starting with Peirce, radically questioned the subjectivist turn in philosophy. They attacked the notion that philosophical reflection begins within the inner chambers of mental episodes. American pragmatists promoted an intersubjectivist turn which highlighted the communal and social character of acquiring knowledge. American process philosophers accented a primordial form of experience, for example, causal efficacy, which disclosed the often overlooked interpretive and abstract status of sense perception.

These two diverse critiques of the fundamental starting point for European Enlightenment philosophy undermined the relational framework of mind-objects-God. The pragmatists' move led toward a focus on the social practices—from verification procedures to communal values—which produced knowledge about minds, objects and God. The process strategy yielded a new complicated vocabulary which rejected lines of demarcation between consciousness, world and the divine. Furthermore, the legacies of both pragmatic and process thought reclaimed the epistemic and scientific status of religious beliefs as well as their practical value. In short, the major movements in the Golden Age of philosophy of religion undercut the three basic pillars of modern European philosophy.

The distinctive feature of the most influential American philosophies of religion—pragmatism and process thought—is that they defend religious experience and beliefs under the banners of radical empiricism, open-ended pragmatism and ethical activism. Radical empiricism tries to stay in tune with the complex plurality and fluid multiplicity of experience on the individual and corporate levels. Open-ended pragmatism accentuates the various problems which motivate logical inquiry and reflective intelligence. Ethical activism links human responsibility and action to the purposeful solving of problems in the personal, cultural, ideological, political, economic and ecological spheres of human and natural activities. In this sense, the major American philosophers prior to World War II did not succumb to the secular insularity of their European counterparts; nor did they cater to the irrational impulses of parochial religious and ideological thinkers. Their plebeian humanism—more democratic than Matthew Arnold's bourgeois humanism and more individualistic than Marx's revolutionary humanism—encouraged them to view sympathetically though critically the lives of common people and hence take religion seriously in their sophisticated philosophical reflection.

The Decline of Philosophy of Religion

As I noted earlier, the Golden Age of philosophy of religion is long past. The flowering of American philosophy—with its deep religious concerns—was cut short. The political and military crisis in Europe resulted in intellectual émigrés to the United States who changed the academic discipline of philosophy. This change was inextricably bound to the increasing professionalization of the discipline of philosophy.

The advent of logical positivism—with its diverse versions of atomism, reductionism and narrow empiricism—put an end to the Golden Age of philosophy of religion. This Viennese-style positivism, though popularized in America by A. J. Ayer's *Language, Truth, and Logic* (1936), brought with it all the old European Enlightenment baggage pragmatism and process thought had discredited: the subjectivist starting point, subject/object relations and the philosophical trashing of religion. As Dewey's long and languishing star faded in New York and Whitehead's legacy courageously persisted in relative isolation at Chicago, the positivism of Rudolf Carnap, Carl Hempel and others spread like wildfire throughout elite graduate schools in philosophy—especially Harvard, UCLA and Minnesota. By the death of Whitehead in 1947, few graduate students in philosophy at the influential schools had heard of Hocking and Brightman, had read Wieman or had grappled with Whitehead (besides, maybe, his *Principia Mathematica*). James was deemed a cultural critic who lacked philosophical rigor; Dewey, a mere social activist with scientistic sentiments and fuzzy philosophical meditations. Technical argumentation, logical notation and rigorous analysis—with their concomitant subfields of logic, epistemology and methodology in the natural sciences—had seized center stage.

To put it crudely, logical positivism was based on three fundamental assumptions. First, it assumed a form of sentential atomism which correlates isolated sentences with either possible empirical confirmation (as in the sciences), logical necessity (as in mathematics and logic) or emotion (as in ethics, religion and the arts). Second, it emerged with a kind of phenomenalist reductionism which translates sentences about physical objects into sentences about actual and possible sensations. Third, it presupposed a version of analytical empiricism which holds observational evidence to be the criterion for cognitively meaningful sentences and hence the final court of appeal in determining valid theories about the world. These crucial assumptions, which constitute independent yet interrelated doctrines, were held at various times by the leading logical positivists. More important, they were guided by fundamental distinctions between the analytic and the synthetic, the linguistic and the empirical, theory and observation.[2]

The immediate consequence of logical positivism on philosophy of religion was the near collapse of the latter as a serious academic discipline, or even a subfield within philosophy. This consequence had a devastating effect: during the early stages of the professionalization of philosophy after World War II, philosophy of religion had little or no academic legitimacy. Therefore most of those interested in philosophy with religious concerns were forced to study in graduate programs of divinity schools or seminaries such as Yale, Chicago or Union. Furthermore, since American philosophies of religion also were forms of social and cultural criticism, the near collapse of philosophy of religion was a symptom of the narrow mode of philosophizing promoted by logical positivists. Needless to say, as philosophers had less and less to say about religion, politics, ethics, the arts and the normative role of science in the world, and more and more to say about analytical sentences, methodological operations in physics and the reducibility of objects to sense data, the literate populace lost interest in the intellectual activity of philosophers. In other words, philosophy in America was losing touch with American philosophy.

The Resurgence of American Philosophy

The major tragedy of contemporary philosophy of religion is that the resurgence of American philosophy occurred at the time when most American theologians were being seduced either by the antiphilosophical stance of Karl Barth or by the then fashionable logical positivism and linguistic analysis. The great contributions of W. V. Quine, Nelson Goodman and Wilfred Sellars, which undermined Viennese-style positivism and Oxford-inspired linguistic philosophy, were made just as A. J. Ayer, J. L. Austin and Ludwig Wittgenstein, or Karl Barth and Emil Brunner were becoming prominent on the American theological scene. The result of this situation is that Quine, Goodman and Sellars are relatively alien to most contemporary religious thinkers, and that either refined forms of German idealism, as with Paul Tillich, heuristic mythological versions of Christianity, as in Reinhold Niebuhr, and indigenous updates of process philosophy, as in Schubert Ogden and John B. Cobb, Jr., constitute the most significant contributions of philosophy of religion in America after World War II.

The resurgence of American philosophy was enacted by the powerful critiques of logical positivism launched by Quine, Goodman and Sellars. Quine's epistemological holism, which heralded systems of sentences (or theories) as opposed to isolated sentences as the basic units of empirical significance, discarded sentential atomism. Furthermore, his methodological monism, which rejected the analytic-synthetic distinction, rendered unacceptable the positivist classificatory criterion for tautological and meaningful sentences.[3] Goodman's postempiricist antireductionism highlighted the theory-laden character of observation and undercut the narrow empiricist standard for adjudicating between conflicting theories of the world. And his ontological pluralism relegated the idea of truth to that of fitness, and promoted diverse true versions of the world instead of a fixed world and unique truth. He thus called into question the monocosmic naturalism of logical positivism (a radical move which even Quine resisted owing to his ontological allegiance to physics— a lingering trace of positivism in the great critic of positivism).[4]

Lastly, Sellars's epistemic antifoundationalism precluded any "given" elements as acceptable candidates which serve as the final terminating point for chains of epistemic justification—thereby condemning any form of empiricist grounding of knowledge claims.[5] The Quine-Goodman-Sellars contributions, though related in complex and often conflicting ways and still questionable in some philosophical circles, signify the American takeover of analytical philosophy—a takeover which has led to the demise of analytical philosophy.[6]

The Quine-Goodman-Sellars insights bear striking resemblances to the viewpoints of earlier American pragmatists. The resurgence of American philosophy is, in part, the recovery of the spirit and temper of American pragmatism reflected in Charles Peirce's first rule of reason: Do not block the way of inquiry.[7] Yet this resurgence is silent regarding the status and role of religion (and social and cultural criticism) in philosophical reflection. Contemporary American philosophy is postanalytic philosophy, with deep debts to pragmatism yet little interest in religious reflection.

This is so principally because postanalytic philosophy has been preoccupied with the secular priesthood, the sacred institution in modern culture: the scientific community and its practice. Thomas Kuhn's influential book *The Structure of Scientific Revolutions* (1962) can be viewed as the grand postanalytic philosophical text written for the positivist philistines—the great popularization of the implications of the Quine-Goodman-Sellars contributions for the paradigm of rationality in modern culture, that is, the practices of scientists. Paul Feyerabend, who describes himself as a "church historian," deepens these implications (in the political and ideological spheres) regarding the demystification of scientific method and practices in *Against Method* (1975) and *Science in a Free Society* (1978). In short, the philosophy and history of science function in contemporary American philosophy as did the philosophy and history of religion in the Golden Age of American philosophy. The gain is a more sophisticated dialogue concerning the content and character of rationality in modernity; the loss is a less engaged relation with the wider culture and society.

This situation is exemplified in Richard Rorty's masterful manifesto of American postanalytic philosophy, *Philosophy and the Mirror of Nature* (1979), and Richard Bernstein's learned meditations on the role of philosophy after Rorty in *Beyond Objectivism and Relativism* (1983). Despite their Kuhnian perspectives regarding the social character of rationality, both focus their philosophical concerns almost exclusively on philosophy of science and say nothing about philosophy of religion. And this latter silence is accompanied by a glaring absence of sustained social and cultural criticism. The salutary contributions of Rorty and Bernstein are that (like Hegel and Marx at their best) they make historical consciousness central to their philosophical reflections, without falling into the transcendentalist trap of making historical consciousness the new candidate for philosophically grounding knowledge claims (as did Hegel and Marx at their worst). Yet Rorty and Bernstein put forward "thin" historical narratives which rarely dip into the complex world of politics and culture. Both remain seduced by a kind of Lovejoy-like history of ideas far removed from concrete historical processes and realities. "Thick" historical narratives, such as those of Karl Marx, Max Weber, Simone de Beauvoir, W. E. B. Du Bois and Antonio Gramsci, elude them.

In other words, Rorty and Bernstein hold at arm's length serious tools of social theory and cultural criticism. Presently, Rorty's self-styled neopragmatism—much like Jacques Derrida's poststructuralism—is creating waves in the academy. But these waves remain

those of departmental internecine struggles between old-style empiricists and new-style pragmatists, argumentative realists and narrati-
vistic historicists, establishmentarian humanists and the professional
posthumanists. These noteworthy conflicts within the discipline of
philosophy in the academy have yet to spill over into serious cultural
and political debates regarding the larger issues of public concern.

The Theological Discovery of History

While professional philosophers lingered under the spell of the
grand Quine-Goodman-Sellars breakthroughs, and academic theologians nested in Barthian cocoons or emulated logical positivists
and linguistic analysts, liberation theologians discovered history.
This discovery did not consist of systematic reflections on historicity,
which has been long a priority of German-trained theologians and
Heideggerian-influenced philosophers, but rather of linking historical processes in society to political praxis. In this sense the theological discovery of history by Gustavo Gutierrez, Mary Daly and James
Cone was qualitatively different from the recovery of historicism
by Richard Rorty and Richard Bernstein.[8] The former was philosophically underdeveloped yet politically engaged and culturally
enlightening; the latter, politically and culturally underdeveloped
and philosophically enlightening. Gutierrez was responding, in part,
to the hegemony of Jacques Maritain's integral humanism among
liberal, Latin American, Catholic elites and the "developmentalism"
of US foreign policy which masks corporate interests and Latin
American social misery. Daly and Cone were recuperating the experiential and activist dimensions of American thought. The early
works of Daly are not simply religious critiques of ecclesiastical
and cultural patriarchy; they also explore—at the behest of
Whitehead and James—primordial forms of female experience
which may empower victims of sexist oppression. Even in her post-
Christian texts, these experiential and activist dimensions remain.
Similarly, the initial works of Cone are not only sustained diatribes

against Euro-American racism; they also probe into the degraded and devalued modes of African American experience that promote and encourage resistance against white-supremacist practices. Yet, for many of us, Daly's neo-Thomist metaphysics loomed too large and Cone's Barthian Christocentrism was too thick—and their early one-dimensional social analyses were too parochial.

Notwithstanding their philosophical and social analytical limitations, liberation theologians put historical processes, social analyses and political praxis at the center of theological discourse in seminaries and divinity schools. Their linking of historical consciousness to present-day political struggles—to anti-imperialist, feminist and black freedom movements—galvanized new intellectual energies throughout the religious academy. This intellectual upsurge caught many neo-orthodox theologians and liberal philosophers of religion unaware and unequipped to respond adequately. Yet it is no accident that the two major theological responses to liberation theology have come from process theologians: Schubert Ogden's *Faith and Freedom* and John B. Cobb, Jr.'s *Process Thought and Political Theology*.

Just as Rorty's and Bernstein's historicism is philosophically groundbreaking yet lacking in serious political substance, Gutierrez's, Daly's and Cone's liberation perspectives are theologically groundbreaking yet lacking in serious philosophical substance. For example, Gutierrez's conception of Marxist science is quite positivist, Daly's ontological arguments often slide into mere cathartic assertions, and Cone's religious claims reek of a hermetic fideism. Unfortunately, the nonexistent dialogue between academic philosophers and theologians nearly ensures an intellectual estrangement which permits the political insouciance of American neopragmatists and promotes the philosophical insularity of liberation theologians. What is needed is a rapprochement of the philosophical historicism of Rorty and Bernstein and the moral vision, social analysis and political engagement of the liberation perspectives of Gutierrez, Daly and Cone.

The Present Need for the Philosophy of Religion

American philosophy at its best has taken the form of philosophy of religion. This is so not because philosophy of religion possesses some special privilege or wisdom as a discipline, but rather because of the particular character of American philosophical thought. For complex national reasons, when American philosophers turn their backs on religion, they turn their eyes toward science. This usually results in muting their social and political concerns. My point here is not that American philosophers become religious, but rather that they once again take religion seriously, which also means taking culture and society seriously.

The contemporary tasks of a responsible and sophisticated philosophy of religion are threefold. First, it must deepen the historicist turn in philosophy by building upon the Quine-Goodman-Sellars contributions, and "thickening" the "thin" historicism of Rorty's and Bernstein's neopragmatism by means of undogmatic social analysis and engaged cultural criticism. Second, it should put forward moral visions and ethical norms which regulate the social analysis and cultural criticism drawn from the best of available religious and secular traditions bequeathed to us from the past. Third, it should scrutinize in a rational manner synoptic worldviews of various religious and secular traditions in light of their comprehensive grasp of the complexity, multiplicity and specificity of human experiences, and their enabling power to motivate human action for the negation and transformation of structures of oppression.

The historicist turn in philosophy of religion must steer clear of the Scylla of transcendental objectivism and the Charybdis of subjectivist nihilism. My particular version of philosophical historicism is neither the neo-Kantian historicism (à la Wilhelm Dilthey) which presupposes a positivist conception of the *Naturwissenschaften* nor the Popperian-defined historicism that possesses magic powers of social prediction and projection. Rather the historicism I promote is one which understands transient social practices, contingent cultural descriptions and revisable scientific theories as the subject matter for philosophical reflection. Hence, social analysis and cultural criticism are indispensable components of such reflection.

On the one hand, transcendental objectivism is precluded by rejecting all modes of philosophical reflection which invoke ahistorical quests for certainty and transhistorical searches for foundations—including most realist moves in ontology, foundationalist strategies in epistemology, and mentalistic discourses in philosophical psychology. On the other hand, subjectivist nihilism is avoided by condemning all forms of philosophical activity that devalue and disregard possibilities, potentialities and alternatives to prevailing practices. Wholesale leveling and trashing of standards, criteria and principles which facilitate dialogue, conversation and exchange result from subjectivist nihilism. Such nihilism is not simply parasitic on the failures of transcendental objectivism; it also shuns historical consciousness and thereby remains captive to the subjectivist turn. In this way transcendental objectivism is delusory though not necessarily socially pernicious, whereas subjectivist nihilism is inescapably insidious.

My version of historicism flows from the tradition of mitigated skepticism signified by Sebastian Castellio of Basel, William Chillingworth and Pascal at the birth of modern conceptions of knowledge and science. It is deepened and enriched by the tempered Pyrrhonism of David Hume, the Hegelian-inspired historicisms of Kierkegaard and Marx, the demystifying perspectivalism of Nietzsche, and the enabling pragmatism of James and Dewey. Like Gadamer, my version of historicism acknowledges the unavoidable character and central role of tradition and prejudice, yet it takes seriously the notion of sound human judgment relative to the most rationally acceptable theories and descriptions of the day. In this way, the historicism I promote is akin to that of Rorty and Bernstein—and especially that of Jeffrey Stout.[9]

My philosophical historicism is inextricably bound to undogmatic social analysis and engaged social criticism, because if one is not nihilistic about history, one must be open to new possibilities, potentialities and alternatives to present practices. In this view, the major role of social analysis and cultural criticism is to understand these practices and discern forces for betterment. Therefore, philosophical historicism—if logically consistent and theoretically coherent—leads to "thick" historicism, to social and heterogeneous narratives which account for the present and project a future.

Although social analysis and cultural criticism play central roles in my historicist philosophy of religion, some forms of such analyses and criticisms are not acceptable. Adequate social analyses and cultural critiques must be regulated by moral visions and ethical norms which are ensconced in religious or secular traditions—shot through with their own set of presuppositions, prejudgments and prejudices. A historicist philosophy of religion is not limited in an a priori manner to religious traditions. Yet in its attempts to take seriously the human dimensions of ultimacy, intimacy and sociality, it usually incorporates elements from religious traditions. Secular traditions are indispensable, yet they have had neither the time nor the maturity to bequeath to us potent cultural forms of ultimacy, intimacy and sociality comparable to older and richer religious traditions.

Acceptable modes of social analysis and cultural criticisms are guided by moral visions and ethical norms which flow from synoptic worldviews, including such crucial matters as the ideal of what it is to be human, the good society, loving relationships and other precious conceptions. These worldviews are to be rationally scrutinized in light of their capacity to illuminate the complexity, multiplicity and specificity of human experiences and their ability to enable oppositional activity against life-denying forces, be they biological, ecological, political, cultural or economic forces.

Since I believe that the major life-denying forces in our world are economic exploitation (resulting primarily from the social logic of capital accumulation), state repression (linked to the social logic of state augmentation), bureaucratic domination (owing to the social logic of administrative subordination), racial, sexual and heterosexual subjugation (due to the social logics of white, male and heterosexual supremacist practices) and ecological subjection (resulting, in part, from modern values of scientistic manipulation), I entertain a variety of social analyses and cultural critiques which yield not merely one grand synthetic social theory but rather a number of local ones which remain international in scope and historical in content. My general social analytical perspective—deeply neo-Gramscian in spirit—is more influenced by the Marxist tradition than by any other secular tradition, but it also acknowledges the severe limitations of the Marxist tradition. By claiming that the Marxist tradition is indispensable yet inadequate, my social analytical perspective is post-Marxist without being anti-Marxist or pre-Marxist; that is, it incorporates elements from Weberian, racial, feminist, gay, lesbian and ecological modes of social analysis and cultural criticism.

I arrive at these analyses because the moral vision and ethical norms I accept are derived from the prophetic Christian tradition. I follow the biblical injunction to look at the world through the eyes of its victims, and the Christocentric perspective which requires that one see the world through the lens of the Cross—and thereby see our relative victimizing and relative victimization. Since we inhabit different locations on the existential, socioeconomic, cultural and political scales, our victim status differs, though we all, in some way, suffer. Needless to say, the more multilayered the victimization, the more suffering one undergoes. And given the predominant forms of life-denying forces in the world, the majority of humankind experiences thick forms of victimization.

The synoptic vision I accept is a particular kind of prophetic Christian perspective which comprehensively grasps and enables opposition to existential anguish, socioeconomic, cultural and political oppression and dogmatic modes of thought and action. I do not believe that this specific version of the prophetic Christian tradition has a monopoly on such insights, capacities and motivations. Yet I have never been persuaded that there are better traditions than the prophetic Christian one.

My acceptance of the prophetic Christian tradition is rational in that it rests upon good reasons. These reasons are good ones not because they result from logical necessity or conform to transcendental criteria. Rather they are good in that they flow from rational deliberation which perennially scrutinizes my particular tradition in relation to specific problems of dogmatic thought, existential anguish and societal oppression.

My reasons may become bad ones. For example, I would give up my allegiance to the prophetic Christian tradition if life-denying forces so fully saturated a situation that all possibility, potentiality and alternatives were exhausted, or if I became convinced that another tradition provides a more acceptable and enabling moral vision, set of ethical norms and synoptic worldview. I need neither metaphysical criteria nor transcendental standards to be persuaded, only historically constituted and situated reasons.

Yet, presently, I remain convinced by the prophetic Christian tradition. Its synoptic vision speaks with insight and power to the multiform character of human existence and to the specificity of the historical modes of human existence. Its moral vision and ethical norms propel human intellectual activity to account for and transform existing forms of dogmatism, oppression and despair. And the historicist turn in philosophy of religion helps us understand that we are forced to choose, in a rational and critical manner, some set of transient social practices, contingent cultural descriptions, and revisable scientific theories by which to live. This historicist stress on human finitude and human agency fits well, though it does not justify, my Christian faith. And, to put it bluntly, I do hope that the historicist turn in philosophy of religion enriches the prophetic Christian tradition and enables us to work more diligently for a better world.

9

The Limits of Neopragmatism

The renaissance of pragmatism in philosophy, literary criticism and legal thought in the past few years is a salutary development. It is part of a more general turn toward historicist approaches to truth and knowledge. I am delighted to see intellectual interest rekindled in Peirce, James, and especially Dewey. Yet I suspect that the new pragmatism may repeat and reproduce some of the blindness and silences of the old pragmatism—most important, an inadequate grasp of the complex operations of power, principally owing to a reluctance to take traditions of historical sociology and social theory seriously. In this essay, my strategy shall be as follows. First, I shall briefly map the different kinds of neopragmatisms in relation to perspectives regarding epistemology, theory and politics. Second, I shall suggest that neopragmatic viewpoints usually fail to situate their own projects in terms of present-day crises—including the crisis of purpose and vocation now raging in the professions. Third, I will try to show how my conception of prophetic pragmatism may provide what is needed to better illuminate and respond to these crises.

Much of the excitement about neopragmatism has to do with the antifoundationalist epistemic claims it puts forward. The idea that there are no self-justifying, intrinsically credible or ahistorical courts of appeal to terminate chains of epistemic justification calls into question positivistic and formalistic notions of objectivity, necessity and transcendentality. In this sense, all neopragmatists are antifoundationalists; that is, the validation of knowledge claims rests on practical judgments constituted by, and constructed in, dynamic social practices. For neopragmatists, we mortal creatures achieve and acquire knowledge by means of self-critical and self-correcting social procedures rooted in a variety of human processes.

Yet all neopragmatists are not antirealists. For example, Peircean pragmatists are intent on sidestepping any idealist or relativist traps and they therefore link a social conception of knowledge to a regulative ideal of truth. This viewpoint attempts to reject metaphysical conceptions of reality *and* skeptical reductions of truth-talk to knowledge-talk. In contrast, Deweyan pragmatists tend to be less concerned with charges of idealism or relativism, owing to a more insouciant attitude toward truth. In fact, some Deweyan pragmatists—similar to some sociologists of knowledge and idealists—wrongly collapse truth claims into warranted assertability claims or rational acceptability claims. Such moves provide fodder for the cannons of not only Peircean pragmatists, but also old style realists and foundationalists. To put it crudely, truth at the moment cannot be the truth about things, yet warranted assertable claims are the only truths we can get. To miss the subtle distinction between dynamic knowledge and regulative truth is to open the door to metaphysics or to slide down the slippery slope of sophomoric relativism. Yet the antifoundationalist claims put forward by neopragmatists are often construed such that many open such doors or slide down such slopes. In short, epistemic pluralism degenerates into an epistemic promiscuity that encourages epistemic policing by realists and foundationalists.

Neopragmatists disagree even more sharply in regarding the role of theory (explanatory accounts of the past and present). All neopragmatists shun grand theory because it smacks of metaphysical posturing. Yet this shunning often shades into a distrust of theory per se—hence a distancing from revisable social theories, provisional cultural theories or heuristic historical theories. This distrust may encourage an ostrichlike, piecemeal incrementalism that reeks of a vulgar antitheoreticism. On this view, neopragmatism amounts to crude practicalism. The grand pragmatism of Dewey and especially

C. Wright Mills rejects such a view. Instead, it subtly incorporates an experimental temper within theory-laden descriptions of problematic situations (for instance, social and cultural crises). Unfortunately, the pragmatist tradition is widely associated with a distrust of theory that curtails its ability to fully grasp the operations of power within the personal, social and historical contexts of human activities.

It is no accident that the dominant form of politics in the pragmatist tradition accents the pedagogical and the dialogical. Such a noble liberalism assumes that vast disparities in resources, enormous polarizations in perceptions or intense conflicts of interests can be overcome by means of proper education and civil conversation. If persuasive historical sociological claims show that such disparities, polarizations and conflicts often produce improper agitation and uncivil confrontation, the dominant form of politics in the pragmatist tradition is paralyzed or at least rendered more impotent than it is commonly believed. One crucial theme or subtext in my genealogy of pragmatism is the persistence of the sense of impotence of liberal intellectuals in American culture and society, primarily because of unattended class and regional disparities, unacknowledged racial and sexual polarizations, and untheorized cultural and personal conflicts that permeate and pervade our past and present. My view neither downplays nor devalues education and conversation; it simply highlights the structural background conditions of pedagogical efforts and dialogical events.

This leads me to my second concern, namely, the relative absence of pragmatist accounts of why pragmatism surfaces now in the ways and forms that it does. Such an account must situate the nature of pragmatist intellectual interventions—their intended effects and unintended consequences—in the present historical moment in American society and culture. I suspect that part of the renaissance of neopragmatism can be attributed to the crisis of purpose and vocation in humanistic studies and professional schools. On this view, the recent hunger for interdisciplinary studies—or the erosion of disciplinary boundaries—promoted by neo-pragmatisms, poststructuralisms, Marxisms and feminisms is not only motivated by a quest for truth, but also activated by power struggles over what kinds of knowledge should be given status, be rewarded and be passed on to young, informed citizens in the next century. These power struggles are not simply over positions and curriculums, but also over ideals of what it means to be humanistic intellectuals in a declining empire—in a first-rate military power, a near-rescinding economic power and a culture in decay. As Henry Adams suggests, the example of a turn toward history is most evident in American culture when decline is perceived to be undeniable and intellectuals feel most removed from the action. Furthermore, pragmatism at its best, in James and Dewey, provided a sense of purpose and vocation for intellectuals who believed they could make a difference in the public life of the nation. And it is not surprising that the first perceivable consequence of the renaissance of neopragmatism led by Richard Rorty echoed James's attack on professionalization and specialization. In this sense, Rorty's *Philosophy and the Mirror of Nature* (1979) not only told the first major and influential story of analytic philosophy, but was also a challenging narrative of how contemporary intellectuals have come to be contained within professional and specialized social spaces, with little outreach to a larger public and hence little visibility in, and minimal effect on, the larger society. Needless to say, Rorty's revival of Jamesian antiprofessionalism—not to be confused with anti-intellectualism or even antiacademicism—has increased intellectuals' interest in public journalism and intensified the tension between journalists and academics.

The crisis of purpose and vocation in humanistic studies and professional schools is compounded by the impact of the class and regional disparities, racial and sexual polarizations, and cultural and personal conflicts that can no longer be ignored. This impact not only unsettles our paradigms in the production of knowledge, but also forces us to interrogate and examine our standards, criteria, styles and forms in which knowledge is assessed, legitimated and expressed. At its worst, pragmatism in the academy permits us to embrace this impact without attending to the implications of power. At its best, pragmatism behooves us to critically scrutinize this impact as we promote the democratization of American intellectual life without vulgar leveling or symbolic tokenism.

But what is this "pragmatism at its best"? What form does it take? What are its constitutive features or fundamental components? These questions bring me to my third point—the idea of a prophetic pragmatist perspective and praxis. I use the adjective "prophetic" in order to harken back to the rich, though flawed, traditions of Judaism and Christianity that promote courageous resistance against, and relentless critiques of, injustice and social misery. These traditions are rich, in that they help keep alive collective memories of moral (that is, anti-idolatrous) struggle and nonmarket values (that is, love for others, loyalty to an ethical ideal and social freedom) in a more and more historically amnesiac society and market-saturated culture. These traditions are flawed because they tend toward dogmatic pronouncements (that is, "Thus saith the Lord") to homogeneous constituencies. Prophetic pragmatism gives courageous resistance and relentless critique a self-critical character and democratic content; that is, it analyzes the social causes of unnecessary forms of social misery, promotes moral outrage against them, organizes different constituencies to alleviate them, yet does so with an openness to its own blindnesses and shortcomings.

Prophetic pragmatism is pragmatism at its best because it promotes a critical temper and democratic faith without making criticism a fetish or democracy an idol. The fetishization of criticism yields a sophisticated ironic consciousness of parody and paralysis, just as the idolization of democracy produces mob rule. As Peirce, James and Dewey noted, criticism always presupposes something in place—be it a set of beliefs or a tradition. Criticism yields results or makes a difference when something significant is antecedent to it, such as rich, sustaining, collective memories of moral struggle. Similarly, democracy assumes certain conditions for its flourishing—like a constitutional background. Such conditions for democracy are not subject to public veto.

Critical temper as a way of struggle and democratic faith as a way of life are the twin pillars of prophetic pragmatism. The major foes to be contested are despair, dogmatism and oppression. The critical temper promotes a full-fledged experimental disposition that highlights the provisional, tentative and revisable character of our visions, analyses and actions. Democratic faith consists of a Pascalian wager (hence underdetermined by the evidence) on the abilities and capacities of ordinary people to participate in decision-making procedures of institutions that fundamentally regulate their lives. The critical temper motivated by democratic faith yields all-embracing moral and/or religious visions that project credible ameliorative possibilities grounded in present realities in light of systemic structural analyses of the causes of social misery (without reducing all misery to historical causes). Such analyses must appeal to traditions of social theory and historical sociology just as visions must proceed from traditions of moral and/or religious communities. The forms of prophetic praxis depend on the insights of the social theories and the potency of the moral and/or religious communities. In order for these analyses and visions to combat despair, dogmatism and oppression, the existential, communal and political dimensions of prophetic pragmatism must be accented. The existential dimension is guided by the value of *love*—a risk-ridden affirmation of the distinct humanity of others that, at its best, holds despair at bay. The communal dimension is regulated by *loyalty*—a profound devotion to the critical temper and democratic faith that eschews dogmatism. The political dimension is guided by *freedom*—a perennial quest for self-realization and self-development that resists all forms of oppression.

The tradition of pragmatism is in need of a mode of cultural criticism that keeps track of social misery, solicits and channels moral outrage to alleviate it, and projects a future in which the potentialities of ordinary people flourish and flower. The first wave of pragmatism foundered on the rocks of cultural conservatism and corporate liberalism. Its defeat was tragic. Let us not permit the second wave of pragmatism to end as farce.

10

On Georg Lukács

The antihistoricist climate of postmodern thought makes a reassessment of Lukács refreshing. Despite his incurable nostalgia for the highbrow achievements of classical bourgeois culture, Lukács remains the most provocative and profound Marxist thinker of this century. His major texts display the richness of the dialectical tradition, a tradition which emerged in figural biblical interpretation, was definitively articulated by Hegel and deepened by Kierkegaard and Marx.

This dialectical tradition differs from humanism and poststructuralism in three basic ways. First, the mode of theoretical activity of dialectical thought is *critique:* the demystifying of an apparent static surface and the disclosing of an underlying process whose emergence negates, preserves and transforms this surface. The corresponding mode of theoretical activity of humanist thought is *criticism:* the "civil" procedure of endless correction while remaining on the surface. That of poststructuralism is *deconstruction:* a potentially radical yet ultimately barren operation of ingeniously dismantling humanist thought and (attempting to) disarm dialectical reflection.

Second, dialectical thought is guided by the rhetorical trope of *synecdoche:* of part-whole relations in which a totality serves as the context within which complex levels are mediated and related. Humanist thought is dominated by the rhetorical trope of *metaphor:* of an unmediated identification and resemblance (between subject and object, ideas and world) in which correspondence is attained and unity is achieved. Poststructuralist thought is regulated by the rhetorical trope of *metonymy:* of the juxaposition or contiguity of the free play of signifiers which preclude correspondence and unity.

Lastly, the basic problematic of dialectical thought is *sociopolitical crisis:* a crisis linked in a complex manner to prevailing structures of domination. The chief aims are to keep alive the notion of a different and better future, to view the present as history, and to promote engagement in transforming this present. The major problematic of humanism is the *exercise of heroic individual will:* an activity deeply shaped by the emergence and decline of modern capitalist civilization. The central aim is to preserve the sanctity of individual achievement and to defend its nobility at nearly any social cost. The principal problematic of poststructuralism is the *philosophical antinomies of humanist thought:* these antinomies constitute an inescapable yet untenable metaphysics of presence. The major aim is to decenter and therefore break "free" from these antinomies, even though this "freedom" results in mere ironic negativity and severe paralysis of praxis.

Lukács deserves our attention not simply because he believed that the dialectical tradition is the most theoretically engaging and politically relevant of the three, but rather, more important, because his major texts enact the most important dialectical reflections in our time. In this essay I will examine Lukács as neither a literary critic nor a political strategist, but primarily as a dialectical philosopher. I will focus on his later ontological writings, especially parts of his *Toward the Ontology of Social Existence.* I will suggest that his rich dialectical textual practice is ultimately deficient, that is, not dialectical enough.

The Early Period

In order to understand more fully the later Lukács, it is necessary to look briefly at his early and middle periods. György (Hungarian for the more widely used German name Georg) Lukács was born in Budapest in 1885, the son of a wealthy banker. Lukács was raised in a flaccid aristocratic milieu, as evidenced by his early use of "von" in his signature of early writings.[1] Lukács's rejection of aristocratic pretense and bourgeois values was inspired by two of the greatest figures in modern Hungarian literature—the novelist Zsigmond Móricz and the poet Endre Ady—as well as the influential progressive thinker Ervin Szabó. Of these three, it was Ady who had the greatest impact on the young Lukács.[2] While obtaining a degree in jurisprudence at the University of Budapest (1902 to 1906), Lukács became deeply involved in literary writing and aesthetic theory. Like Ady, he was of "two souls": scornful of the privileged class, hence a bourgeois-democratic revolutionary, and nostalgic for a heroic life of authenticity, therefore of antibourgeois artistic temperament. This predicament led to Lukács's adoption of a tragic view of the world—a moralistic revolt against a corrupt bourgeoisie, opportunist progressive movement and insecure urban intelligentsia. In his noteworthy 1909 essay on Ady, Lukács described the despair of himself and his revolutionary comrades:

> Ady's public is absurdly touching. It consists of men who feel that there is no way out except revolution . . . who see that everything in existence is bad, cannot be corrected, and must be destroyed to make room for new possibilities. The need for a revolution does exist, but it is impossible to hope that one could be attempted even in the distant future.[3]

At this point in Lukács's career, he considers socialism to be the only alternative to the present order, but he cannot yet believe in socialism.

> The only possible hope would be the proletariat and socialism . . . [but] socialism does not appear to have the religious power capable of filling the entire soul—a power that used to characterize early Christianity.[4]

Lukács is not so much in search of a religion as he is trying to get in touch with that which religion promises: coherence, wholeness and meaning in life. His attendance at Georg Simmel's seminars in Berlin (1909 to 1910) and Windelband's and Rickert's lectures in Heidelberg (1912 to 1915), and his incessant discussions with Emil Lask and Max Weber, would only shape the form which this quest for coherence, wholeness and life-meaning would take. In short, Lukács's early writings—from his first book, *A History of the Development of Modern Drama* (1909, published in 1911), through *The Soul and the Forms* (1910), *The Philosophy of Art* (1912 to 1914), *Heidelberg Aesthetics* (1916 to 1918) to *The Theory of the Novel* (1916)—were neo-Kantian in character and existentialist in content. These works were preoccupied with the clash between the life-world of authenticity, nobility, clarity, honesty and that of inauthenticity, vulgarity, ambiguity and dishonesty. At times, Lukács posits a mediation between these life-worlds, a mediation which takes the form of a mode of cultural objectifications in the world (such as forms in *The Soul and the Forms* and works in the *Heidelberg Aesthetics*). Yet Lukács ultimately rejects such reconciliation and is left with sheer existential despair.

For example, in his poignant collection of essays on such bourgeois, anticapitalist, romantic figures as Novalis, Kierkegaard, Theodor Storm, Stefan George and Paul Ernst in *The Soul and the Forms,* Lukács presented a dialectical yet ahistorical, that is, tragic, vision of modern life. Fueled by a Kantian dualism of subjective intention and objective causation and filtered through a Kierkegaardian quest for a heroic and authentic life-gesture, Lukács promoted (much like the later Heidegger) a project of passivity, a patient Beckett-like waiting. The only authentic alternatives were a religious expectation of divine grace, or suicide.

This either-or framework—with either passive or destructive results—is best seen in Lukács's crucial 1912 "literary" work, "On Poverty of Spirit" (considered by Max Weber to be on the same par with *The Brothers Karamazov*). The central issue is suicide; the form is that of a letter and dialogue. After the suicide of his lover, the protagonist eventually commits suicide as the enactment of his genuine rejection of the inauthenticity and vulgarity of modern life.[5] For the young Lukács, the intractability of capitalist society, the arbitrariness of human existence and the failure of modern culture to project a realizable future of wholeness yield existential despair. This worldview results in what Agnes Heller has called "a peculiar mixture of proud aristocratism and submissive humility."[6] Lukács's *The Theory of the Novel*—in response to World War I and the collapse of the Second International, and conceived as the introduction to a book on Dostoevsky—attempted to specify the literary content of his nostalgia for a heroic, authentic life, examine its demise and explore its future possibilities. In short, Lukács's quest for wholeness and totality becomes a search for holistic, totalizing narrative.[7] He finds this ideal state of affairs represented by the Greek epic, namely, Homer's poetic narrative. He briefly and therefore crudely sketches the degeneration of this narrative into the modern novel (from Cervantes to Flaubert) in light of the rise of modern experiences of individualism, alienation and time. With the ending of the age of the novel, "the epoch of complete sinfulness" (in Fichte's words), a revised form of the epic poem, of totalizing narrative arrives in the work of Tolstoy and, particularly, of Dostoevsky. As Lukács clearly—hence uncharacteristically—put it in the last paragraphs of this book:

> In Tolstoy, intimations of a breakthrough into a new epoch are visible; but they remain polemical, nostalgic and abstract. It is in the works of Dostoevsky that this new world, remote from any struggle against what actually exists, is drawn for the first time simply as a seen reality. . . . Dostoevsky did not write novels. . . . He belongs to the new world. Only formal analysis of his works can show whether he is already the Homer or the Dante of that world or whether he merely supplies the songs which, together with the songs of other forerunners, later artists will one day weave into a great unity: whether he is merely a beginning or already a completion. It will then be the task of historico-philosophical interpretation to decide whether we are really about to leave the age of absolute sinfulness or whether the new has no

other herald but our hopes: those hopes which are signs of a world to come, still so weak that it can easily be crushed by the sterile power of the merely existent.[8]

What is at stake here is not simply a new totalizing narrative nor a new holistic world, but also a new socioeconomic order. And, more important, the ethical means to bring it about. Dostoevsky's formulation of "everything is permitted if God is dead" and his probing portrayal of terrorism—in addition to Friedrich Hebbel's *Judith,* in which the tyrant Holophernes is murdered and the justification is explored—signify a shift in Lukács's thought from existential concerns to more focused ethical matters. This shift was accelerated by the Russian Revolution. Yet even Marxist revolutionary ideology for the young Lukács lacked an indispensable element— a genuine ethic:

> The ideology of the proletariat, its understanding of solidarity, is still so abstract that—whatever importance we attach to the military arm of the class struggle—the proletariat is incapable of providing a real ethic embracing all aspects of life.[9]

This ethical problematic—the is/ought issue and the immoral means to moral ends—plagued Lukács the rest of his writing career. In his equivocal, neo-Kantian essay of 1918, "Bolshevism as a Moral Problem," Lukács held to a rigid dichotomy of social facts and human values, empirical reality and utopian human will. On the one hand, he agreed with Marxism: "The victory of the proletariat is, of course, an indispensable precondition if the era of true freedom, with neither oppressor nor oppressed, is at last to become a reality." On the other hand, he disagreed: "But it cannot be more than a precondition, a negative fact. For the era of freedom to be attained, it is necessary to go beyond those mere sociological statements of facts and those laws from which it can never be derived: it is necessary to will the new, democratic world."[10]

For the young Lukács, the Marxist attempt at a unity of facts and values, reality and human will, is illusory. It tends to elide the differences—moral and empirical ones—in the real world. In this pivotal essay, Lukács ambiguously applauded the proletariat as "the bearer of the social redemption of humanity" and the legatee of German classical philosophy. Yet he questioned whether the proletariat was really "a mere ideological envelope for real class interests, distinct from other interests not by their quality or moral force, but only by their content."[11] His left neo-Kantianism culminated in his treatment of violence. Reminiscent of John Dewey's critique of Trotsky, Lukács asked whether good can be achieved through evil means, whether capitalist terror can be abolished by means of proletarian terror. Similar to Dewey, Lukács replied:

> I repeat, Bolshevism rests on the metaphysical hypothesis that good can come out of evil, that it is possible, as Razumikhin puts it in *Crime and Punishment,* to attain the truth with a lie. The author of these lines cannot share this belief, and that is why he sees an insoluble moral dilemma in the very roots of the Bolshevik mentality.[12]

The Middle Period

Lukács's middle period begins with his December 1918 conversion to Marxism—he was thirty-three years old. His friend Anna Lesznai noted that Lukács's "conversion took place in the interval between two Sundays: from Saul came Paul."[13] In this period—more accessible and hence well-known to American audiences—Lukács's writings were dialectical in character and political in content. Yet this fundamental shift from neo-Kantianism to Marxism, from existential concerns to political ones, pivoted on the ethical problematic (his first essay as a Bolshevik was "Tactics and Ethics"). In his autobiographical testament, he noted:

> This key decision for my worldview brought about a change in the whole way of life. . . . Ethics (behavior) no longer involved a ban on everything our own ethics condemned as sinful or abstentionist, but established a dynamic equilibrium of praxis in which sin (in its particularity) could sometimes be an integral and ines-

capable part of the right action, whereas ethical limits (if regarded as universally valid) could sometimes be an obstacle to the right action. Opposition: complex: universal (ethical) principles versus practical requirements of the right action.[14]

Yet what was new and striking about Lukács's middle period—and decisive in his later works—was his obsession with the scientific status of Marxist dialectics, the objective character of Marxist theory. As the Bolshevik Lukács crept toward Leninism—through ethical ultraleftism, political ultraleftism and left Bolshevism—he became more captive to a Marxist version of scientism. Lukács's newly acquired political faith had to be grounded in the nature of social and historical reality. His conversion to Marxism was neither simply a Kierkegaardian leap of faith nor a Pascalian wager on history. Rather it was accompanied by an increasingly intense belief in the scientificity of Marxist dialectics and in the certainty of a totality-in-history.

Lukács's classic work *History and Class Consciousness* (1923) was a thoroughly political work focussed on proletarian revolutionary activity against capitalist reification. But one misses a crucial aspect of this masterpiece if one overlooks its philosophical dimension: the attempt to put forward a philosophical foundation for this proletarian revolutionary activity. Lukács's grand attempt to achieve a dialectical synthesis of is and ought, facts and values, politics and ethics, immediate circumstances and final telos, material conditions and human will, object and subject, rests upon claims about the fundamental nature of social and historical reality. And, ironically, these claims rest upon an unarticulated correspondence theory of truth, namely, a theory which invokes agreement with "reality" as the court of appeal for adjudicating between conflicting theories about the world.

On the one hand, it seems as if Lukács recognizes that the theory-laden character of observations relativizes talk about the world, such that realist appeals to "the world" as a final court of appeal to determine what is true can only be viciously circular. He appears to realize that we cannot isolate "the world" or "reality" from theories about the world or reality, then compare these theories with a theory-free world or theory-free reality. Since we cannot compare theories with anything that is not a product of another theory, any talk about "the world" or "reality" is relative to the theories available. At times, Lukács affirms this Peircean-like pragmatic viewpoint:

> The historical process is something unique and its dialectical advances and reverses are an incessant struggle to reach higher stages of the truth and of the (societal) self-knowledge of man. The "relativisation" of truth in Hegel means that the higher factor is always the truth of the factor beneath it in the system. This does not imply the destruction of "objective" truth at the lower stages but only that it means something different as a result of being integrated in a more concrete and comprehensive totality.[15]

On the other hand, Lukács's realist roots come to light when he admits: "It is true that reality is the criterion for the correctness of thought."[16] And his Hegelian metaphysical biases are revealed when he states:

> Thus thought and existence are not identical in the sense that they "correspond" to each other, or "reflect" each other, that they "run parallel" to each other or "coincide" with each other (all expressions that conceal a rigid duality). Their identity is that they are aspects of one and the same real historical and dialectical process. What is "reflected" in the consciousness of the proletariat is the new positive reality arising out of the dialectical contradictions of capitalism.[17]

This philosophical juggling of dialectical pragmatism, philosophical realism and Hegelian idealism breeds confusion. The notion of truth as that-which-holds-in-the-long-run is logically independent of the notion of truth as that-which-reality-determines. And both notions of truth fly in the face of identity-claims about thought and existence within a dialectical process. Lukács's gallant response to neo-Kantian idealism is provocative, but, on a philosophical level, incoherent.

Lukács's attempt to ground the scientificity of Marxist dialectics led him to adopt a form of epistemological foundationalism and philosophical realism. He wanted not only assurance that reality is independent of human consciousness, but also certainty that this reality is inherently dialectical. And the intratheoretic status of the latter claim simply did not satisfy his need to be scientific, that is, certain. For example, he characterized class consciousness and the Communist Party as objective possibilities, yet he also set out to show that the dialectical development of social and historical reality held out the promise of the realizable actualization of them. In short, the basic philosophical contradiction in Lukács's thoroughly Leninist classic is that the historicity of Marxist methodology precludes the kind of scientificity of Marxist dialectics he wants. The bugbear of relativism made Lukács tremble, and his response to it was a creative Hegelian Marxist conception of scientific dialectics. To put it crudely, Lukács replaced the prevailing forms of positivistic scientism with a Hegelian form of scientism in the Marxist tradition.

The result of Lukács's appropriation of Hegel in his own work was twofold. First, it facilitated the most powerful theoretical reading of cultural life in capitalist society, thereby bursting out of the economistic straitjackets of the Second International. Second, it promoted Lukács's own valorizing of Hegel's notion of reconciliation (*Versöhnung*). This valorizing—intimated in "Moses Hess and the Problems of Idealist Dialectics" (1926) and articulated in "Hölderlin's Hyperion" (1935)—led to Lukács's radical antiutopianism, "realism," and thereby his surrender to Stalinism. Of course, it is difficult to determine the extent of Lukacs's actual belief in Stalinism, yet in light of his practice and support, for instance, his 1929 hypocritical rejection of the "Blum Theses," it seems as if his defense of Hegel's antiutopianism and realism justified his own reconciliation with Stalinism.[18]

Lukács's vast intellectual productions between 1926 and 1955 (part of this time he was forced to live in the Soviet Union) primarily consisted of literary criticism and intellectual history. Lukács's novel conception of literary critical realism—enacted by writers such as Scott, Goethe, Balzac, Tolstoy, Dostoevsky, Sholokhov, Gorky and Mann—his rich inquiry into the young Hegel, and his hyperbolic history of European Romanticism were his major projects during this period. Despite great energy and scope, these works display a nagging rigidity, reflective of the Stalinist ethos under which he labored.

The Later Period

In 1955, after the initiation of de-Stalinization in the Soviet Union and just prior to the Soviet repression of democratic forces in his own Hungary (which resulted in his expulsion from the Party and retirement from the University of Budapest), Lukács stated: "I only began my real oeuvre at the age of seventy."[19] For the first time in over thirty years, he engaged in sustained philosophical reflection. In 1963, he published more than 1700 pages entitled *The Specific Nature of the Aesthetic* (and projected two more volumes) and in 1976 (five years after his June 1971 death) another 1700 pages appeared under the title *Toward the Ontology of Social Existence* (he also had promised an Ethics). Both of these not-yet-digested works are dialectical in character and philosophical in content: they present a Marxist epistemology and a Marxist social ontology, respectively. In short, they are Lukacs's most ambitious philosophical works.

These texts initially strike one as strange, primarily because they are written in a philosophical style and terminology reminiscent of pre–World War II Germany. Admittedly, and understandably, Lukács failed to stay in tune with the latest developments in contemporary Anglo-American and Continental philosophy. For example, despite the avalanche of devastating criticisms by Wittgenstein, Heidegger and Quine of reflection theory in epistemology, Lukács adopts in his *Aesthetics* the conception of art as a kind of reflection (*Widerspiegelung*), copy (*Abbild*) or imitation (*Nachahmung*) of reality. In this regard, his homage to Lenin's reflection theory in *Materialism and Empirio-Criticism* is embarrassing. Yet Lukács's philosophical realist position in search of ontological grounding led him to the neglected though most fascinating ontological defense of realism in twentieth-century German philosophy: the prodigious corpus of Nicolai Hartmann.

Hartmann plays a central role in Lukács's later ontological writings. Like Lukács, Hartmann's major shift was a revolt against the neo-Kantianism of his youth. This shift consisted primarily of a move from transcendental idealism to ontology, from schemas which constitute the objective (not real) world to phenomenological descriptions of a multitude of modes and strata of Being. In retrospect, it is important to note that it was Hartmann's *Outlines of a Metaphysic of Knowledge* (1921)—not Heidegger's *Sein und Zeit* (1927)—which initiated the Continental renaissance of ontology, principally by arguing that epistemology is based on ontology. Furthermore, again like Lukács, Hartmann grappled seriously with ethical issues, eventually arriving at the notion in his magnum opus *Ethics* (1926) that the task of ethics is to enable persons to discern objective values in the world, thereby putting ethical values on the level of science (this strategy was adopted ingeniously by the American realist W. M. Urban). Lastly, Hartmann's conception of the teleological character of human activity expounded in his work *Teleological Thought* (1951) serves as a major pillar of Lukács's understanding of human labor.

The significance of Lukács's ontological works is twofold. First, it raises the most fundamental questions regarding the status of Marxist discourse. Is Marxism an ontology, epistemology, science and/or theory? How does one justify one's choice among the possible points of theoretical departure—among class, capital formation, reification, contradiction, overdetermination, mode of production and others—in Marxism? To what extent can Marxism reject a priori formulations of its central notions and remain Marxism? Second, Lukács's ontological work—much like that of the later Wittgenstein, J. L. Austin and Heidegger—conceives the problem of everyday life as worthy of philosophical attention. His Marxist heritage compels him to understand everyday life as a historical product, hence a dynamic form of social existence. Similar to Lefebvre and the later Sartre, Lukács is sensitive to the kind of everyday life in late capitalist society and raises this issue to a philosophical plane. In other words, beneath the dense ontological inquiry in his later works lurks a central concern which guided his classic *History and Class Consciousness:* a theoretical reading of cultural life in capitalist society.

Yet Lukács's importance lies more in raising questions than providing answers. His ontological writings are to the Marxist tradition what Whitehead's are to bourgeois philosophy: rich in metaphysical speculation, full of fascinating insights, innovative in historical reconstruction of major philosophers, yet difficult to take seriously as contemporary philosophical inquiry. It is not simply that his later writings are antiquated or outdated. Rather it is that, despite their length, they lack the appropriate patience and thorough stick-to-itness requisite for coming to terms with the fundamental issues they raise.

For example, it is in no way obvious that there is or can be such a thing as a Marxist ontology or even a Marxist epistemology. After incomplete starts, hints and intimations, Lukács never directly engages this central query in a serious and sustained manner. He shows in a persuasive fashion how Hegel bases his dynamic ontology on his dialectical logic. Lukács then assumes that Marx's historicizing of Hegel's ontology—by concretely contextualizing human labor—yields a social ontology.

It is quite plausible to argue that Marx's critique of Hegel's ontology does not simply reject Hegel's logical foundations but, more important, calls into question the very notion of ontology. *Ontologia* as a philosophical term (coined by scholastic writers in the seventeenth century) was canonized by the German rationalist Christian Wolff (the writer responsible for Kant's "dogmatic slumber" prior to his awakening by Hume).[20]

What Wolff had in mind was a deductive method by which the single sense of Being could be disclosed. In our own time, Hartmann and Heidegger breathed new life into the term by both historicizing it and situating it in relation to scientific inquiry. Lukács makes it clear that his ontology is a science: "the science of objective dialectics manifesting itself in reality."[21] He goes as far as to try to revive a dynamic conception of substantiality. Yet Marx's critique of Hegel's ontology was precisely that historical consciousness, understood concretely, shifted pontifical ontological pronouncements on Being to engaged theoretical discourse about reality. In short, methodological issues and theoretical considerations replace ontological and metaphysical ones. Reality indeed is "outside" of theories, but claims about reality are intratheoretic. And, given the concrete historical character of theories, the clash of major social theories constitutes clashes between historical forces.

In other words, Marx's critique of Hegel's ontology not only puts an end to ontological inquiries but, more important, opens the door to self-reflective methodological considerations on the ideological character of scientific theories. Marx did not explore this path in any systematic way—with the major exception being his demystification of bourgeois scientific theories in political economy. Yet he surely precluded the kind of ontological investigation Lukács attempts.

Why then did Lukács—the greatest Marxist thinker of this century—pursue such a futile project? Chiefly because he never really took the historicist turn that Marx, Nietzsche and others initiated. Notwithstanding his fifty-three years in the Marxist camp, Lukács remained, in a fundamental way, true to his neo-Kantian idealist problematic. He remained in search of certainty, in need of philosophical foundations. He had to find a secure grounding for his belief in the objective possibility of wholeness and life-meaning.

The central problem for neo-Kantian idealism is agnosticism about reality. Lukács spent most of his life trying to supplant this agnosticism with the Marxist faith that reality is not only "there" but also going "somewhere." Therefore Lukács's historicism did not cut deep enough—at the bottom of it still sat Kant. In fact, Lukács's ontological writings can best be seen as the culmination of his lifelong quarrel with Kant, aided by Hegel, Marx and Hartmann.

If Lukács's profound formulations of Marx's social ontology are viewed as deliberations on the complexity of Marx's theoretical methodology, we can more fully appreciate his contribution to contemporary Marxist discourse and praxis. For instance, he demythologizes the Althusserian reduction of Hegelian totality to expressive causality:

> If we now attempt to summarize what is most essential in Hegel's ontology from what has so far been obtained, we arrive at the result that he conceives reality as a totality of complexes that are in themselves, thus relatively, total, that the objective dialectic consists in the real genesis and self-development, interaction and synthesis of these complexes, and that therefore the absolute itself, as the epitome of these total movements, can never reach a standstill of removed indifference towards concrete movements, that it is rather itself movement, process, as the concrete synthesis of real movements—without prejudice to its absolute character, and that the original form of the Hegelian contradiction, the identity of identity and non-identity, remains insurpassably effective in the absolute too. This dialectical ontological core of Hegel's philosophy stands in evident contrast to the logically hierarchical construction of his system.[22]

In contrast to Althusser's claims, Lukács shows how Hegel enables Marx to arrive at an overdetermined conception of contradiction, a flexible yet firm explanatory framework for social activities:

> The opposition between "elements" and totality should never be reduced to an opposition between the intrinsically simple and the intrinsically compound. . . . Every "element" and every part, in other words, is just as much a whole; the "element" is always

a complex with concrete and qualitatively specific properties, a complex of various collaborating forces and relations. However, this complexity does not negate its character as an "element."[23]

In fact, Lukács echoes Althusser's sophisticated conception of totality:

> Marx warns against making the irreducible, dialectical and contradictory unity of society, a unity that emerges as the end product of the interaction of innumerable heterogeneous processes, into an intrinsically homogeneous unity, and impeding adequate knowledge of this unity by inadmissable and simplifying homogenizations. . . . Two things follow from this. Firstly, each element retains its ontological specificity . . . secondly, these interrelations are not equal value, either pair by pair or as a whole, but they are rather all pervaded by the ontological priority of production as the predominant moment.[24]

Lukács's treatment of Hegel is unique in that he highlights the role of the reflection determinations in the transition from understanding (*Verstand*) to reason (*Vernunft*). This is not surprising given Lukács's attempt to reply to Kant and arrive at reality. This focus enables Lukács to put forward a novel approach to an old Marxist problem: the problem of the relation of essence to appearance:

> Hegel's philosophical revolution, his discovery of and focussing on the reflection determinations, consists above all in the ontological removal of the chasm of absolute separation between appearance and essence. In so far as the essence is conceived neither as existing and transcendent, nor as the product of a process of mental abstraction, but rather as a moment of a dynamic complex, in which essence, appearance and illusion continuously pass into one another, the reflection determinations show themselves in this new conception as primarily ontological in character. . . . That essence and illusion, irrespective of their sharp contrast, belong inseparably together, and that the one can in no way exist without the other, provides the ontological foundation for the epistemological path from understanding to reason; the former remains impris-

oned at the level of the immediate givenness of contradiction, which is however itself an ontological property of the complex, while the latter gradually raises itself up to comprehend the complex as a dialectical totality via a series of transitions.[25]

This passage disarms any catechistic Marxist formulations of rigid oppositions between essence and appearance (based on the famous quotation in Volume III of *Das Capital*). It also situates the philosophical predicament and ontological motivation of Paul de Man's obsession with the symbiotic relationship between truth and error, insight and blindness—a predicament which can only repeat itself and a motivation any Derridean should scorn.

The grandiose conclusions Lukács draws from focusing on the reflection determinations, from following the move from understanding to reason, are exorbitant:

> If we consider Hegel's epistemological path from understanding to reason, its epochal significance is easy to make clear. In contrast to earlier thinkers, or to his contemporaries, Hegel managed to lay the foundations for knowledge of a complex, dynamically contradictory reality, consisting of totalities, something that had defeated the epistemology of his predecessors. He applied the higher level of reason that was now attainable to the entire area of knowledge; he did not remain, as did the Enlightenment, at the level of the understanding; he did not shift rational knowledge, as Kant did, to the unknowable realm of the thing-in-itself, and his criticism of the understanding did not lead him, with Schelling and the Romantics, into the nebulous realm of irrationalism. It is thus quite justifiable to say, with Lenin, that the dialectic is a theory of knowledge. But Marxist epistemology, as a theory of the subjective dialectic, simultaneously always presupposes an ontology, i.e. a theory of the objective dialectic in reality.[26]

If Lukács took historicism seriously, his own conception of ontology as a scientific theory of reality itself would fall prey to the reflection-determination machinery. That is, it would include itself in the process of negation, preservation and transformation. Whether the result is post-Marxism, anti-Marxism or neo-Marxism is an open question—with crucial political consequences.

The two linchpins of Lukács's Marxist ontology are his philosophical realist position and his conception of science. Both lead him to conceive of philosophical discourse as a metadiscourse (ontology and epistemology) which grounds the master discourse (Marxist theory) of modern capitalist societies. His philosophical realist position—much like that intimated in *History and Class Consciousness* after the Hegelian smoke cleared—rests upon an "epistemology of mimesis" in which "agreement with reality is the sole criterion of correct thought."[27]

This realist position undergirds Lukács's conception of science as disinterested and objective. His clearest statements about science are found in his *Aesthetics:*

> The de-anthropomorphising of science is an instrument by which man masters the world: it is a making-conscious, a raising up to a method, that form of conduct which, as we have shown, begins with work that differentiates man from animal and which helps make him into a man. Work and the highest conscious form which grows out of work, scientific conduct, is in this case not only merely an instrument for mastering the world, but in its very nature is a detour which enables a rich discovery of reality which enriches man himself and makes him more complete and more humane than he could be otherwise.[28]
>
> Science focuses on Being as such and seeks to re-produce it in its purest possible form which is freed from all subjective additions.[29]

This veneration of science rivals that of the old positivists. And the claim about the humanizing effects of science is a throwback to pre–World War I bourgeois optimism. Lukács remains absolutely silent about the technological character of science and the ideological character of technology.

Lukács's view of science has dire consequences for art and he candidly accepts them: art cannot give knowledge. Science discovers general laws, whereas art discloses a specialness (*Besonderheit*). This specialness consists of an absolute and complete totality; it involves a "return" to the self after acquiring a self-consciousness of the social world. Unlike science, art is anthropomorphic; it begins and ends with the subject while transcending mere subjectivity. Unlike religion, art is this-worldly (*diesseitig*); it makes no claims about transcendent reality or otherworldly redemption.

Lukács's neo-Kantian roots are quite apparent in his view of science: particularly the fundamental distinction between *Geisteswissenschaften* and *Naturwissenschaften*. Despite his attempt to reformulate Engels's dialectics of nature and thereby overcome this distinction, his neo-Kantian perspective remains in his crucial dichotomy of natural causation and labor teleology:

> A real ontology of social being is not possible without a correct contrasting of natural casuality and labour teleology, without the presentation of their concrete dialectical interconnections.[30]

Lukács relates these two processes in a less rigid and more sophisticated manner than any of the neo-Kantians, including the renegade Hartmann:

> The value of this differentiation made by Hartmann should not be underestimated. Separation of the two acts, the positing of the goal and the investigation of the means, is of the highest importance for an understanding of the labour process, and particularly for its significance in the ontology of social being. Precisely here, we can see the inseparable connection of two categories that are in themselves antithetical, and which viewed abstractly are mutually exclusive: causality and teleology.[31]

Natural causality and labor teleology are central categories for Lukács because in the latter lies the uniqueness of human beings. He considers "the genetic leap" (his phrase)—the move from animals to human beings—to have been achieved by conscious, goal-directed action:

The overcoming of animality by the leap to humanization in labour, the overcoming of the epiphenomenal consciousness determined merely by biology, thus acquires, through the development of labour, an unstayable momentum, a tendency towards a prevalent universality.[32]

For Lukács, Kant provided the proper starting point on this issue and Marx (mediated by Hegel) arrived at the acceptable answer:

By defining organic life as "purposiveness without purpose," he [Kant] hit on a genial way to describe the ontological essence of the organic sphere. His correct criticism demolished the superficial teleology of the theodicists who preceded him, and who saw the realization of a transcendent teleology even in the mere usefulness of one thing for another. He thereby opened the way to a correct knowledge of this sphere of being . . . but when Kant is analyzing human practice, he directs his attention exclusively to its highest, most subtle and most socially derived form, pure morality, which thus does not emerge for him dialectically from the activities of life (society), but stands rather in an essential and insuperable antithesis to these activities. . . . [Hence] Kant had to speak— of course in his epistemologically oriented terminology—of the incompatibility of causality and teleology. But once teleology is recognized, as by Marx, as a really effective category, exclusive to labour, the concrete real and necessary coexistence of causality and teleology inexorably follows.[33]

Lukács seeks to avoid an old-style teleology which posits a goal for both nature and history while promoting a teleology in the social world. Ironically, his subtle analysis of the interrelation and interpenetration of natural causality and labor teleology is such that he can be accused of a creeping overarching teleology—with the goal of ever-broadening socialization and humanization:

There can be no economic arts—from rudimentary labour right through to purely social production—which do not have underlying them an ontologically immanent intention towards the humanization of man in the broadest sense, i.e., from his genesis through all his development. This ontological characteristic of the economic sphere casts light on its relationship with the other realms of social practice. . . . This contention is in itself completely value-free.[34]

Lastly, Lukács's philosophical realist position and his conception of science result in his view of philosophical discourse as a metadiscourse which supports the master discourse on modern capitalist societies. At this point, the parallel with Kant is irresistible. To put it crudely, just as Kant's aim was to secure the scientificity of Newtonian physics and leave room for moral action, so Lukács's aim was to secure the scientificity of Marxist dialectics and leave room for political praxis. Both projects assume an uncritical attitude toward the status of their own discourse and an unwavering acceptance of the "sciences" to be legitimated.

What is at issue here is not whether Marxist theory is *the* master discourse on modern capitalist societies. Despite its rich explanatory power, there is little doubt that Marxist theory is not the master discourse on modern forms of oppression. For example, Marxist discourse has no acceptable theory of the specificity of racial or sexual oppression. The major concern here is the relation between believing in *the* master discourse and justifying that belief by concocting a metadiscourse to ground *the* master discourse. This operation is, in essence, a theological one: an attempt to provide philosophical foundations for a leap of faith or present ontological grounds for a wager on reality. Such leaping and wagering is unavoidable, but the operation itself is deceptive and dishonest. My aim here is not to make us all religionists, but rather to accent the dimension of risk and uncertainty in our most fundamental commitments and convictions.

What is disturbing about Lukács is his reluctance to admit this dimension of risk and uncertainty within his Marxist faith. This reluctance, I suggest, flows from his intense existential bout with neo-Kantian agnosticism about reality; it also reflects a deeply bourgeois worldview, in which the slightest acknowledgment of uncertainty and arbitrariness signifies fundamental crisis. This bourgeois worldview—which encompasses many perspectives—consists of a broad set of values and sensibilities over which hangs a heavy cloud of utmost seriousness. Like Nietzsche's "spirit of gravity," it invokes privileged beneficiaries of capitalist fruits making life-and-death decisions in the solitude of their finely decorated writing rooms:

> 15 December. The crisis seems to be over. . . . But I look on my "life," my "capacity to go on living" as a kind of Decadence: if I had committed suicide, I would be alive, at the height of my essence, consistent. Now everything is just pale compromise and degradation.[35]

What is missing in Lukács's Marxism is a sense of fundamental openness and flexibility—a protean outlook which embodies the risks and uncertainties which permeate the life-worlds of the oppressed peoples for whom he struggled. This outlook is absent partly because Lukács's central neo-Kantian problematic—against which he struggled most of his life—was defined initially in a bourgeois, academic milieu, in a highbrow, aristocratic ambience where proletarian culture dare not tread. Like Sartre, Lukács remained rooted in his intellectual, bourgeois beginnings; unlike Sartre, he rarely explored how these beginnings shaped the long and winding Marxist path he blazed.

11

Fredric Jameson's American Marxism

Fredric Jameson is the most challenging American Marxist hermeneutic thinker on the present scene. His ingenious interpretations (prior to accessible translations) of major figures of the Frankfurt School, Russian formalism, French structuralism and poststructuralism as well as of Georg Lukács, Jean-Paul Sartre, Louis Althusser, Max Weber and Louis Marin are significant contributions to the intellectual history of twentieth-century Marxist and European thought. Jameson's treatments of the development of the novel, the surrealist movement, of Continental writers such as Honoré de Balzac, Marcel Proust, Alessandro Manzoni and Alain Robbe-Grillet, and of American writers, including Ernest Hemingway, Kenneth Burke and Ursula Le Guin, constitute powerful political readings. Furthermore, his adamantly antiphilosophical form of Marxist hermeneutics puts forward an American *Aufhebung* of poststructuralism that merits close scrutiny.

In this chapter I shall highlight Jameson's impressive intellectual achievements, specific theoretical flaws, and particular political shortcomings by focusing on the philosophical concerns and ideological aims in his trilogy.[1] Jameson is first and foremost a loyal, though critical, disciple of the Lukács of *History and Class Consciousness,* in the sense that he nearly dogmatically believes that commodification—the selling of human labor power to profit-maximizing capitalists—is the primary source of domination in capitalist societies and that reification—the appearance of this relation be-

tween persons and classes as relations between things and prices—
is the major historical process against which to understand norms,
values, sensibilities, texts and movements in the modern world.[2]
The central question that haunts Jameson is "How to be a
sophisticated Lukácsian Marxist without Lukács's nostalgic historicism and highbrow humanism?" A more general formulation of
this question is "How to take history, class struggle and capitalist
dehumanization seriously after the profound poststructuralist deconstructions of solipsistic Cartesianism, transcendental Kantian-
ism, teleological Hegelianism, genetic Marxism and recuperative
humanism?" In Anglo-American commonsense lingo, this query
becomes "How to live and act in the face of the impotence of irony
and the paralysis of skepticism?" The pressing problem that plagues
Jameson is whether the Marxist quest for totalization—with its
concomitant notions of totality, mediation, narrative (or even universal) history, part/whole relations, essence/appearance distinctions and subject/object oppositions—presupposes a form of philosophical idealism that inevitably results in a mystification which
ignores difference, flux, dissemination and heterogeneity. Jameson's
work can be read as a gallant attempt at such a quest, which hopes
to avoid idealist presuppositions and preclude mystifying results.

Jameson initiates this quest by examining the major European
Marxist thinker for whom this problematic looms large: Jean-Paul
Sartre.[3] Yet Jameson's project takes shape in the encounter with
the rich German tradition of Marxist dialectical thought best exemplified in the works of Adorno, Benjamin, Marcuse, Bloch and, of
course, Lukács. His dialectical perspective first tries to reveal the
philosophical and political bankruptcy of modern Anglo-American
thought. In the preface to *Marxism and Form* he writes:

> Less obvious, perhaps, is the degree to which anyone presenting
> German and French dialectical literature is forced—either implic-
> itly or explicitly—to take yet a third national tradition into ac-
> count, I mean our own: that mixture of political liberalism, empiri-
> cism, and logical positivism which we know as Anglo-American

philosophy and which is hostile at all points to the type of thinking outlined here. One cannot write for a reader formed in this tradition—one cannot even come to terms with one's own historical formation—without taking this influential conceptual opponent into account; and it is this, if you like, which makes up the tendentious part of my book, which gives it its political and philosophical cutting edge, so to speak. (MF x)

Jameson's battle against modern Anglo-American thought is aided by poststructuralism in that deconstructions disclose the *philosophical* bankruptcy of this bourgeois humanist tradition. Yet such deconstructions say little about the *political* bankruptcy of this tradition; further, and more seriously, deconstructions conceal the political impotency of their own projects. In short, Jameson rightly considers poststructuralism an ally against bourgeois humanism yet ultimately an intellectual foe and political enemy. His tempered appreciation and subsequent rejection of structuralism and poststructuralism are enacted in his superb critical treatment of their roots and development in *The Prison-House of Language*. For example, he writes in the preface of this text:

My own plan—to offer an introductory survey of these movements which might stand at the same time as a critique of their basic methodology—is no doubt open to attack from both partisans and adversaries alike. . . . The present critique does not, however, aim at judgments of detail, nor at the expression of some opinion, either positive or negative, on the works in question here. It proposes rather to lay bare what Collingwood would have called the "absolute presuppositions" of Formalism and Structuralism taken as intellectual totalities. These absolute presuppositions may then speak, for themselves, and, like all such ultimate premises or models, are too fundamental to be either accepted or rejected. (PHL x)

Jameson's first lengthy treatment of the Marxist dialectical tradition focuses on the most intelligent thinker and adroit stylist of that tradition: Theodor Adorno.[4] Adorno presents Jameson with his most formidable challenge, for Adorno's delicate dialectical acrobatics embark on the quest for totalization while simultaneously calling such a quest into question; they reconstruct the part in light of the whole while deconstructing the notion of a whole; they devise a complex conception of mediation while disclosing the idea of totality as illusion; and they ultimately promote dialectical development while surrendering to bleak pessimism about ever attaining a desirable telos. In short, Adorno is a negative hermeneutical thinker, a dialectical deconstructionist par excellence: the skeleton that forever hangs in Jameson's closet.

In this way, Adorno is the most ingenious and dangerous figure for Jameson. Adorno ingeniously makes and maintains contact with the concrete in a dialectical demystifying movement that begins with the art object and engages the psychological, that moves from the psychological and implicates the social, and then finds the economic in the social. Yet he refuses to ossify the object of inquiry or freeze the concepts he employs to interrogate the object. This intellectual energy and ability is characterized by Jameson in the following way:

> It is to this ultimate squaring of the circle that Adorno came in his two last and most systematic, most technically philosophical works, *Negative Dialectics* and *Aesthetic Theory*. Indeed, as the title of the former suggests, these works are designed to offer a theory of the untheorizable, to show why dialectical thinking is at one and the same time both indispensable and impossible, to keep the idea of system itself alive while intransigently dispelling the pretentions of any of the contingent and already realized systems to validity and even to existence. . . . Thus a negative dialectic has no choice but to affirm the notion and value of an ultimate synthesis, while negating its possibility and reality in every concrete case that comes before it . . . . negative dialectics does not result in an empty formalism, but rather in a thoroughgoing critique of forms, in a painstaking and well-nigh permanent destruction of every possible hypostasis of the various moments of thinking itself. (MF 54–55, 56)

Adorno is dangerous for Jameson because his deconstructionist strategies and political impotence resemble the very poststructuralism with which Jameson wrestles. Jameson never adequately settles this deep tension with Adorno. In his later work, he circumvents this tension by reducing Adorno's negative dialectics to an aesthetic ideal, and this reduction minimizes Adorno's philosophical challenge to Jameson's own antiphilosophical hermeneutics. Jameson tries to disarm Adorno's position by construing it as a perspective that reconfirms that status of the concept of totality by reacting to and deconstructing "totality."[5] In Jameson's view, the antitotalizing deconstructionist strategies of Jacques Derrida and Paul de Man also "confirm" the status of the concept of totality, since such strategies "must be accompanied by some initial appearance of continuity, some ideology of unification already in place, which it is their mission to rebuke and to shatter" (PU 53). Jameson seems to be employing a rather slippery notion of how the idea of totality is confirmed, since powerful projects which "rebuke" and "shatter" this idea appear to "confirm" it. On this crucial point, Jameson presents neither a persuasive argument against deconstructionists nor a convincing case for his own position, but rather a defensive recuperative strategy that co-opts the deconstructionists in a quest for totality unbeknownst and unrecognizable to them. This ad hoc strategy reflects Jameson's unsettled tension with Adorno and his reluctance to come to terms with Paul de Man's rigorous version of deconstruction.[6]

Yet what is missing in Adorno, Jameson finds in Benjamin, Marcuse and Bloch: a theoretical mechanism that sustains hope and generates praxis in the present moment of the historical process. Such hope and praxis are promoted by a *politicized notion of desire* that is sustained by a "nostalgia conscious of itself, a lucid and remorseless dissatisfaction with the present on the grounds of some remembered plenitude" (MF 82). For example, Jameson is attracted to Benjamin primarily because Benjamin's conception of nostalgic utopianism as a revolutionary stimulus in the present delivers Jameson from the wretched pessimism of Adorno.

For Jameson, Benjamin's notion of nostalgic utopianism—best

elucidated in his masterful essay on Nikolai Leskov, "The Story-teller"—unfolds as storytelling that does justice to our experience of the past, as nonnovelistic (hence, nonindividualistic) narrative that makes contact with the concrete, with an authentic form of social and historical existence quickly vanishing owing to the reification process in late monopoly capitalism. Following Benjamin, Jameson holds that reification destroys the conditions for storytelling, for meaningful destinies and common plots that encompass the past, present and future of the human community. Therefore one-dimensional societies do not simply domesticate their opposition; they also deprive such opposition of the very means to stay in touch with any revolutionary past or visionary future. Such societies present no stories, but rather "only a series of experiences of equal weight whose order is indiscriminately reversible" (MF 79).

Jameson conceives the politicized notion of desire—found first in Friedrich Schiller and then more fully in Herbert Marcuse—as the transformative élan repressed and submerged by the reification process in late monopoly capitalism. This conception of desire constitutes the central component of Jameson's notion of freedom, a notion that he argues can never be conceptually grasped but rather symptomatically displayed in the dissatisfaction of the present, in a Faustian Refusal of the Instant, or in a Blochian ontological astonishment that renders us aware of the "not-yet" latent in the present. To put it crudely, Jameson's politicized notion of desire promises access to a revolutionary energy lurking beneath the social veil of appearances, an energy capable of negating the reified present order.

This notion of freedom—or negational activity motivated by the desire for freedom—serves as the "center" that Jameson's Marxist hermeneutics dialectically discloses and decenters. This is what makes his viewpoint *political* and *hermeneutical* as opposed to *idealistic* and *philosophical*. For example, he states,

> For hermeneutics, traditionally a technique whereby religions recuperated the texts and spiritual activities of cultures resistant to them, is also a political discipline, and provides the means for

maintaining contact with the very sources of revolutionary energy during a stagnant time, or preserving the concept of freedom itself, underground, during geological ages of repression. Indeed, it is the concept of freedom which . . . proves to be the privileged instrument of a political hermeneutic, and which, in turn, is perhaps itself best understood as an interpretive device rather than a philosophical essence or idea.[7] (MF 84)

Jameson's totalizing impulse is seen quite clearly in his claim that this political hermeneutic approach is the "absolute horizon of all reading and all interpretation" (PU 17). This approach preserves, negates and transcends all prevailing modes of reading and interpreting texts, whether psychoanalytic, myth-critical, stylistic, ethical, structural or poststructural. Jameson unequivocally states,

One of the essential themes of this book will be the contention that Marxism subsumes other interpretive modes or systems; or, to put it in methodological terms, that the limits of the latter can always be overcome, and their more positive findings retained, by a radical historicizing of their mental operations, such that not only the content of the analysis, but the very method itself, along with the analyst, then comes to be reckoned into the "text" or phenomenon to be explained. (PU 47)

This totalizing impulse can be best understood in the crucial links Jameson makes among the notions of desire, freedom and narrative. In a fascinating and important discussion of André Breton's *Manifesto,* Jameson writes,

It is not too much to say that for Surrealism a genuine plot, a genuine narrative, is that which can stand as the very *figure* of Desire itself: and this not only because in the Freudian sense pure physiological desire is inaccessible as such to consciousness, but also because in the socioeconomic context, genuine desire risks being dissolved and lost in the vast network of pseudosatisfactions which makes up the market system. In that sense desire is the form taken by freedom in the new commercial environment, by a freedom we do not even realize we have lost unless we think of it in terms, not only of the stilling, but also of the awakening, of Desire in general. (MF 100–101)

In Jameson's sophisticated version of Lukácsian Marxism, narrative is the means by which the totality is glimpsed, thereby preserving the possibility of dialectical thinking. This glimpse of totality—disclosed in a complex and coherent story about conflicting classes and clashing modes of production—constitutes the "very figure of Desire" in the present, a desire that both enables and enacts the negation of the present. Jameson understands this notion, unlike the function of the notion of desire in poststructuralism, to result in a will to freedom, not in a will to presence. In fact, Jameson's conception of the function of desire is much closer to the Christian view of a will to salvation than the deconstructionist "will to presence"; that is, Jameson's perspective more closely resembles a transcendental system which regulates human action than a rhetorical system which circumscribes epistemological moves.

Jameson's American Marxist *Aufhebung* of poststructuralism posits the major terrain—the primal scene—of contemporary criticism not as epistemology, but as ethics. Instead of focusing on the numerous Sisyphean attempts to construct a metaphysics of presence, he highlights the various efforts to negate the present and shows how such negations point toward a society of freedom. For example, Jacques Derrida, the preeminent deconstructionist, brilliantly unmasks the binary oppositions in traditional and contemporary Western thought, such as speech and writing, presence and absence and so forth. Yet Derrida remains oblivious to similar binary oppositions in ethics such as good and evil.

> To move from Derrida to Nietzsche is to glimpse the possibility of a rather different interpretation of the binary opposition, according to which its positive and negative terms are ultimately assimilated by the mind as a distinction between good and evil. Not metaphysics but ethics is the informing ideology of the binary opposition: and we have forgotten the thrust of Nietzsche's thought and lost everything scandalous and virulent about it if

we cannot understand how it is ethics itself which is the ideological vehicle and the legitimation of concrete structures of power and domination. (PU 114)

Jameson's attempt to shift the fierce epistemological and metaphysical battles in contemporary Continental philosophy and criticism to ethics is invigorating and impressive. This shift is prompted by his de-Platonizing of the poststructuralist notion of desire—which freely floats above history like a Platonic form only to be embodied in various versions of metaphysics of presence—and his placing it in the underground of history which emerges in the form of a negation of the present, as an "ontological patience in which the constraining situation itself is for the first time perceived in the very moment in which it is refused" (MF 84–85). Of course, Jameson recognizes that this shift replaces one metaphysical and mythical version of desire with his own. Yet, in his view, his politicized notion of desire has crucial historical consequences and therefore it is more acceptable than the poststructuralist conception of desire.

> Yet, it will be observed, even if the theory of desire is a metaphysic and a myth, it is one whose great narrative events—repression and revolt—ought to be congenial to a Marxist perspective, one whose ultimate Utopian vision of the liberation of desire and of libidinal transfiguration was an essential feature of the great mass revolts of the 1960s in Eastern and Western Europe as well as in China and the United States. (PU 67)

Jameson's project of politicizing the notion of desire is rooted in Schiller's *Letters on the Aesthetic Education of Mankind,* which sidesteps the Kantian epistemological question of the necessary conditions for the possibility of experience, and instead raises the more political question of the speculative and hypothetical (or utopian) conditions for the possibility of a free and harmonious personality. In attempting to answer this question, Schiller presents analogies between the psyche and society, between the mental divisions of impulses (*Stofftrieb, Formtrieb* and *Spieltrieb*) and the social divisions of labor (Work, Reason and Art). In the same vein, Jameson's reading of Marcuse's *Eros and Civilization* sees Marcuse as replacing Freud's inquiry into the structure of actual mental phenomena with an inquiry into the speculative and hypothetical conditions for the possibility of an aggression-free society in which work is libidinally satisfying. As in Benjamin's nostalgic utopianism, the primary function of memory is to serve the pleasure principle; the origin of utopian thought resides in the remembered plenitude of psychic gratification. Jameson quotes Marcuse's famous formulation of the origins of thought. "The memory of gratification is at the origin of all thinking, and the impulse to recapture past gratification is the hidden driving power behind the process of thought."[8] Jameson then adds,

> The primary energy of revolutionary activity derived from this memory of a prehistoric happiness which the individual can regain only through its externalization, through its reestablishment for society as a whole. The loss or repression of the very sense of such concepts as freedom and desire takes, therefore, the form of a kind of amnesia or forgetful numbness, which the hermeneutic activity, the stimulation of memory as the negation of the here and now, as the projection of Utopia, has as its function to dispel, restoring to us the original clarity and force of our own most vital drives and wishes. (MF 113–14)

It should be apparent that Jameson is, in many ways, a traditional hermeneutical thinker; that is, his basic theoretical strategy is that of recuperation, restoration and recovery.[9] Furthermore, his fundamental aim is to preserve the old Christian notion—and Marxist affirmation—that history is meaningful:

> Only Marxism can give us an adequate account of the essential *mystery* of the cultural past, which, like Tiresias drinking blood, is momentarily returned to life and warmth and allowed once more to speak, and to deliver its long-forgotten message in surroundings utterly alien to it. This mystery can be reenacted only if the human adventure is one. . . . These matters can recover their original

urgency for us only if they are retold within the unity of a single
great collective story; only if, in however disguised and symbolic
form, they are seen as sharing a single fundamental theme—for
Marxism, the collective struggle to wrest a realm of Freedom from
a realm of Necessity; only if they are grasped as vital episodes in
a single vast unfinished plot.[10] (PU 19–20)

Jameson recognizes the deep affinity of his Marxist project with
religious *Weltanschauungen*. And since he is not afflicted with the
petty, antireligious phobia of scientistic Marxists, Jameson develops
his affinity by juxtaposing the medieval Christian allegorical method
and Northrop Frye's interpretive system with his own project.[11] In
fact, the system of four levels—the literal, allegorical, moral and
anagogical levels—of medieval Christian allegorical interpretation
constitutes a crucial component of his theoretical framework. This
model provides him a means by which to come to terms with the
persistent problem for Marxism: the problem of mediation, the task
of specifying the relationship between various levels and of adapting
analyses from one level to another in light of a meaningful story of
the past, present and future of the human community.

The first (or literal) level permits Jameson to retain the historical
referents of events and happenings—such as human suffering, domination and struggle—and the textual referents of books and
works—such as conflict-ridden historical situations, class-ridden
social conditions and antinomy-ridden ideological configurations.
In this way, Jameson accepts the antirealist arguments of poststructuralists, yet rejects their textual idealism.[12] He acknowledges that
history is always already mediated by language, texts and interpretations, yet he insists that history is still, in some fundamental sense,
"there." He conceives of history as an "absent cause" known by
its "formal effects." In the crucial paragraph that directly replies
to textual idealists and completes his theoretical chapter in *The
Political Unconscious* he writes,

> History is therefore the experience of Necessity, and it is this alone
> which can forestall its thematization or reification as a mere object

of representation or as one master code among many others. Necessity is not in that sense a type of content, but rather the inexorable *form* of events; it is therefore a narrative category in the enlarged sense of some properly narrative political unconscious which has been argued here, a retextualization of History which does not propose the latter as some new representation or "vision," some new content, but as the formal effects of what Althusser, following Spinoza, calls an "absent cause." Conceived in this sense, History is what hurts, it is what refuses desire and sets inexorable limits to individual as well as collective praxis, which its "ruses" turn into grisly and ironic reversals of their overt intention. But this History can be apprehended only through its effects, and never directly as some reified force. This is indeed the ultimate sense in which History as ground and untranscendable horizon needs no particular theoretical justification: we may be sure that its alienating necessities will not forget us, however much we might prefer to ignore them. (PU 102)

The second (or allegorical) level sets forth the interpretive code, which is for Jameson the mediatory code of the reification process in capitalist societies.[13] This mediatory code takes the form of a genealogical construction characterized by neither genetic continuity nor teleological linearity, but rather by what Bloch called *Ungleichzeitigkeit* or "nonsynchronous development." This conception of history and texts as a "synchronic unity of structurally contradictory or heterogeneous elements, genetic patterns, and discourses" allows Jameson to identify and isolate particular aspects of the past as preconditions for the elaboration of reifying elements in the present.[14]

The third (or moral) level constitutes an ethical or psychological reading in which, following Althusser's conception of ideology, representational structures permit individual subjects to conceive their lived relationships to transindividual realities such as the destiny of humankind or the social structure. The fourth (or anagogical) level—which is inseparable from the third level—provides a political reading for the collective meaning of history, a characterization of the transindividual realities that link the individual to a fate, plot and story of a community, class, group or society.

Jameson's appropriation of the medieval system leads him to redefine the activity of interpretation in allegorical terms; that is, his own political allegorical machinery, with its aims of ideological unmasking and utopian projection, dictates the way in which interpretation and criticism ought to proceed.

> We will assume that a criticism which asks the question "What does it mean?" constitutes something like an allegorical operation in which a text is systematically *rewritten* in terms of some fundamental master code or "ultimately determining instance." On this view, then, all "interpretation" in the narrower sense demands the forcible or imperceptible transformation of a given text into an allegory of its particular master code or "transcendental signified": the discredit into which interpretation has fallen is thus at one with the disrepute visited on allegory itself.
>
> Yet to see interpretation this way is to acquire the instruments by which we can force a given interpretive practice to stand and yield up its name, to blurt out its master code and thereby reveal its metaphysical and ideological underpinnings. (PU 58)

Jameson's redefinition of the allegorical model also draws him closer to Northrop Frye. In *Marxism and Form*, Jameson invokes, in a respectful yet somewhat pejorative manner, Frye's interpretive system as "the only philosophically coherent alternative" to Marxist hermeneutics.[15] In a later essay, "Criticism in History," Jameson harshly criticizes Frye's system as ahistorical and guilty of presupposing an unacceptable notion of unbroken continuity between the narrative forms of "primitive" societies and those of modern times.[16] Yet in *The Political Unconscious*, there is some change of heart.

> In the present context, however, Frye's work comes before us as a virtual contemporary reinvention of the four-fold hermeneutic associated with the theological tradition. . . .
>
> The greatness of Frye, and the radical difference between his work and that of the great bulk of garden-variety myth criticism,

lies in his willingness to raise the issue of community and to draw
basic, essentially social, interpretive consequences from the nature
of religion as collective representation. (PU 69)

In fact, Jameson's central concept of the political unconscious—
though often defined in Lévi-Straussian language as a historical
pensée sauvage and influenced by the Feuerbachian and Durkheim-
ian conceptions of religion—derives from Frye's notion of literature
(be it a weaker form of myth or a later stage of ritual) as a "symbolic
meditation on the destiny of community."[17] What upsets Jameson
about Frye is no longer simply Frye's ahistorical approach, but,
more important, Frye's Blakean anagogy—the image of the cosmic
body—which Jameson claims privatizes a political anagogy and
hence poses the destiny of the human community in an individualistic manner, in terms of the isolated body and personal gratification.[18]

Frye's conflation of ethics and politics gives Jameson the opportunity both to congratulate and to criticize him. Jameson congratu-
lates Frye—the North American liberal version of structuralism—
because Frye conceives the central problematic of criticism to be
not epistemological but rather ethical, namely the relation of texts
to the destiny of human communities. In this sense, Frye is preferable
to the French structuralists and poststructuralists, since he understands that there is a crucial relationship among desire, freedom
and narrative.

Jameson criticizes Frye because Frye understands this relationship too idealistically and individualistically. In this sense, Frye
stands halfway between the *Platonized* notion of desire employed
by those who deconstruct the metaphysics of presence and the *politicized* notion of desire promoted by Jameson's Marxist hermeneutics.
Frye's *moralized* notion of desire dictated by his "anatomy of romance" (to use Geoffrey Hartman's phrase) constitutes a halfway
house.[19] As Jameson notes,

> Frye's entire discussion of romance turns on a presupposition—
> the ethical axis of good and evil—which needs to be historically

problematized in its turn, and which will prove to be an ideologeme that articulates a social and historical contradiction. (PU 110)

By contrast, the principal attraction of Jameson to the project of Gilles Deleuze and Félix Guattari in *Anti-Oedipus* is precisely their *politicized* notion of desire, which does not simply relegate it to the subjective and psychological spheres. Jameson acknowledges that the

> thrust of the argument of the *Anti-Oedipus* is, to be sure, very much in the spirit of the present work, for the concern of its authors is to reassert the specificity of the political content of everyday life and of individual fantasy-experience. (PU 22)

But Jameson objects to their Nietzschean perspectivist attack on hermeneutic or interpretive activity, and hence their antitotalizing orientation and micropolitical conclusions.

The major problem with Jameson's innovative Marxist hermeneutics is that, like Frye's monumental liberal reconstruction of criticism or M. H. Abrams's magisterial bourgeois reading of romanticism, his viewpoint rests on an unexamined metaphor of translation, an uncritical acceptance of transcoding. In this sense, Geoffrey Hartman's incisive criticisms of Frye and J. Hillis Miller's notorious attack on Abrams render Jameson's project suspect.[20] In an interesting manner, the gallant attempts of Frye to resurrect the romance tradition and the Blakean sense of history, of Abrams to recuperate the humanist tradition and the bourgeois conception of history, and of Jameson to recover the Marxist tradition and the political meaning of history, all ultimately revert to and rely on problematic methodological uses of various notions of analogy and homology.[21]

For example, Jameson presupposes homologous relations between ethics and epistemology. This presupposition permits him to distinguish himself from Frye by articulating the differences between moralizing and politicizing the notion of desire. As I noted earlier, Jameson ingeniously shifts the primal scene of criticism from epistemology to ethics. Yet his attempt to historicize the moralistic elements of Frye encourages him to follow the Nietzschean strategies of the poststructuralists in the realm of ethics. Therefore he arrives at the notion that he must go beyond the binary opposition of good and evil in order to overcome ethics and approach the sphere of politics. This notion leads him to the idea that such overcoming of ethics is requisite for a "positive" hermeneutics and a nonfunctional or anticipatory view of culture.

Three principal mistakes support Jameson's presupposition that analogous and homologous relations obtain between ethics and epistemology. First, he believes that the epistemological decentering of the bourgeois subject can be smoothly translated into the moral sphere as an attack on individualistic ethics of bourgeois subjects. This plausible case of analogy seems to warrant, in his view, more general considerations about the homologous relation between ethics and epistemology. Second, he assumes that the poststructuralist attacks on epistemological and metaphysical binary oppositions can be simply transcoded en bloc to ethical binary oppositions. This assumption rests on the notion that these attacks are merely "misplaced"[22] rather than misguided. Third, Jameson misreads three important moments in modern philosophy, namely, Nietzsche's ill-fated attempt to go beyond good and evil, Hegel's critique of Kantian morality and Marx's rejection of bourgeois ethics.

There is a fundamental link between the epistemological decentering of the subject and an attack on the individualistic ethics of bourgeois subjects, for the arguments by Spinoza and Hegel against individualistic ethics were accompanied by epistemological hostility to the isolated subject. And as Jameson rightly argues, the distinctive Marxist contribution to the current discourse, which takes "decentering" as its center, is to show that both the subject decentered and the decentering itself are modes of ideological activity that are always already bound to particular groups, communities and classes at specific stages of capitalist development.

In my view, Jameson goes wrong in trying to relate epistemological moves to ethical ones in ideological terms without giving an account of the collective dynamics that accompany these moves. From the Marxist perspective, all metaphysical, epistemological and ethical discourses are complex ideological affairs of specific groups, communities and classes in or across particular societies. These discourses must not be understood in their own terms (which Jameson rightly rejects), nor may one discourse become primary and consequently subordinate other discursive nets (which Jameson often insinuates). Rather, the Marxist aim is to disclose the ideological function and class interest of these evolving discourses in terms of the collective dynamics of the pertinent moment in the historical process. Jameson moves two steps forward by eschewing the metaphysical and epistemological terrains of the poststructuralists; his strategy discredits rather than defeats them, which is appropriate since poststructuralist defeatism is impossible to defeat on its own grounds. Yet Jameson moves a step backward by shifting the battleground to ethics. This shift, as I shall show later, prevents him from employing the Marxist logic of collective dynamics and leads him to call for a "new logic of collective dynamics" (PU 294).

Jameson's second mistake is to believe that the poststructuralist attacks on binary oppositions are enacted in the wrong terrains, rather than being wrong attacks. Instead of calling into question the very theoretical attitude or unmasking the ideological activity of "going beyond" binary oppositions, Jameson appropriates the same machinery and directs it to ethical binary oppositions. In this way, his project is akin to poststructuralist ones in the bad sense—or akin to idealist projects, in the Marxist sense. Jameson mistakenly does not object to deconstructionist strategies but rather to where they have been applied. In short, his critique does not go deep enough; that is, he does not disclose *the very form of the strategies themselves as modes of ideological activity* that both conceal power relations and extend mechanisms of control by reproducing the ideological conditions for the reproduction of capitalist social arrangements.

Jameson's third mistake is a threefold misreading: of Nietzsche's attempt to go beyond good and evil, of Hegel's critique of Kantian morality and of Marx's rejection of bourgeois ethics. For Jameson, Nietzsche's attempt to go beyond good and evil is the ethical analogue to the poststructuralist attempt to go beyond the binary oppositions in metaphysics and epistemology. But surely this is not so. Nietzsche's attempt to go beyond good and evil is, as the subtitle of his text states, "Vorspiel einer Philosophie der Zukunft" (Prelude to a Philosophy of the Future). Nietzsche hardly rests with the aporias of deconstructionists, but rather aligns himself with the genealogical concerns of the "historically minded" in order to get his own positive project off the ground. His profound transvaluation of values is not enacted in order to transcend the moral categories of good and evil, but rather to unmask them, disclose what they conceal, and build on that which underlies such categories. And for Nietzsche, the "reality" that lies beneath these categories is the will to power. *Ressentiment* is one particular expression of the will to power of the weak and oppressed toward the strong and oppressor within traditional Judeo-Christian culture and, to a certain extent, modern, bourgeois, European culture.[23] Unlike the deconstructionists, Nietzsche aims is to debunk and demystify in order to build anew—and the springboard for his "countermovement," his "new gospel of the future," is the will to power.

> Suppose, finally, we succeeded in explaining our entire instinctive life as the development and ramification of *one* basic form of the will—namely, of the will to power, as *my* proposition has it; suppose all organic functions could be traced back to this will to power and one could also find in it the solution of the problem of procreation and nourishment—it is *one* problem—then one would have gained the right to determine *all* efficient force univocally as—*will to power.* The world viewed from inside, the world defined and determined according to its "intelligible character"— it would be "will to power" and nothing else.[24]

Jameson's emulation of poststructuralist strategies in the realm of ethics leads him to root Nietzsche's project in the isolated subject of bourgeois epistemology and to offer the doctrine of eternal recurrence as the Nietzschean solution to the problem of good and evil. He writes,

> Briefly, we can suggest that, as Nietzsche taught us, the judgmental habit of ethical thinking, of ranging everything in the antagonistic categories of good and evil (or their binary equivalents), is not merely an error but is objectively rooted in the inevitable and inescapable centeredness of every individual consciousness or individual subject: what is good is what belongs to me, what is bad is what belongs to the Other. . . . The Nietzschean solution to this constitutional ethical habit of the individual subject—the Eternal Return—is for most of us both intolerable in its rigor and unconvincingly ingenious in the prestidigitation with which it desperately squares its circle. (PU 234)

It is necessary to note four points against Jameson, however. First, like Marx, Nietzsche realizes that all ethical discourse is a communal affair; ethics is a group response to particular historical circumstances. Therefore, bourgeois ethics (tied to the individual subject) is but one communal response among others and certainly not identical or even similar to expressions of traditional Christian morality.[25] Second, Nietzsche's doctrine of eternal recurrence grounds his affirmative attitude toward life (an alternative to that of Christianity, in his view); it is itself an expression of his will to power, but not a "solution" to the binary opposition of good and evil. Third, Nietzsche acknowledges that his "going beyond" good and evil does not result in transcending morality, but rather in establishing a new morality that rests upon precisely that which former moralities concealed and precluded: a will to power that generates a creative, self-transforming, life-enhancing morality. Fourth, Nietzsche, again like Marx, holds that "going beyond" good and evil is not a philosophical or even hermeneutical issue, but rather a genealogical matter linked to a historical "countermovement" that contains a vision of the future. Going beyond good and evil will not result in finding new categories untainted by the double bind, but rather new distinctions of good and evil tied to building new communities or, for Nietzsche, building new "selves."

This building of new communities leads us directly to Jameson's misunderstanding of Hegel's critique of Kantian morality and Marx's rejection of bourgeois ethics. Jameson rightly notes that

> one of the great themes of dialectical philosophy, the Hegelian denunciation of the ethical imperative, [is] taken up again by Lukács in his *Theory of the Novel*. On this diagnosis, the *Sollen*, the mesmerization of duty and ethical obligation, necessarily perpetuates a cult of failure and a fetishization of pure, unrealized intention. For moral obligation presupposes a gap between being and duty, and cannot be satisfied with the accomplishment of a single duty and the latter's consequent transformation into being. In order to retain its own characteristic satisfactions, ethics must constantly propose the unrealizable and the unattainable to itself. (PU 194)

But Jameson then problematically adds that dialectical philosophy addresses itself to the matter of "going beyond" good and evil and, in contrast to Nietzsche, "proposes a rather different stance (this time, outside the subject in the transindividual, or in other words in History) from which to transcend the double bind of the merely ethical" (PU 235).

The problem here is that Jameson reads Hegel through post-structuralist lenses in which "the double bind of the merely ethical" is a philosophical problem that demands categorical transcendence, rather than through Marxist lenses in which "the double bind of the merely ethical" is an ideological activity to unmask and transform by collective praxis. This Marxist reading of Hegel is necessary in order to grasp the depths of Marx's rejection of bourgeois ethics. Hegel's disenchantment with Kant's morality was not simply because he believed that the categorical imperative was empty or that the moral ought was unattainable. But rather, more important, Hegel was disenchanted because the way in which Kant separates the real from the ideal requires a philosophical projection of an impossible ideal that both presupposed and concealed a particular social basis, namely, Kant's own specific time and place.[26] In other words, Hegel saw Kant's morality as a *Moralität*—a first-personal matter—that was derivative from a *Sittlichkeit*—a communal matter.

The Hegelian critique of Kantian morality opens the door to a Marxist viewpoint on ethics in two respects. First, it rejects the Kantian conception of what a theory about the nature of ethics must be. Second, it imposes severe limits on the role and function of ethical discourse (which is not reducible to moral convictions) in social change. As David Hoy rightly points out, "in giving up the Kantian metaphilosophical view about what theories of morality can and should do, Hegel is giving up the dream of ideal resolutions of moral conflicts. Conflicts are matters of weighing obligations, and moral obligations have no automatic priority."[27]

On this view, Marx's rejection of bourgeois ethics bears little resemblance to poststructuralist attempts to go beyond good and evil. Rather, Marx's rejection is based on giving up the Kantian dream of ideal resolutions of moral conflicts, giving up the Hegelian dream of philosophical reconciliation of the real and the ideal, and surrendering the poststructuralist dream of philosophical transcendence of metaphysical, epistemological and ethical double binds.[28] The Marxist concern is with practically overcoming historical class conflicts. Therefore, the Marxist rejection of bourgeois ethics has less to do with attacks on binary oppositions such as good and evil, and more to do with the Hegelian subordination of *Moralität* to *Sittlichkeit*. The Marxist aim is to discern an evolving and developing *Sittlichkeit* in the womb of capitalist society, a *Sittlichkeit* whose negative ideal is to resist all forms of reification and exploitation, and whose positive ideals are social freedom and class equality.

The Marxist lesson here is that only if one has taken metaphysics, epistemology and ethics seriously will one be attracted by Heideggerian rhetoric about going beyond metaphysics or Nietzschean rhetoric about going beyond good and evil. If one instead takes history seriously—as do Marx after 1844 and American pragmatism at its best—then metaphysics, epistemology and ethics are not formidable foes against which to fight, nor are the Ali-like shuffles of the deconstructions that "destroy" them impressive performances. On this view, deconstructionists become critically ingenious yet politically deluded ideologues, who rightly attack bourgeois humanism, yet who also become the ideological adornments of late monopoly capitalist academies.

Analogies and homologies, no matter how sophisticated and refined between epistemology and ethics, metaphysics and morals, make sense as long as one clings to the notion that there are two such interrelated yet distinct spheres, disciplines or discourses. One rejects this notion neither by enabling interdisciplinary moves nor by questing "beyond" both spheres, but rather by viewing the historical process outside the lenses of traditional or contemporary metaphysical, epistemological and ethical discourses. That is, our history has not posed metaphysical, epistemological and ethical problems that need to be solved or "gone beyond"; rather, it has left us these problems as imaginative ideological responses to once-pertinent but now defunct problematics.

To resurrect the dead, as bourgeois humanists try to do, is impossible. To attack the dead, as deconstructionists do, is redundant and, ironically, valorizes death. To "go beyond" the dead means either surreptitiously recuperating previous "contents" of life in new forms (Nietzsche) or else deceptively shrugging off the weight of the dead, whether by promoting cults of passive, nostalgic "dwelling" (Heidegger) or by creative self-rebegetting and self-redescribing (Emerson, Harold Bloom, Richard Rorty).

What is distinctive about the Marxist project is that it neither resurrects, attacks nor attempts to "go beyond" metaphysical, epistemological and ethical discourses. It aims rather at transforming present practices—the remaining life—against the backdrop of previous discursive and political practices, against the "dead" past. Marxism admonishes us to "let the dead bury the dead"; acknowledges that this "dead" past weighs like an incubus upon prevailing practices; and accents our capacities to change these practices. Marx ignores, sidesteps and avoids discussions of metaphysical, epistemological and ethical issues not because he shuns his inescapable imprisonment in binary oppositions, remains insulated from metaphysical sedimentations, or hesitates to make knowledge claims and moral judgments, but rather because, for him, the bourgeois forms of discourse on such issues are "dead," rendered defunct by his particular moment in the historical process. The capitalist mode of production—with its own particular mystifying forms of social relations, technologies and bureaucracies and its aim of world domination—requires forms of theoretical and practical activity, and modes of writing, acting and organizing heretofore unknown to the "dead" past.

From this Marxist view, the deconstructionist disclosing and debunking of the binary oppositions in the Western philosophical tradition is neither a threat to European civilization nor a misplaced critique better enacted against the binary oppositions in ethics. Rather, deconstructions are, like the left-Hegelian critiques of Marx's own day, interesting yet impotent bourgeois attacks on the forms of thought and categories of a "dead" tradition, a tradition that stipulates the lineage and sustains the very life of these deconstructions. My claim here is not simply that these attacks valorize textuality at the expense of power, but more important, that they are symbiotic with their very object of criticism: that is, they remain alive only as long as they give life to their enemy. In short, deconstructionist assaults must breathe life into metaphysical, epistemological and ethical discourses if their critiques are to render these discourses lifeless.[29]

The major ideological task of the Marxist intervention in present philosophical and critical discussions becomes that of exposing the reactionary and conservative consequences of bourgeois humanism, the critical yet barren posture of poststructuralist skepticism and deconstructionist ironic criticism, and the utopian and ultimately escapist character of the Emersonian gnosticism of Bloom and the Emersonian pragmatism of Rorty. The negative moment of Jameson's Marxist hermeneutics initiates this urgent task. The basic problem with the positive moment in his project is precisely its utopianism, especially in linking the Nietzschean quest beyond good and evil to Marxist theory and praxis. In a crucial passage, Jameson writes,

> It is clear, indeed, that not merely Durkheim's notion of collective "consciousness," but also the notion of "class consciousness," as it is central in a certain Marxist tradition, rests on an unrigorous and figurative assimilation of the consciousness of the individual subject to the dynamics of groups. The Althusserian and post-structuralist critique of these and other versions of the notion of a "subject of history" may readily be admitted. The alternatives presented by the Althusserians, however . . . have a purely negative or second-degree critical function, and offer no new conceptual categories. What is wanted here—and it is one of the most urgent tasks for Marxist theory today—is a whole new logic of collective dynamics, with categories that escape the taint of some mere application of terms drawn from individual experience (in that sense, even the concept of praxis remains a suspect one). (PU 294)

It comes as little surprise that Jameson's plea for a "new logic" resembles Jacques Derrida's call for a "new reason," since Jameson enacts the deconstructionist strategy of going beyond binary oppositions. At this level of comparison, the major difference is that Jameson banks his positive hermeneutics on this "new logic," whereas Derrida merely invokes "new reason" in his rhetoric before returning to his negative antihermeneutical activity. Yet, from a Marxist perspective, Jameson's basis for a positive hermeneutics is utopian in the bad sense; for it is a utopianism that rests either on no specifiable historical forces potentially capable of actualizing it or on the notion that every conceivable historical force embodies it. Jameson clearly favors the latter formulation.

> The preceding analysis entitles us to conclude that all class consciousness of whatever type is Utopian insofar as it expresses the

unity of a collectivity; yet it must be added that this proposition is an allegorical one. The achieved collectivity or organic group of whatever kind—oppressors fully as much as oppressed—is Utopian not in itself, but only insofar as all such collectivities are themselves *figures* for the ultimate concrete collective life of an achieved Utopian or classless society. Now we are in a better position to understand how even hegemonic or ruling-class culture and ideology are Utopian, not in spite of their instrumental function to secure and perpetuate class privilege and power, but rather precisely because that function is also in and of itself the affirmation of collective solidarity. (PU 290–91)

This exorbitant claim illustrates not only utopianism gone mad, but also a Marxism in deep desperation, as if any display of class solidarity keeps alive a discredited class analysis. Even more important, this claim, similar to the thin historicism and glib optimism of Bloom's Emersonian gnosticism and Rorty's Emersonian pragmatism, reflects the extent to which Jameson remains within the clutches of American culture. Given the barbarous atrocities and large-scale horrors inflicted by hegemonic ruling classes in Europe, Africa, Asia and Latin America, only a Marxist thinker entrenched in the North American experience could even posit the possibility of ruling-class consciousness figuratively being "in its very nature Utopian" (PU 289). Benjamin's tempered utopianism or Bloch's doctrine of hope certainly do not support such Marxist flights of optimism or lead to such an American faith in the future.

Jameson's bad utopianism is but a symptom of the major political shortcoming of his work: his texts have little or no political consequences. On the one hand, his works have little or no political praxis as texts; that is, they speak, refer or allude to no political movement or formation in process with which his texts have some connection.[30] They thus remain academic Marxist texts which, for the most part, are confined to specialists and antispecialists, Marxists and anti-Marxists, in the academy. On the other hand, his works have little or no political praxis in yet another sense: they provide little or no space for either highlighting issues of political praxis within its theoretical framework or addressing modes of political praxis in its own academic setting.[31]

Jameson's works are therefore too theoretical; his welcome call for a political hermeneutics is too far removed from the heat of political battles. By their failure sufficiently to reflect, and reflect on, the prevailing political strife, Jameson's works reenact the very process of reification that they condemn. Surely, the present fragmentation of the North American left, the marginalization of progressive micropolitical formations, and the rampant mystification of North American life and culture impose severe constraints on Jameson's textual practice; nonetheless, more substantive reflections on "practical" political strategies seem appropriate. My plea here is not anti-intellectual or antitheoretical, but rather a call for more sophisticated theory aware of and rooted in the present historical and political conjuncture in American capitalist civilization.

Of course, Jameson's own social positioning—an American professor of French writing Marxist hermeneutical works—solicits expectations of self-obsession, political isolation and naive optimism. Yet Jameson's texts are not self-obsessed, though his style of elusive, elliptical sentences (which appear more contrapuntal than dialectical) borders on a Frenchifying of English prose. Jameson's texts are not isolated, monadic works, despite the consistent absence of any acknowledgments to fellow critics or colleagues in his prefaces, yet they direct us to look at France rather than at ourselves. Hence his critical treatments of Sartre, Lévi-Strauss, Althusser, Lacan, Bénichou, Deleuze, Guattari and Lyotard are nearly hermetic and he is relatively silent on distinguished American critics such as his former Yale colleague Paul de Man, or noteworthy historically minded critics like R. P. Blackmur, Philip Rahv or Irving Howe. Jameson is not a naive optimist, but his sophisticated utopianism finally seems to be part and parcel of the American penchant for unquenchable faith in history and irresistible hope for romantic triumph.

My main point here is not simply that Jameson should write less Frenchified, expand his fascinating Marxist discourse to include talented American friends and foes, and situate himself more clearly within the American Marxist tradition. Rather, Jameson's own historical predicament—his own conceptual tools, academic audience, utopian proclivities and political praxis—should become more an object of his dialectical deliberations. Nevertheless, Jameson has done more than any other American hermeneutical thinker in achieving intellectual breakthroughs and accenting theoretical challenges of the Marxist tradition in our postmodern times. The path he has helped blaze now awaits those, including himself, who will carry on with the urgent tasks not simply of taking seriously history and politics, but more specifically, of taking seriously our intellectual, American and socialist identities as writers of texts, shapers of attitudes, beneficiaries of imperialist fruits, inheritors of hegemonic sensibilities and historical agents who envision a socialist future.

Law and Culture

12

Reassessing the Critical Legal Studies Movement

Much of Western European history conditions us to see human differences in simplistic opposition to each other: dominant/subordinate, good/bad, up/down, superior/inferior. In a society where the good is defined in terms of profit rather than in terms of human need, there must always be some group of people who, through systematized oppression, can be made to feel surplus, to occupy the place of the dehumanized inferior. Within this society, that group is made up of black and third world people, working class people, older people and women.

Institutionalized rejection of *difference* is an absolute necessity in a profit economy which needs outsiders as surplus people. As members of such an economy, we have *all* been programmed to respond to the human differences between us with fear and loathing and to handle that difference in one of three ways: ignore it, and if that is not possible, copy it if we think it is dominant, or destroy it if we think it is subordinate. But we have no patterns for relating across our human differences as equals. As a result, those differences have been misnamed and misused in the service of separation and confusion.

Audre Lorde
Sister Outsider

A specter is haunting American legal education—the specter of critical legal studies. This rapidly expanding reform movement within elite institutions of legal pedagogy is principally a significant response to the crisis of purpose among law professors and students. Like liberation theologians in seminaries, social medicine proponents in medical schools, radical deconstructionists in university literature departments and opposition postmodern critics in the arts, critical legal theorists fundamentally question the dominant and usually liberal paradigms prevalent and pervasive in American culture and society. This thorough questioning is not primarily a constructive attempt to put forward a conception of a new legal and social order. Rather, it is a pronounced disclosure of the inconsistencies, incoherences, silences and blindness of legal formalists, legal positivists and legal realists in the liberal tradition. Critical legal studies is more a concerted attack and assault on the legitimacy and authority of pedagogical strategies in law schools than a comprehensive announcement of what a credible and realizable new society and legal system would look like.

In this essay, I shall situate the critical legal studies movement within the context of the larger crisis of purpose among intellectuals and academicians in contemporary American society. I will examine the critical legal studies movement as a significant and insightful, though flawed, response to this crisis of purpose. Then I shall suggest how the critical legal studies movement can become a more effective prophetic force in our time.

Allan Bloom's bestseller, *The Closing of the American Mind*—a nostalgic and, for some, a seductive depiction of the decline and decay of the elitist, highbrow, classical humanist tradition in institutions of higher education—and Russell Jacoby's *The Last Intellectuals*—a sentimental requiem for leftist public intellectuals—are both emblematic symptoms of the larger crisis of purpose in the academy.[1] For Bloom, critical legal studies would be viewed as an attempt to highlight the racism, patriarchy and class-skewed character of the classical tradition that he defends. Critical legal studies for Bloom would be simply another instance of what he calls the "Nietzschenization of the American left"—his way of describing the American left as an irrational movement.[2] For Jacoby, critical legal studies constitutes an example of academic leftists who refuse to intervene into the larger public conversation concerning the destiny of the country. Yet both Bloom and Jacoby are silent on the major challenge of academic left subcultures like critical legal studies: the complex operations of power enacted in the styles and standards, values and sensibilities, moods and manners, grids of seeing and structures of feelings, into which students are socialized and acculturated.

Critical legal theorists focus on the kinds of dispositions and the forms of discourse: but where do these forms gain their legitimacy? What makes them more acceptable than other kinds of styles, other kinds of grids, other kinds of structures of feelings[3] in the culture of critical discourse?

Based in part on the pioneering work of Michel Foucault, oppositional intellectuals, including critical legal theorists, are not simply contesting prevailing paradigms in the academy, they are also investigating the historical origins and social functions of the kinds of standards and criteria used to evaluate paradigms, arguments and perspectives in the culture of critical discourse. They must be able to construct a genealogy of the culture of critical discourse itself: when it emerges, what justifies the kind of standards invoked, and how those standards have changed over time. They are not merely displacing prevailing paradigms with new ones, but are raising deeper questions about the very standards and criteria themselves. These investigations highlight the often concealed ideological assumptions, the exclusions of certain styles of argument,[4] and the arbitrary character of the concrete results (as embodied in curricula and enshrined in exemplary legal scholarship). This kind of intellectual interrogation is, in many ways, unprecedented in the academy, because it not only criticizes paradigms, arguments and perspectives but, more pointedly, it calls into question the very grounds upon which acceptable paradigms, good arguments and legitimate perspectives are judged. This radical questioning views the present institutional arrangements of legal scholarship and education, along with their mediated link to the liberal status quo, as themselves impediments to the production of new perspectives and paradigms which are worthy of acceptance.

In short, academic left subcultures such as critical legal studies put forward metaphilosophical and metainstitutional inquiries that cast suspicion on the capacity of the academy to satisfy the conditions required for undistorted dialogue and uncoerced intellectual exchange. This incapacity exists precisely because of the ways in which the culture of critical discourse is already implicated in the ideological battles raging in society at large, ensconced in the political struggles of the day and partisan in these battles and struggles. These metaphilosophical and metainstitutional inquiries are primarily attempts to show how the forms of rationality dominant in the academy—and regulating of the practices of most academicians—are value-laden, ideologically loaded, and historically contingent. In this way, critical legal theorists highlight the arbitrary content and character of the standards, styles, curricula, concepts (for example, rules of law) and conclusions of legal scholarship and education.

Like Foucault, critical legal theories examine diverse and multiple "micro-physics of power"—Foucault's term for the ways in which societies preserve themselves partly by encouraging intellectuals to be unmindful of how they are socialized and acculturated into the prevailing "regimes of truth."[5] They overlook and ignore the ways in which the prevailing culture of critical discourse remains uncritical about itself, the ways in which the very invoking of relentless criticism, and how, in fact, the predominant quest for truth remains untruthful about itself. A first step toward a more thorough critique and a more truthful quest for truth is to accent the way dominant discourses construct regulative identities, forms of argument, modes of presentation and ideological outlooks that preclude taking seriously alternative, and especially oppositional, identities, types of augmentation and political perspectives held by those viewed as other, alien, marginal and unconventional.

This unprecedented kind of critique of the culture of critical discourse in the academy promotes a full-fledged historicist orientation and an explicit encounter with social theory. By historicist orientation, I mean the provisional, tentative and revisable character of formulations that reflect the state of political and ideological conflict in society at a particular moment. (For example, the reason that a greater number of women attend law school today as opposed to previously reflects the larger political and ideological struggles that have transpired since the 1960s.) By an explicit encounter with social theory, I mean the particular understandings of the structural constraints—those of the state, economy and culture—that shape and are shaped by legal practices. Needless to say, the critical legal studies movement focuses on how the undeniable realities of class exploitation, racial subjugation, patriarchal domination and homophobic marginalization affect the making and enforcement of legal sanctions. Until now, legal discourse has not really focused on these issues. In the name of criticism, it has remained silent about objects that require serious critical investigation—the way in which the law has been shaped by Jim Crowism, the way it has been shaped by patriarchal forms of relations both in the private sphere and in the public sphere, and the way it has been shaped by the marginalization of gays and lesbians and so forth.

In the past, legal formalism and legal positivism have resisted the serious challenge of this kind of historicist and theoretical focus. Legal realism—that powerful pragmatic perspective inaugurated by Oliver Holmes and enacted in the works of Felix Cohen and others—took an important step in this historicist and theoretical direction. Yet its amorphous notion of "experience" remained confined to immediate problems and practical solutions, rather than the structural deficiencies and fundamental transformative possibilities of society. In this way, critical legal studies goes far beyond earlier attempts to highlight the contingent character of the law.

Academic left subcultures like critical legal studies tend to respond to the crisis of purpose among intellectuals by projecting the role of social critic within critical discourse. Such a role requires that one be equipped not only with a sense of history, but also with a broad knowledge of history—especially the new social histories that focus on those on the underside of traditional views of history. To be a social critic in legal discourse also requires that one be well-grounded in the classical and oppositional traditions of social theory—Marx, Weber, Durkheim, Simmel, Lukács, de Beauvoir, Du Bois, Parsons, Gouldner, Habermas, and others. And, of course, one must be well-versed in the past and present forms of legal discourse.

I find the notion of legal scholar as social critic—best seen in the works of the late Robert Cover[6]—to be highly attractive. Yet to be a sophisticated and effective social critic requires intellectual and existential sources that fall far outside those provided by a typical elite undergraduate education and law school training. The major flaws of most of the work done by critical legal studies can be attributed to this truncated education and training. I shall examine briefly three basic flaws in the critical legal studies movement: the first is a dominant tendency to "trash" liberalism (by which I mean the tendency to delegitimate and demystify it and to describe it as just a cover for power); the second, a refusal to come to terms with tradition as both an impediment and impetus to social change; and the third, cultural distance from nonacademic prophetic and progressive organized efforts to transform American culture and society.

I have never fully understood the animosity and hostility toward liberalism displayed in much of the writing of critical legal theorists. (I am thinking here, for example, of the works of Duncan Kennedy, David Trubeck, and Mark Tushnet.) I find many of their criticisms of liberalism persuasive—such as the ways in which the language of impartiality, objective due process, and value-free procedure hides and conceals partisan operations of power and elite forms of social victimization. Yet the hostility may itself conceal a deeper existential dimension of the critical legal studies movement: namely, the degree to which it is a revolt against the liberalism of elite law schools. To put it more pointedly, most first-generation critical legal theorists are rebellious students of major liberal legal thinkers. And, as in all such affairs, the central object of critique implicitly affects the very critique itself. My hunch is that one discernible effect is to fan and fuel, accentuate and exaggerate the ideological distance between the fathers and the progeny.

This distance has now become a rather nasty point of contention and confrontation due to the political polarization between the critical legal scholars and their critics in many law schools. What was once a rather mild Oedipal family romance has turned into a Clausewitzian affair, given the fierce struggle over tenure slots, administrative power, curriculum and influence. The "trashing" of liberalism has played a noteworthy role in this escalating battle.

On the other hand, serious conflict and contestation is inevitable between those who question the very rules of the game and those who claim that this interrogation itself is a rejection of the noble ends and aims of legal education. (For example, Richard Posner, Robert Bork and others view critical legal studies as calling into question the very ends of Western civilization and the ends of traditional legal education. Thus, they conclude it ought to be pushed outside the academy completely.) In this sense, academic left subcultures of any sort are critical of the liberal academy. On the other hand, to "trash" liberalism as a political ideology in the modern world is to overlook its revolutionary beginnings and opposition potential—despite its dominant versions and uses to preserve the status quo. To ignore the ambitious legacy of liberalism and thereby downplay its grand achievements is to be not only historically forgetful but also politically naive. It is not only to throw the baby out with the bathwater, but also to pull the rug from under the very feet of those who are struggling for prophetic social change. While liberalism in America is associated with the status quo, in South Africa, for example, it is still a revolutionary ideology. Crucial aspects of liberalism inform and inspire much of the oppositional left activities here and around the world. To see solely the ways in which dominant versions of liberalism domesticate and dilute such oppositional activities is to view liberalism in too monolithic and homogeneous a manner.[7]

Despite the powerful yet unpersuasive antiliberal perspectives of Alasdair MacIntyre and the insightful yet unclear postliberal viewpoints of many critical legal theorists, I simply cannot conceive of an intellectually compelling, morally desirable and practically realizable prophetic social vision, strategy and program that does not take certain achievements of liberalism as a starting point. A reconceptualization of political obligation, participatory citizenship and redistribution of wealth by civil and legal means indeed is required in a revising of this liberal starting point—yet this constitutes a radical democratic interpretation of liberalism, not a total discarding of it. In this sense, liberalism is an unfinished project arrested by relatively unaccountable corporate power, a passive and depoliticized citizenry and a cultural conservatism of racism, patriarchy, homophobia and narrow patriotism or neonationalism. In other words, leftist oppositional thought and practice should build on the best of liberalism, yet transform liberalism in a more democratic and egalitarian manner.

In *Whose Justice? Which Rationality?* Alasdair MacIntyre laments the fact that "the contemporary debates within modern political systems are almost exclusively between conservative liberals, liberal liberals and radical liberals. There is little place in such political systems for the criticism of the system itself, that is, for putting liberalism in question" (p. 392). Yet after his interesting and insightful reconstruction of the conceptions of practical rationality that inform the notions of justice in the Aristotelian, Augustinian, Thomistic and Humean traditions, MacIntyre provides us with no clue as to what a constructive antiliberal proposal for justice would be like. Similarly, much of the provocative and penetrating criticisms of liberalism put forward by critical legal theorists gives us little sense of what a desirable postliberal society would look like. The trilogy of Roberto Unger, published as *Politics Toward a Reconstructive Social Theory,* indeed attempts to meet this challenge—and it is not surprising that he dubs his project a "superliberal" one which tries to capture the utopian, experimental and democratic impulse that informed the early stages of liberal thought and practice.[8]

The second criticism of critical legal studies is its refusal to acknowledge the equivocal character of tradition. The powerful demystifying and deconstructive strategies of critical legal theorists tend to promote and encourage Enlightenment attitudes toward tradition—that is, the notion that tradition is to be exclusively identified with ignorance and intolerance, prejudice and parochialism, dogmatism and docility. Yet as Hans-Georg Gadamer, Edward Shils, Antonio Gramsci and Raymond Williams have shown, tradition can also be a source for insight and intelligence, rationality and resistance, critique and contestation. Partly owing to the available options in legal education, critical legal theorists tend to respond to liberalism's hegemony in the academy by disclosing the various exclusions of the liberal traditions, rather than reconstructing the creative ways in which oppressed and marginalized persons have forged traditions of resistance by appropriating aspects of liberalism for democratic and egalitarian ends. These appropriations not only force us to acknowledge the dynamic, malleable and revisable character of a diverse liberal tradition, they also compel us to accent the way in which this tradition is fused with other oppositional traditions such as the civic republican, communitarian and democratic socialist traditions of subaltern peoples. In this regard, the relative silence of critical legal theorists regarding the constructive attempts of serious left thinkers in oppositional traditions—as opposed to the deconstruction of the canonical texts of the white liberal fathers—is quite revealing. Needless to say, both activities are needed—yet a balance is required.

This imbalance is related to my third criticism: the paucity of sustained reflection by critical legal theorists regarding strategies and tactics for effective social change in the larger culture and society. By remaining captive to an implicit Foucaultian outlook— namely, enacting resistance in the form of incisive genealogies of the emergence of partisan and power-concealing liberal legal discourses that purport to be impartial, objective and fair—critical legal thinkers usually have little to say about how this resistance can be linked to struggles for social change outside of the academy. As Foucaultian "specific intellectuals" who rest content with contesting the prevailing "regimes of truth" within their academic context, critical legal theorists do not specify how their significant effects of pedagogical reform are related to progressive activities of struggling peoples in nonacademic contexts. My claim is simply that the relative neglect of interest in, and the interrogation of traditions of resistance of, subaltern peoples encourages a lack of concern about and attention to strategies of social change beyond the academy. Note that I am not describing the intentions and aspirations of the critical legal studies movement, but rather the dominant practices of most of its figures.

My criticisms of this movement—put forward in a spirit of intellectual sympathy and political support—reflect a disenchantment with its Foucaultian orientation. These criticisms can be met best by a broadening of this orientation into a Gramscian perspective. Such a perspective requires that critical legal theorists become public intellectuals—that is, thinkers who make significant interventions into the larger conversation that bears more directly on the destiny of American society. For too long critical legal theorists have put forward primarily academic critiques of the academy—critiques that further extend the authority of the academy while they attempt to delegitimate the academy. The paradoxical effects of these critiques inscribe the critical legal studies movement more deeply within the limits of the very academic styles and ethos it purports to change. There surely is some significance to these critiques, yet they remain highly limited without elaboration of their implications in the public sphere of intellectual exchange. Such an elaboration would result in the emergence of visible critical legal studies figures comparable to Noam Chomsky or Edward Said—that is, figures who put forward views with which the larger society would have to reckon.

A Gramscian perspective also would require that critical legal studies attempt to become more grounded in the progressive sectors of the black, Latino, feminist, gay, lesbian and trade union resistance efforts. This attempt to become more organic with traditions of resistance should be a mutually critical and empowering process. My hunch and hope is that one significant result of this process is that the critical legal studies movement will become more conscious of race and gender bias, homophobia and nonacademic political struggle (as well as more appreciative of the oppositional potential of the liberal tradition) and that progressive black, Latino, feminist, gay, lesbian and trade union groups will become more cognizant of demystifying, deconstructive and class strategies of thought and action. This kind of mutual learning and solidarity building facilitates the shedding of intellectual parochialism and the overcoming of political isolation—a plight and predicament shared by most progressive groups and academic left subcultures like the critical legal studies movement.

In conclusion, a Gramscian perspective is more easily enunciated than enacted, and the implicit Foucaultian orientation of most critical legal studies figures impedes such an enactment. Furthermore, the vast depoliticization of the American populace and the minimal financial resources for creating and sustaining mobilizing and organizing efforts contribute to the unlikelihood of the emergence of insurgent progressive social movements. Yet the prevailing desperation and even desolation of the American left—both in and out of the academy—is no excuse for isolation and insularity. Rather, it makes even more imperative efforts regulated by a Gramscian perspective.

The critical legal studies movement is one sign of hope in a period of widespread narrow conservatism, nationalism, cynicism and defeatism. But its intellectual and political potential remains truncated as long as it refuses to make a Gramscian leap into an unpredictable future.

13

Critical Legal Studies and a Liberal Critic

The battle now raging in the legal academy between the critical legal studies movement (CLS) and its critics has taken a decisive turn. Battles over decisions not to hire or give tenure to scholars associated with CLS have been front-page news in the academic community, and the tone of scholarly discussion has become decidedly negative. Much of the criticism has been aimed at one person often considered a guru to CLS, Roberto Unger. His work has inspired sharply negative commentary both here and abroad, and his most recent work, *Politics,* has received several scathing reviews.

William Ewald's evaluation of Unger's philosophy is the latest salvo in the offensive against Unger and, through him, against CLS. Ewald throws down the gauntlet in the name of logical rigor and analytical precision, historical accuracy and argumentative soundness, looking closely at " 'the sheer breadth of Unger's knowledge and the unrelenting force of his analysis.' Neither," Ewald concludes, "is as great as his followers believe."[1] Consequently, Ewald argues, both Unger's credibility as a scholar and the quality of his philosophical contribution to CLS as a whole should be seriously questioned.

CLS is indeed in need of serious and thorough treatment by left, liberal and conservative legal scholars. The sooner, the better; the more, the merrier. In the recent wave of commentary, unfortunately, hostile gut reactions have replaced guarded respectful responses; passionate political and cultural evaluations have supplanted balanced intellectual assessments. Nowhere is this more apparent than in Ewald's essay.

The overall impression the essay leaves is not one of fruitful critique but rather one of a mean-spirited academic put-down. This is apparent from Ewald's strategy, which is to devote more than half of his long article to a few pages of *Knowledge and Politics*. Ewald apparently believes that Unger's work can be dismissed because a close reading of Unger's first book, published in 1975, discloses an objectionable interpretation here and a contestable reading there. He then proceeds to view Unger's later books through the narrow and often blinding lens of this first youthful effort.

This fundamental mistake regulates Ewald's overall strategy: He refuses to acknowledge the "epistemological break" between Unger's first book (*Knowledge and Politics*) and his later work (*The Critical Legal Studies Movement* and *Politics*). By "epistemological break" (Gaston Bachelard's term popularized by Louis Althusser's interpretation of Marx), I mean Unger's crucial historicist turn in his work from a self-styled neo-Aristotelian perspective (or a teleological and essentialist view) to a full-blown antifoundational orientation. This basic shift has three major consequences in Unger's work. First, he gives up the unpersuasive talk about "intelligible essences," and moves toward immanent critiques of the rhetoric and practice of democracy and freedom in contemporary societies. Second, he abandons "total criticism" and links his immanent critiques to concrete historical investigations and specific programmatic formulations. Third, he rejects his ahistorical "trashing" of liberalism and puts forward his new project in the name of superliberalism.

Ewald's efforts are faulty, in that they assume that there is a smooth linear progression from the early to the later Unger. This unwarranted assumption leads him to conclude that *Knowledge and Politics* is the core of Unger's corpus and that the later works are mere embellishments and elaborations of the early book. Ewald is blind to the shift in Unger's work, and adduces no textual evidence that this shift does not occur. Therefore his detailed criticisms of Unger's early work are interesting—a few even convincing—yet the grand claims he makes about what these criticisms imply regarding Unger's overall philosophy and project are bloated. The edifice Ewald believes he has dismantled is not a palatial mansion in which CLS dwells, but rather an old decrepit doghouse abandoned by Unger long ago. If Ewald's criticisms are to have the broad implications he wants to draw, he must engage in a detailed reading of Unger's later philosophy with the same tenacity with which he examines Unger's early philosophy, and then show that Unger's own self-criticisms of his earlier work do not prefigure the more significant points made by his critics. Until Ewald puts forward such an account, he commits the fallacy he accuses Unger of: the fallacy of agglomeration, of treating clashing and contradictory bodies of thought (that is, early and later Unger) as if they were a single body of coherent and consistent thought.

Ewald's essay not only fans and fuels an immobilizing ideological polarization, but also hides the basic issues at stake between CLS and mainstream legal scholarship. Ewald's dismissive approach—which vents its undeniable venom behind a "disinterested" critique of microanalytic units of Unger's texts—forces us to raise fundamental questions regarding the complex relations between scholarship, ideology and philosophy in the legal academy. Within the limited confines of this essay, I shall address some of these issues.

There is a special irony in Ewald's efforts to "trash" Unger, in that they violate the very standards of academic objectivity and scholarly care he lauds. Ronald Dworkin—for whose *Law's Empire* Ewald has the distinction of having written many of the nontextual footnotes—has argued that CLS theorists are not entitled to claim that liberal legal texts and doctrines embody "fundamental contradictions" unless they can justly

> claim to have looked for a less skeptical interpretation and failed. Nothing is easier or more pointless than demonstrating that a flawed and contradictory account fits as well as a smoother and

more attractive one. The internal skeptic must show that the flawed and contradictory account is the only one available. (*Law's Empire*, p. 274n4)

Dworkin's persuasive point here is simply that we must try to present the most subtle and sympathetic interpretations of an opponent's viewpoints before we uncharitably "trash" them. And we must ask: Has Ewald followed his mentor's sound advice and shown that his reading of Unger as a flawed, vague and contradictory philosopher is the only one available? I suspect not, and I wager that most readers of Ewald's article will agree. If so, then the razor-sharp blade Dworkin uses on uncharitable readers is double-edged—cutting both "trashers" within CLS or a trasher of the trashers like Ewald. Vigorous criticism rises above the level of trashing when it locates and appreciates both insights and blindnesses, tensions and inconsistencies within the views of a worthy opponent. Dworkin's remarks simply restate the sensible morality of public discussion articulated in Chapter II of John Stuart Mill's *On Liberty* and affirm Nietzsche's endeavor of proving that one's opponent "did you some good." Like the trashing wing of CLS, Ewald fails to meet these intellectual standards.

These introductory metacritical remarks suggest two types of response to Ewald. One is a microanalytical approach that examines a few specific criticisms he makes of Unger, assessing the accuracy of his critiques, agreeing if warranted or offering competing readings if not. These indeed are important exercises—already enacted in the early versions and rewritings of his essay in light of early drafts of this essay. Yet, given the limited space, I find it more important to show that a more useful reading of Unger is available—a reading that is both critical and sympathetic. I shall attempt to lay bare the nature of the larger CLS project, discern the specific role and function of Unger's still-developing work in this larger project, understand why Unger's texts are so seductive to some law students and professors, and then put forward some objections to these texts in light of my own agreements and disagreements with various aspects of the CLS project.

CLS bears the marks of its birth in elite law schools, and its members are exorbitantly preoccupied with the liberalism of the legal academy, that is, the liberalism of their teachers in elite law schools. They thus see as especially important those works, such as Unger's, that combat the theory of their teachers on the theoretical turf their teachers had for so long claimed as their own. Thus, the extravagant praise of Unger by some CLS members cited by Ewald is a truthful reflection of the movement's reaction to those works. It is, however, only a partial truth. People attracted to CLS are also motivated by concern for specific sorts of injustices, and they recognize that theoretical works such as Unger's can provide at best indirect and obscure guidance in their search for answers to these more specific problems. What is important in CLS is the nature of the relationship between theory and practice—theorists do not tell those with more practical interests what to do, but rather their theory amplifies the lessons of practice, pointing to ways that deviations from the norms of behavior and institutional organization can be viewed as norms that can serve as bases for new forms of social organization. This is what Unger sees as the focus of his notion of "deviationist doctrine," an idea Ewald sees as primarily an odd form of unprofessional behavior. This view of the relationship between theory and practice implies that the demise of theory will not undermine practice in the way it might seem to in a more traditional academic movement: Theory is a form of practice in CLS, and, while other forms of practice can learn from it, they are not dependent upon it. Members of CLS are clearly aware of this. For example, James Boyle, whose praise of Unger Ewald refers to several times in the essay, has also explained the limited role Unger's theoretical work plays in the broader project of CLS:

> Unger's *Knowledge and Politics* gives us a total critique of liberalism that tells us nothing about sexual harassment in the workplace,

racial discrimination in the classroom, or the multiple oppressions
of a welfare office. . . . It takes apart the formalized structure
behind liberal political discourse, and liberal political discourse
is narrow. . . .

So Unger's total critique is best read as a *local* critique because
it is (and must be) implicated in the artificial categories it helps
to explode. Of course, there are teachers, editorial writers, politicians, people involved in ethical arguments, who produce the
mode of discourse that Unger deconstructs. But the claim to "totality" can be misunderstood because of the strong prejudice that
emanates from within liberal thought—the prejudice that the
deepest and most important level of what is going on is the theory
of the state with its attendant moral, psychological, and legal
postulates. The point is that such a structural prejudice, and the
diminished visibility that it implies for all the other little exercises
of power going on in the world, is part of the *problem* and not
the *solution*.[2]

It is of course possible that Ewald could reconcile the ideas in this
quotation with his implication that criticizing Unger undermines
CLS. What is shocking, however, is that he fails even to point to
this passage. As a result, the praise of Unger he quotes so liberally
presents at best a partial picture. The very sources he quotes deny
precisely the link between Unger and CLS he describes them as
exemplifying. Is this "up to the mark both in its historical assertions
and in its reasoning?"[3]

To take another example, consider Ewald's "meritocratic" challenge to Unger's theory of organic groups. Ewald argues that Unger's
theory is unworkable because it fails to consider seriously the importance of efficiency and meritocratic criteria in the operation of key
desirable institutions. Ewald suggests that the staff of a large urban
hospital simply could not operate in an acceptable manner (that is,
could not care for the hospital's patients) based on Unger's "non-
meritocratic" viewpoint.[4] Too much democracy in the name of
"eradicating domination" fails to acknowledge the high level of
skill and knowledge requisite for effective physicians; too much

"meritocratic hierarchy" precludes the kind of radical democratic arrangements Unger's theory promotes.

Ewald's example is ingeniously misleading in three ways. First, a hospital is an institution that renders desirable services to human beings, rather than a production site in which people produce inanimate commodities, as in a large factory. Unger's formulations focus on the latter.[5] Both hospitals and factories indeed constitute present-day workplaces of importance, yet Unger makes it clear that his remarks pertain more to a goods-producing context than to a service-rendering one. Nevertheless, his three institutional principles of organic groups—the community of life, the democracy of ends and the division of labor—do apply to all contexts of the workplace in modern society, so at this point Ewald's example is slightly uncharitable but warranted.

Second, Ewald's characterization of Unger's "non-meritocratic" hospital—an example Unger does not use—relies principally upon the first two institutional principles of organic groups. It is highly revealing that Ewald quotes liberally from the sections on the community of life, the democracy of ends and the state. And when Ewald mentions Unger's understanding of the role of the division of labor in organic groups, he claims it to be vacuous.[6] Yet his criticism of Unger relies principally on Unger's inability to balance democracy and meritocracy, people's control with the specialization and differentiation of indispensable and desirable labor tasks. When we actually look at what Unger has to say about the division of labor in organic groups (hospital or factory), we discover that "though the principle of the division of labor requires that specialization be tempered, it does not prescribe that it be abolished." Hence Unger's imaginary hospital is not "non-meritocratic" but rather a place where the high level of skill and knowledge of doctors, nurses and maintenance staff is best put to use in order to cure patients under maximally communal and democratic conditions. Unger states explicitly, "the organic group must start by combining a standard of merit with one of need." On the one hand, "the mere possession of skills can never in itself justify material advantages or the exercise of power. On the other hand, "a relentless insistence on deciding collectively all significant matters . . . would undetermine the possibility of a division of labor in which the talents of each could be brought to fruition, for specialization allocates meritorious power. Unger then significantly though vaguely suggests that the route between the Scylla of pure meritocracy and the Charybdis of inefficient democracy "must be resolved by prudential judgment."[7] Hence Unger rejects exactly the simplistic viewpoint that Ewald attributes to him. And Ewald's claim about the emptiness of "prudential judgment" is based on Unger's incomplete elaboration, not his lack of insight.

Last, Ewald holds that the positive program outlined in the theory of organic groups is "little more than a blur."[8] But Unger makes it clear that he is no utopian radical democrat. He knows that his organic groups will not "eradicate domination." He repeatedly reminds us that his ideals are "incapable of being completely realized in history." Therefore, his aim of creating a universal community "is meant to serve as a regulative ideal rather than as the description of a future society."[9] Thus, again, Ewald's attempt to link Unger's failure to put forward a detailed description of a social world of organic groups to naive utopian sensibilities is unconvincing.[10] Rather, Unger's religious realism leads him to reject naive utopianism; just as his open-endedness leaves him reluctant to predetermine the concrete arrangements of the desirable society.

Also troubling is Ewald's criticism of how Unger uses the word "liberalism." (Indeed, to signal his distaste he puts the word in a special type face, suggesting thereby that Unger's use of the word deviates from usual practice.) All Ewald's talk about how to define "liberalism" would seem to be more the subject of lexicographic squabbles than legal scholarship, were it not for the fact that on the meaning of "liberalism" turns the viability of Ewald's most important criticism of Unger. Ewald's central claim is that Unger is able to find contradictions in liberalism only because he defines the term so as to lump together thinkers who disagree with one another. By "agglomerating" thinkers whose thoughts clash, Unger has, according to Ewald, put the rabbit into his hat, all so he could feign surprise when the contradictions came jumping out of it. In fact it may be Ewald who is guilty of smuggling presuppositions into his definition of the term. He assumes that the term "liberalism" must refer to something that could be recognized as a coherent, internally consistent body of thought that is defined in terms of the rigorous logical standards he espouses. For his own purposes in the common rooms at Oxford, such standards may be appropriate. But Unger is not interested in debunking the claims of philosophers to have found a "liberalism" that is not internally contradictory. He is instead interested in the connection between types of knowledge and the exercise of political power—hence the title of the book, *Knowledge and Politics*. The "liberalism" he criticizes is the set of those ideas that have routinely been used as justifications for the use of power by politicians and their apologists since the seventeenth century. These people have confronted different situations, their purposes have differed from one another's, and the ideas they have used differ accordingly. Yet the leaders of Western societies have tried over the last one hundred and fifty years, almost without exception, to describe their policies as "liberal." The term "liberalism" thus has come to us with no unitary meaning, but instead with a dynamic and flexible "open-textured" quality[11] that developed from the diverse and contesting influences acting upon it. It is therefore perfectly acceptable for Unger to point out that, over the years, the term has been used to justify the exercise of power in ways that contradict one another, and that its value as a legitimating force for using power is now useful only insofar as people do not see that it can be used for both every situation and its opposite. In doing so, he takes advantage of common uses of the term liberalism. There is no agglomeration here, at least not by Unger.

Ewald misses the basic issue dividing CLS and its liberal critics. He invokes criteria, such as "historical accuracy" and "soundness of argument," as if they are not being contested on a deeper intellectual and institutional level. Such an appeal may be heartwarming and image-boosting to one's peers, but it does not meet the fundamental critique CLS is putting forward against mainstream legal scholarship. CLS neither rejects appeals to historical accuracy nor abandons sound argumentation. Rather, it probes the ways in which such criteria have been and are deployed in order to preclude certain kinds of appeals to historical accuracy to delegitimate specific forms of argumentation. The premature—and usually ideologically motivated—attempt to view such intellectual probing as irrational is both untrue and unfair. In fact, such a misleading characterization of the intellectual work of CLS reflects a refusal of liberal legal scholars to engage at a deeper level of theoretical exchange. There is no doubt that legal liberalism can put forward a plausible reply to this CLS critique, but it must be done on the metaphilosophical and metainstitutional levels—that is, reflections that seriously interrogate and justify the kind of prevailing standards, the present institutional arrangements of legal scholarship and education, and their link to the liberal legal status quo. It is quite telling that no liberal legal theorist has yet done this in response to CLS. Instead we get implicit appeals to the sheer facticity and entrenched immovability of the present conditions of legal scholarship and education or, as with Ewald, pronouncement of the supposedly self-evident standards of the liberal consensus. Yet as the power and potency of CLS escalates, such sophisticated liberal defenses will come—for thoughtful proponents of a status quo always emerge when they feel it is sufficiently threatened.

The first basic issue dividing CLS and mainstream legal scholarship has to do with the cultural context in which legal scholarship and education take place. This is why Ewald's attempt to invoke criteria of historical accuracy and soundness of argument as if they are context-free, universal standards untainted by ideological prejudgments and outside of power struggles and political conflict is problematic. The commonsensical reply to such suspicion is that without these standards we are left with a nihilistic epistemic situation in which "anything goes," or in which "might determines right," and so on. Such a reply misses the point. The issue here is not the nonexistence of standards, but rather the way in which prevailing standards are part and parcel of a larger form of life— a cultural context of legal scholarship and education with great authority and power that invokes its standards, in part, in order to reproduce itself. This reproduction marginalizes and devalues certain perspectives, orientations, questions, answers, styles and persons. If we view this complex process of reproduction as a thoroughly historical and political affair—from the kind of standards invoked to the type of members admitted—we are forced to become more relentlessly critical and self-critical of its results.

Surely the efforts to create the present cultural context of legal scholarship and education constitute a long and arduous battle. Both the liberal rule of law and civilian government—two grand achievements of most advanced capitalist societies—result from much bloodshed; bloodshed from those who fought and fight to create and sustain them, as well as bloodshed from those who have been and are victimized by their flaws, imperfections and structural deficiencies. Given this crucial link between legal systems and their regulatory impact on the legitimate instrumentalities of violence, as well as legal systems' crucial role in inhibiting or enhancing the well-being of the populace, CLS begins with a historical and social analysis of the present cultural context of legal scholarship and education. This analysis—aided but not dictated by theorists such as Marx, Weber, Foucault, Du Bois, de Beauvoir and others—leads CLS to contest its own context while finding a place within it. The aim of this critique is not simply to understand better how the cultural context of legal scholarship and education is reproduced, but also to change this context. This change is promoted on the intellectual plane by means of a thorough questioning of the assumptions and presuppositions of the kind of standards invoked, the role these standards play in encouraging certain viewpoints and discouraging others, and the way in which these standards legitimate the deployment of key notions such as impartiality, disinterestedness, objective due process and value-free procedure. These key notions of liberal perspectives have indeed contributed greatly to minimizing bloodshed and enhancing the welfare of the populace. But they also hide and conceal systemic relations of power that continue to encourage bloodshed and inhibit people's well-being.

A basic purpose of CLS is to disclose the degree to which liberal perspectives are unable to be truthful about themselves owing to the blindnesses and silences reinforced by their assumptions and presuppositions. The "standards" of judgment that shape liberal discourse make it difficult and even *illegitimate* to discuss certain issues—especially those that contest the very "impartiality" and "objectivity" that hide the operations of power in liberal discourses. Those liberal standards of judgment are especially delegitimating to those who contest them in an interrogative and visionary style which differs from the traditional propositional form of professional journals. Like Foucault, some members of CLS—especially Unger— try to show the complex ways in which partiality and partisanship are at work in the dispassionate styles and forms of liberal discourse, including their implicit silences, blindnesses and exclusions. These blindnesses and silences are not simply logical contradictions and analytical paradoxes. Rather, they are unintentional turns away from or intentional justifications of operations of power that scar human bodies, delimit life-chances for many and sustain privilege for some. This point is made forcefully in a contemporary classic essay by Robert Cover.[12] Within the cultural context of legal scholarship and education—a context parasitic on contexts in the large society, such as multinational corporations, and profoundly conditioning for other contexts—serious reflections on these operations of power have been taboo.[13] Like the recent work of Jacques Derrida in literary studies, Richard Rorty and Paul Feyerabend in philosophy, Catherine MacKinnon and Mary Daly in women's studies, Edward Said in Middle Eastern studies, Noam Chomsky on United States foreign policy and Maulana Karenga in black studies, the intent of CLS to contest its context requires that scholars make the very operations of power in their own academic milieu an object of investigation—in the name of intellectual integrity, critical intelligence and moral responsibility. This means creating and sustaining new subcultures of critical discourse within the very contexts one is contesting. This practical strategy is not a crude Leninist tactic of boring from within, because CLS has no group, party or organization outside of its own milieu. Rather, CLS feeds on the very constituency it both is and wants to convince.

The second basic issue between CLS and its liberal critics has to do with the role of historical consciousness and theoretical reflection in legal scholarship. CLS does not simply view law as politics, but rather tries to show how and why dominant legal practices support a particular kind of politics—namely, a liberal politics unmindful of its contradictions and deficiencies and unwilling to question thoroughly its theoretical limitations and social shortcomings. By means as diverse as the controversial "fundamental contradiction" thesis of Duncan Kennedy and the provocative historicist claims of Roberto Unger, CLS thinkers have forced legal scholars to grapple with the complex links between law and structural constraints imposed on it by contingent dynamics in the state, economy and culture—links often concealed by liberal versions of legal formalism, legal positivism and even much of legal realism. This salutary stress on the worldliness of legal operations has rudely awakened many law students and professors from their procedural slumber and persuaded them to read pertinent texts in historiography, social theory and cultural criticism. (CLS is principally responsible for the recent refreshing appearances of Christopher Hill, E. P. Thompson, Eugene Genovese, Sheila Rowbotham and other social historians in the pages of major law journals.) Such an awakening may indeed lend itself to a shallow dilettantism—yet it also undeniably broadens and enriches rather insular legal discourses in exciting and relevant ways, for it links legal studies to instructive and insightful discourses in the humanities and social scientific disciplines too often ignored by legal scholars.

Historical consciousness in Anglo-American legal thought for too long has been associated with the legal realists' limited appeal to experience and with the narrow institutional concerns of the law and economics school. CLS helps us perceive legal systems as complicated structures of power which both shape and are shaped by weighty historical legacies of class exploitation, racial subjugation and gender subordination. The type of historical consciousness promoted by CLS is inseparable from theoretical reflection because attention to structures of power over time and space requires description and explanation of the dynamics of these structures. Such a requirement pushes one into the frightening wilderness of social, political and cultural theory. Unfortunately, "theory" has often been simplistically invoked as a mere weapon with which to beat legal formalists and positivists over the head. A more subtle grasp of the role of theory discloses the degree to which ideological frameworks circumscribe the options of legal scholars, and the way in which intellectual consensus on prevailing paradigms prohibits reflection about the function of authority and power in legal discourses. In this way, CLS has justified the centrality of Marx, Weber, Durkheim, Simmel, Lukács, Foucault and other social theorists in contemporary legal scholarship.

Ewald's essay does not touch on any of these contributions of CLS to legal studies. Instead he views CLS as some foreign intrusion into the civil conversation of properly trained liberal legal thinkers. His approach implies that CLS is but a morbid symptom—perpetrated by ex–New Leftists—of muddleheadedness to be exorcised by means of logic, scholarship and good sense. In light of recent tenure denials and battles over CLS scholars at such liberal bastions as the Harvard Law School and the University of Pennsylvania Law School, we must ask whether Ewald's rhetorical strategy is to legitimate the use of power in law school faculties against the placement and retention of CLS professors and to promote the authority of legal liberalism in contemporary ideological debates. My general complaint about Ewald's readings is that he makes Unger appear less intelligent, learned and sensible than Unger actually is. And, by implication, Ewald suggests that those attracted to Unger's work have been duped. Yet Ewald gives us no account of why so many law students and professors have been misled. Surely, it is not simply because they have rejected Ewald's criteria of historical accuracy and sound argumentation. There are two main reasons for which some of the brightest law students and young law professors pay attention to CLS in general and to Unger in particular. First, there is a widespread disenchantment with the curriculum in elite law schools. The older legal pedagogical methods are viewed by many as boring, tedious and irrelevant. Law classes are viewed as tangentially interesting academic hoops through which one must jump in order to pursue a careerist and private quest for money, position and status in the conservative world of corporate law practice. Many law students and professors who fuse broad intellectual curiosity with progressive political commitment not only find this quest problematic, but also find CLS attractive.

Second, CLS serves as a kind of shortcut to the classics of left social theory, cultural criticism and philosophy. By this I mean that CLS often serves as a kind of overnight education in those oppositional intellectual traditions—Marxism, feminism, black radicalism—which are marginal or absent in law schools. Indeed, much of both the intellectual creativity *and* the theoretical mediocrity of CLS thinkers is due, in large part, to the self-taught character of these thinkers. This character is accentuated by the process by which law students become law professors—a process that provides little time for serious and sustained reflection and research prior to appointment. Therefore, few CLS figures are thoroughly grounded in the very traditions of left thought they propound. Instead, they are forced to play catch-up while they simultaneously wean themselves from and furiously attack the liberal tradition in which they have been taught.

The role of Unger's texts is instructive in this regard. They are seductive to many CLS people precisely because they combine painstaking research, passionate commitment, aversion to classic liberalism, prophetic vision and exposition of left intellectual traditions. Unger's work provides instruction *and* inspiration to young prospective CLS people. And for the less disciplined ones, his texts serve as a substitute for homework. In this way, Unger's work—though some of the most significant and provocative thought on the left today—is overrated by some CLS people. This is understandable given the grand contribution Unger's texts make to the intellectual formation of people who are bursting out of the insular and parochial constraints of legal education. Furthermore, Unger's literary style stands in stark contrast to the bureaucratic prose of much of legal scholarship. As a social theorist, intellectual historian, political activist *and* prophetic visionary, Unger speaks to the head and heart of his CLS sympathizers. There is no doubt that he is a towering figure in CLS—though he is not the paradigmatic or exemplary one.

Despite his unique style and distinctive perspectives (especially his religious sensibilities), the work of the early Unger (now corrected in his later work) shares some of the intellectual limitations and political shortcomings of his fellow CLS thinkers. The major issue here evolves around CLS's thoroughly negative attitude toward liberalism. This attitude has an intramural character that tends to ignore the historically ambiguous legacy of liberalism, and thereby to downplay some of its grand achievements. To minimize the importance of these achievements—a strong motif in CLS work—is to be historically amnesiac and politically naive. Such a view overlooks liberalism as an ideology which informs and inspires crucial aspects of oppositional left movements. Instead, CLS sees almost exclusively the crucial ways in which liberalism serves as a brake on such movements. This seamy side of liberalism is hidden by the liberal scholars who are hegemonic in legal education—as CLS thinkers rightly emphasize. Yet outside elite law schools and inside concrete movements for social change in the larger society, the ambiguous role of liberalism looms large. There simply is no intellectually acceptable, morally preferable and practically realizable left social vision and program that does not take liberalism as a starting point in order to rethink, revise and reform it in a creative manner. The kind of basic problems to which liberalism is a response must be reconceptualized and retheorized in light of both the grand achievements and structural deficiencies of liberalism. Since I view the latter as (to put it crudely) the inability of liberal *capitalist* practices to take seriously the ideals of individual liberty, citizen participation and democratic checks and balances over forms of collective power that affect the populace, liberalism is not so much a culprit (as CLS thinkers argue) but rather an incomplete historical project impeded by powerful economic interests (especially corporate interests), and culturally circumscribed institutional structures like racism, patriarchy and homophobia. I find it ironic that as a black American, a descendant of those who were victimized by American liberalism, I must call attention to liberalism's accomplishments. Yet I must do so—not because liberal thinkers have some monopoly on rigor and precision—but rather because these historic accomplishments were achieved principally by the blood, sweat and tears of subaltern peoples. Liberalism is not the possession of white, male elites in high places, but rather a dynamic and malleable tradition, the best of which has been made vital and potent by struggling victims of class exploitation, racist subjugation and patriarchal subordination. In this regard, liberalism signifies neither a status quo to defend (as with Ewald) nor an ideology to trash (as with some of CLS), but rather a diverse and complex tradition that can be mined in order to enlarge the scope of human freedom. In other words, the United

States Constitution lends itself to a perennial struggle for legitimation—with contested interpretations the primary motor in this struggle.

My kind of left oppositional thought and practice builds on and goes beyond liberalism as a kind of *Aufhebung* of liberalism. And, I believe, deep down in the CLS project there is the notion that the most desirable society will look liberal in some crucial ways. Yet the intramural character of CLS forces it to be excessively rebellious against the truncated liberalism of its fathers in order to sustain much of its *élan vital*. Intellectual integrity and political urgency force me to sidestep such childish games. This is why, though I find CLS intellectually exciting and politically inspiring, I prefer the democratic socialism of John Dewey and R. H. Tawney, the cultural criticism of C. Wright Mills and Thorstein Veblen, the political economy of Paul Sweezy and Alec Nove, and the antiracist, antisexist and antihomophobic perspectives of W. E. B. Du Bois, Sheila Rowbotham, and Audre Lorde over that of most of CLS.

The thoroughgoing negativism of much CLS scholarship leaves the legal left with little to do other than occupy slots and challenge the curriculum in the legal academy; that is, it tends to limit its political praxis to pedagogical reform in elite law schools. This indeed is a noble endeavor, but it channels intellectual and political energy away from constructive proposals and programs for the larger society and culture. More pointedly, it relieves CLS of the burden of specifying and consolidating linkages with other oppositional forces in the United States and abroad. Because it lacks this kind of self-reflection on how to contribute to the building of a broad progressive movement at this particular historical moment— beyond that of legal pedagogical reform—CLS remains an isolated and insulated oppositional affair within the ivy halls of elite law schools that displays the major features of a Freudian family romance. Ewald's essay is a less-than-powerful response in defense of the liberal fathers. I am sure more serious ones will follow. Yet to remain inscribed within this intramural affair by mere negativistic trashing of the liberal fathers is to remain too enamored of their power, influence, status and authority. To ignore the liberal fathers is indeed foolhardy—but the aim is to link rebellion in the legal household to social change in the larger polis. It is time for CLS to both grow up and grow out by historically situating the contributions and shortcomings of its liberal fathers in relation to their project, and by politically situating their own breakthroughs and blindnesses in relation to the progressive struggles in this country and in the rest of the world.

14

Charles Taylor and the Critical Legal Studies Movement

The increasing interest in Hegel among legal scholars can be attributed to three recent developments. First, there is a slow but sure historicist turn in legal studies that is unsettling legal formalists and positivists. This turn—initiated by legal realists decades ago and deepened by the critical legal studies movement in our own time—radically calls into question objectivist claims about procedure, due process and the liberal view of law. Second, there is a growing number of serious reexaminations of the basic assumptions and fundamental presuppositions of dominant forms of liberalism, not only among critics but also by many prominent liberal thinkers themselves. These reexaminations take the form of immanent critiques of liberalism as well as creative revisions of liberalism. Third, a new emerging subject matter has seized the imagination of some legal theorists: the complex *cultures* of liberal societies (including the *subcultures* of the liberal legal academy). For the first time in American legal studies, the crucial roles of race and especially gender are receiving wide attention as legitimate spheres of legal inquiry into what constitutes the ways of life that circumscribe the operations of power in the legal systems of liberal societies.

In this context, Hegel emerges as an enabling figure principally owing to his profound historicist sense, his penetrating critique of liberalism and his illuminating insights about the kinds of *Sittlichkeit* requisite for a stable and harmonious modern society. Needless to say, Hegel provides no panaceas for the concerns of contemporary legal thinkers, but he does make available valuable resources. Further, in our efforts to build on these resources, we must avoid certain seductive ideas that would render our turn to Hegel tendentious. The first such idea is that liberalism consists of a body of ideas or set of practices that is *inherently* ahistorical. This academicist understanding of liberalism holds only if one's gaze remains fixated on the prevailing versions of liberalism promulgated and promoted by many (but not all) American law professors. A deeper grasp of the complex history of liberalism reveals that Burkean, Humean or Deweyan versions of liberalism can be just as historicist as are Hegel's critique of Kantian or Smithian interpretations of liberalism. The second such idea is that communitarian or civic humanist conceptions of legal practices are *necessarily* historicist. This also is a false academicist prejudice that is often parasitic on the notion that liberalism is inherently ahistorical. Hegel's version of civic humanism indeed is historicist, yet it in no way exhausts the forms of communitarian or civic humanist views in the past or present. Of course, I am simply stating the obvious, yet in moments of intellectual recovery the obvious is often overlooked.

I need not remind Professor Taylor of such matters. In his essay, we see what we have come to expect of him—lucid, subtle, and provocative formulations of the current debate in political philosophy that focuses on Hegel, a figure about whom Taylor has written with great insight. In fact, Taylor's magisterial scholarship has contributed greatly to the historicist turn, the problematizing of liberalism and the critical inquiry into the cultures of liberal societies. Taylor is a unique figure in political philosophy, in that he is deeply grounded in the Hegelian tradition without being a Hegelian and profoundly committed to liberal values of individuality and tolerance without being a liberal. So Marxists, communitarians and civic republicans view him as a friend, and discerning liberals (who, for example, welcome his critiques of Hegel) see him as a distant yet courteous fellow traveller.

I consider Taylor to be a highly creative updated Anglo-Ameri-

can version of T. H. Green—with much more depth and scope—
who fuses Hegelian historicism with liberal values about the uniqueness and dignity of the individual. In other words, his insistence on
the historical and social character of how bodies become individuals
and subjects links him to Hegel, and his basic concern with the
self-realization of distinctive persons ties him to liberal notions of
freedom and equality. In his essay, this hybrid Green-like position
is clear. On the one hand, Taylor has little patience for liberal
theories that put a priority of the right over the good, yet he has
liberal suspicions of those communitarian theories that too easily put
a priority of the good over the right. The specter of authoritarianism
rightly frightens him. On the other hand, Taylor realizes that if he
is to mobilize resources from Hegel it must be done alongside some
significant elements of liberalism. Taylor's ingenious alternative is
to put forward a conception of the good that consists roughly of
citizens' common allegiance to a set of particular and concrete
institutions, traditions and histories (not simply universal moral
principles) that bond people together.[3] Taylor is aware of the major
liberal objection to this position, namely that such a conception of
the good tends to *bound* rather than *bond* people or that it bounds
some while it bonds others. So the problem of disagreement about
conceptions of the good still haunts Taylor's alternative. In this
sense, some liberals view Taylor as a closet liberal—since he does
endorse liberal values like diversity and individuality—who remains
unduly nostalgic for the common bonds of older *Gemeinschaften*
no longer applicable in modern *Gesellschaften:* hence his preoccupation with the limits and faults of liberalism along with his strong
rejection of authoritarian illiberalism.

Taylor's attempt to walk the slippery tightrope between Hegel
and liberalism—much like T. H. Green's, though better—seems to
be motivated by his dual allegiance to two distinct traditions of
political philosophy. But I suggest that in his case the motivations
are primarily *metaphysical,* not political; that is, Taylor is first and
foremost a proponent of a specific hermeneutical conception of

persons, rather than a defender of a hybrid political perspective. The latter is a consequence of the former. To put it bluntly, Taylor's bedrock commitment is to a conception of personhood grounded in the very nature of language and, more important, to the intersubjective, that is, public character of human individuality. From the very beginning of his career, Taylor has been espousing a nuanced notion of human beings as self-interpreting animals. This notion is inextricably tied to a radical antireductionist sensibility that resists any attempts to confine the self-realizing and self-determining capacities of persons. Those capacities are, for Taylor, created, constituted and cultivated in interaction with other persons. Hence, the centrality of reciprocal recognition and evaluation, that is, public space, in his work. His major problem with liberalism rests with its philosophical anthropology; that is, at its best, liberalism distrusts this public space, and at its worst, it dispenses with it. In this way, Taylor argues that liberalism downplays or undermines the very conditions for the individuality it heralds. This is why he makes the strong Hegelian claim that liberal societies cannot be free societies without this public space, rather than the weaker claim that liberal societies are partially free but would be more free if they were, for example, more egalitarian, less racist and less sexist. In short, Taylor has metaphysical reasons why he criticizes liberal societies, in addition to his political commitments.

As a thoroughgoing historicist, I have always been critical of Taylor's realist position in the philosophy of science. He has spent much time opposing the arguments of Mary Hesse, Thomas Kuhn and others. Yet I understand this realism as a consequence of the radical split he makes between Nature and History—a split motivated by his hermeneutical perspective. In this regard, I view Taylor as making a limited historicist turn, that is, hermeneutical turn, not a full-fledged historicist one. Interpretation remains an affair of *Geisteswissenschaften* while representation holds for *Naturwissenschaften*. My basic claim is that Taylor's hermeneutical perspec-

of individuality. Yet the jump from this kind of intersubjectivity to public space for political bonding of citizens in societies occurs too quickly in Taylor's argument. To use a favorite Hegelian term, much more "mediation" must take place before such a jump is warranted. The kind of intersubjectivity needed for individuality and the sort of public space requisite for political identity are two moments on a social spectrum, but they are not the same thing and, in fact, exist on two different levels in regard to the operations of power, be those powers rhetorical, political or social. For those of us who take seriously the centrality of race, gender and class—not simply as phenomena to morally condemn but also as structures of domination to theoretically comprehend—it is one thing to side with Taylor and Hegel about the crucial role of reciprocal recognition in subject-formations and another thing to leave open-ended connections between the truncated public sphere in liberal societies to pervasive structures of racism, sexism and class that circumscribe the cultures of these societies. In this regard, my disagreement with Taylor is not a fundamental one, yet it does encourage him to downplay his metaphysical conception of persons and deepen his structural analytical connections between the limited public space in liberal societies and the defects of the structures of racism, patriarchy and class. My position, indeed, may have to spend more time grappling with the faulty conceptions of personhood highlighted by Taylor. And my acceptance of a historical dialectic of reciprocal recognition and valuation—already accented by pragmatists like George Herbert Mead and John Dewey—is a gesture in that direction. But I refuse to make this the main pillar of my critique of dominant forms of liberalism in our time. Instead, I start precisely where Taylor never arrives, namely, with the way in which structures of racism, patriarchy and class delimit the very public sphere Taylor wants. Ironically, my own normative commitments to the desirable society look very much like Taylor's democratic socialist one, with broad egalitarian and liberal arrangements. The recovery of Hegel in legal studies can be quite helpful in moving in the direction of my own position—and away from many of the ahistorical forms of liberalism that Taylor is rightly critical of—yet without Marx, Gramsci, Du Bois, de Beauvoir, Lorde, and others, *we* remain in a limited public dialogue about our truncated public space in liberal societies.

15

The Role of Law in Progressive Politics

WHAT is the role and function of the law in contemporary progressive politics? Are legal institutions crucial terrain on which significant social change can take place? If so, how? In which way? What are progressive lawyers to do if they are to remain relatively true to their moral convictions and political goals?

In this essay I shall attempt to respond to these urgent questions. This response will try to carve out a vital democratic left space between the Scylla of upbeat liberalism that harbors excessive hopes for the law and the Charybdis of downbeat leftism that promotes exorbitant doubts about the law. My argument rests upon three basic claims. First, the fundamental forms of social misery in American society can be neither adequately addressed nor substantially transformed within the context of existing legal apparatuses. Yet serious and committed work within this circumscribed context remains indispensable if progressive politics is to have any future at all. Second, this crucial work cannot but be primarily defensive unless significant extraparliamentary social motion or movements bring power and pressure to bear on the prevailing status quo. Such social motion and movements presuppose either grass-roots citizens' participation in credible progressive projects or rebellious acts of desperation that threaten the social order. Third, the difficult task of progressive legal practitioners is to link their defensive work within the legal system to possible social motion and movements that attempt to fundamentally transform American society.

Any argument regarding the role of law in progressive politics must begin with two sobering historical facts about the American past and present. First, American society is disproportionately shaped by the outlooks, interests and aims of the business community—especially that of big business. The sheer power of corporate capital is extraordinary. This power makes it difficult to even imagine what a free and democratic society would look like (or how it would operate) if there were publicly accountable mechanisms that alleviated the vast disparities in resources, wealth and income owing, in part, to the vast influence of big business on the US government and its legal institutions. This is why those who focus on forms of social misery—like the ill-fed, ill-clad and ill-housed—must think in epochal, not apocalyptic, terms.

The second brute fact about the American past and present is that this society is a *chronically* racist, sexist, homophobic and jingoistic one. The complex and tortuous quest for American identity from 1776 to our own time has produced a culture in which people define themselves physically, socially, sexually and politically in terms of race, gender, sexual orientation and "anti-American" activities. One unique feature of the country among other modern nations—with the embarrassing exceptions of South Africa and Hitler's Germany—is that race has served as the linchpin in regulating this national quest for identity. A detailed genealogy of American legal discourse about citizenship and rights—as initiated by the late Robert Cover of Yale—bears out this inescapable reality. The historical articulation of the experiential weight of African slavery and Jim Crowism to forms of US patriarchy, homophobia and anti-American (usually Communist and socialist) repression and/or surveillance yields a profoundly conservative culture.

The irony of this cultural conservatism is that it tries to preserve a highly dynamic, corporate-driven economy, a stable, election-centered democracy, and a precious, liberties-guarding rule of law. This irony constitutes the distinctive hybridity of American liberalism (in its classical and revisionist versions) and the debilitating dilemma of American radicalism (in its movements for racial, class and/or sexual equality). In other words, American liberalism diffuses the claims of American radicals by pointing to long-standing democratic and libertarian practices, despite historic racist, sexist, class and homophobic constraints. Hence, any feasible American radicalism seems to be but an extension of American liberalism. Needless to say, the sacred cow of American liberalism—namely, economic growth achieved by *corporate* priorities—is neither examined nor interrogated. And those that do undertake such examinations are relegated to the margins of the political culture.

My first claim rests upon the assumption that the extension of American liberalism in response to movements for racial, class and sexual equality is desirable yet insufficient. This is so because the extension of American liberalism leaves relatively untouched the fundamental reality that undergirds the forms of social misery: *the maldistribution of resources, wealth and power in American society.* Yet the extension of American liberalism in regard to race, labor, women, gays, lesbians and nature *appears* radical on the American ideological spectrum principally because it goes against the deeply entrenched cultural conservatism in the country. In fact, this extension—as seen for example in the 1930s and 1960s—takes place by means of insurgent social motion and movements convincing political and legal elites to enact legislation or judicial decrees over against and imposed on the majority of the population. In short, the very extension of American liberalism has hardly ever been popular among the masses of American people primarily owing to a pervasive cultural conservatism.

The law has played a crucial role in those periods in which liberalism has been extended precisely because of the power of judicial review and an elected body of officials responding to social movements—not because cultural conservatism has been significantly weeded out. The effects of these laws and policies have over time attenuated some of the more crude and overt expressions of cultural conservatism—yet the more subtle expressions permeate the culture. The existing legal apparatuses cannot adequately address or substantially transform the plight of the racially and sexually skewed ill-fed, ill-clad or ill-housed not only because of the marginalizing of perspectives that highlight the need for a redistribution of resources, wealth and power, but also because of the perception that the extension of American liberalism is the most radical option feasible within American political culture.

Is this perception true? Is it the case that all workable radical alternatives must presuppose economic growth achieved by corporate priorities? These questions are especially acute given the collapse of social Keynesianism in the mid-1970s—that "magic" Fordist formula of mass production undergirded by mass consumption, alongside government provisions to those with no access to resources, that sustained economic growth in the postwar period. The conservative project of supply-side economics and military Keynesianism of the eighties yielded not simply a larger gap between the haves and have-nots, but also a debt-financed public sphere and a more corporate-dominated economy—in the name of "free enterprise."

If the extension of American liberalism is the only feasible radical option within American political culture, then the defensive role of progressive lawyers becomes even more important. Their work constitutes one of the few buffers against a cultural conservatism that recasts the law more in its own racist, sexist, antilabor and homophobic image. Furthermore, the work within the existing legal system helps keep alive a memory of the social traces left by past progressive movements of resistance—a memory requisite for future movements. This defensive work, though possibly radical in intent, is *liberal* practice in that it proceeds from within the legal system in order to preserve the effects of former victories threatened by the conservative offensive. Yet this same defensive work has tremendous radical potential—especially within the context of vital oppositional activity against the status quo. This is why the distinction between liberal and radical legal practice is not sharp and rigid;

rather it is fluid and contingent, due to the ever-changing larger social situation. Needless to say, the crucial role of this kind of legal practice—be it to defend the rights of activists, secure permits to march, or dramatize an injustice with a class suit—is indispensable for progressive politics. Yet in "cold" moments in American society—when cultural conservatism and big business fuse with power and potency—radical lawyers have little option other than defensive work. This work is often demoralizing, yet it serves as an important link to past victories and a basis for the next wave of radical action.

In our present period, radical legal practice takes two main forms: theoretical critiques of liberal paradigms in the academy that foster subcultures of radical students and professors, or participation in radical organizations that engage extraparliamentary social motion. It is no accident that the first form consists of a pedagogical reform movement within elite institutions of the legal academy. This critical legal studies (CLS) movement is symptomatic of a pessimism regarding feasible radical options in American political culture, and a distance between radical legal critiques and radical legal action vis-à-vis the courts. This sense of political impotence, and the gulf between radical professors of law and radical lawyers, results not because CLS consists of insular bourgeois theorists with little grasp of political reality. In fact, their understanding of this reality is often acute. Yet some of the CLS "trashing" of liberalism at the level of theory spills over to liberal legal practice. This spillover is myopic—for it "trashes" the only feasible progressive practice for radical lawyers vis-à-vis the courts. This myopia becomes downright dangerous and irresponsible when aimed at civil rights lawyers for whom the very effort to extend American liberalism may lead to injury or death in conservative America.

Is there any way out of this impasse? Can progressive legal practice be more than defensive? My second claim holds that there are but two ways out. In situations of sparse resources along with degraded self-images and depoliticized sensibilities, one avenue for poor people is existential rebellion and anarchic expression. The capacity to produce social chaos is the last resort of desperate people. It results from a tragic quest for recognition and for survival. The civic terrorism that haunts our city streets and the criminality that frightens us is, in part, poor people's response to political neglect and social invisibility. Like most behavior in US society, it is directly linked to market activity—the buying and selling of commodities. In this case, the commodities tend to be drugs, alcohol and bodies (especially women's bodies). These tragic forms of expression have yet to take on an explicitly political character—yet they may in the near future. If and when they do, the prevailing powers will be forced to make *political* responses—not simply legal ones that lead to prison overcrowding.

One major challenge for progressive politics is to find a way of channeling the talent and energy of poor people into forms of social motion that can have an impact on the powers that rule. This second way out of the impasse is the creation of citizens' organized participation in credible progressive projects. Yet American political culture mitigates against this. The status quo lives and thrives on the perennial radical dilemma of disbelief: it is hard for ordinary citizens to believe their actions can make a difference in a society whose resources, wealth and power are disproportionately held by the big-business community.

The best project progressive politics offered in the eighties was the courageous and exciting presidential campaigns of the charismatic spokesperson seeking acceptance and respect within the Democratic Party: the prophetic witness of the Reverend Jesse Jackson. Yet his two campaigns reveal the weakness of American progressive politics: the obsession with televisual visibility alongside little grassroots organizing beyond elections, and the inability to generate social motion outside electoral politics. In Jackson's case, it also discloses the refusal to promote democratic practices within one's own organization. Jackson has had a significant and, for the most part, salutary effect on American progressive politics. The major contribution of his effort is that it is the first serious attempt since

Martin Luther King, Jr.'s Poor Peoples' Campaign to constitute a multiracial coalition to raise the issue of the maldistribution of resources, wealth and power. Yet, unlike King, Jackson's attempt to highlight this crucial issue is often downplayed or jettisoned in favor of his quest for entry into the elite groupings of the centrist Democratic Party. Social motion and movements in America tend to be neither rooted in nor sustained by campaigns for electoral office—no matter how charismatic the leader.

There can be no substantive progressive politics beyond the extension of American liberalism without social motion or movements. And despite the symbolic and cathartic electoral victories of liberal women and people of color, all remain thoroughly shackled by corporate priorities in the economy and by debt-ridden administrations. Under such conditions, the plight of the ill-fed, ill-clad and ill-housed tends to get worse.

With the lethargic electoral system nearly exhausted of progressive potential—though never to be ignored owing to possible conservative politicians eager for more power—we must look toward civil society, especially to mass media, universities, religious and political groupings and trade unions. Despite the decline of popular mobilization and political participation, and the decrease of unionized workers and politicized citizens, there is a vital and vibrant culture industry, religious life, student activism and labor stirrings. In the midst of a market-driven culture of consumption—with its spectatorial passivity, evasive banality and modes of therapeutic release—there is an increasing sense of social concern and political engagement. These inchoate progressive sentiments are in search of an effective mode of organized expression. Until we create some channels, our progressive practice will remain primarily defensive.

How do we go about creating these channels of resistance and contestation to corporate power? What positive messages do we have to offer? What programs can we put forward? This brings me to the third claim regarding the role of law in progressive politics. In a society that suffers more and more from historical amnesia—

principally due to the dynamic, past-effacing activities of market forces—lawyers have close contact with the concrete traces and residues of the struggles and battles of the past. This is, in part, what Alexis de Tocqueville had in mind when he called the legal elites America's only aristocracy. Needless to say, he understood continuity with the past in terms of social stability. I revise his formulation to connect continuity with the memory of the effects of progressive victories of the past inscribed in the law of society whose link with the past is tenuous, and whose present is saturated with flashing images, consumer and hedonistic sensibilities and quick information (much of it disinformation dispensed by unreliable corporate cartels).

The role of progressive lawyers is not only to engage in crucial defensive practices—liberal practice vis-à-vis the courts—but also to preserve, recast and build on the traces and residues of past conflicts coded in laws. This latter activity is guided by a deep historical sensibility that not only deconstructs the contradictory character of past and present legal decisions, or demystifies the power relations operative in such decisions; it also concocts empowering and enabling narratives that cast light on how these decisions constitute the kind of society in which we live, and how people resist and try to transform it. Progressive lawyers can be politically engaged narrators who tell analytically illuminating stories about how the law has impeded or impelled struggles for justice and freedom. Like rap artists of the best sort, progressive lawyers can reach out to a demoralized citizenry, to energize them with insights about the historical origins and present causes of social misery in light of visions, analyses and practices to change the world. Lawyers can perform this role more easily than others due to the prestige and authority of the law in American society. Progressive lawyers can seize this opportunity to highlight the internal contradictions and the blatant hypocrisy of much of the law in the name of the very ideals—fairness, protection, formal equality—heralded by the legal system. This kind of progressive legal practice, narrative in character and radical in content, can give visibility and legitimacy to issues neglected by and embarrassing to conservative administrations, as well as exposing and educating citizens regarding the operations of economic and political powers vis-à-vis the courts. In this regard, historical consciousness and incisive narratives yield immanent critiques, disclose the moral lapses and highlight the structural constraints of the law while empowering victims to transform society.

Without this kind of historical consciousness and analytical storytelling, it is difficult to create channels for resistance and challenge to corporate power. In addition, there must be an accent on the moral character of the leaders and followers in the past and present who cared, sacrificed and risked for the struggle for justice and freedom. Progressive lawyers must highlight the *ethical* motivations of those who initiated and promoted the legal victories that further struggles for racial, sexual and class equality within the limiting perimeters of American law.

The critical legal studies movement is significant primarily because it introduces for the first time in legal discourse a profoundly historicist approach and theoretical orientation that highlight *simultaneously* the brutal realities of class exploitation, racial subordination, patriarchal domination, homophobic marginalization and ecological abuse in the American past and present. By historicist approach, I mean a candid recognition that the law is deeply reflective of—though not thoroughly determined by—the political and ideological conflicts in American society. By theoretical orientation, I mean a serious encounter with social theories that accent the structural dynamics—of the economy, state and culture—that shape and are shaped by the law.

Legal formalism, legal positivism and even legal realism have remained relatively silent about the brutal realities of the American past and present. This silence helped American liberalism remain for the most part captive to cultural conservatism. It also limited radical alternatives in legal studies to extensions of American liberalism. The grand breakthrough of CLS is to expose the intellectual *blinders* of American liberal legal scholarship, and to link these blinders to the actual blood that has flowed owing to the realities hidden. CLS calls attention to the human costs paid by those who suffer owing to the institutional arrangements sanctioned by liberal law in the name of formal equality and liberty.

Yet CLS cannot be more than a progressive movement within a slice of the professional managerial strata in American society without connections to other social motions in American society. Academic left subcultures have a crucial role to play, yet they do not get us beyond the impasse.

It may well be that American culture does not possess the democratic and libertarian resources to bring about racial, sexual and class equality. Its cultural conservatism and big-business influences may impose insurmountable constraints for such a radical project. Lest we forget, there are roughly three reactionaries (KKK, John Birchites and so on) for every leftist in America. Yet it is precisely this kind of cynical—or realistic?—outlook that often confines radicalism to extensions of American liberalism. How does one combat or cope with such an outlook?

There is no definitive or decisive answer to this question. The enabling and empowering response that avoids illusions is to sustain one's hope for social change by keeping alive the memory of past and present efforts and victories, and to remain engaged in such struggles owing principally to the *moral* substance of these efforts. As Nietzsche noted (with different aims in mind), subversive memory and other-regarding morality are the principal weapons for the wretched of the earth and those who fight to enhance their plight. This memory and morality in the United States consists of recurring cycles of collective insurgency and violent repression, social upsurge and establishmentarian containment. The American left is weak and feeble during periods of social stability owing to the powers of big business and cultural conservatism; it surfaces in the form of social movements (usually led by charismatic spokespersons) to contest this stability due to their *moral* message that borrows from the nation's collective self-definition (as democratic and free), and due to cleavages within big business and culturally conservative groups. The social movements do not and cannot last long; they indeed change the prevailing status quo, but rarely fundamentally rearrange the corporate priorities of American society. In this regard, American radicalism is more than an extension of American liberalism when it constitutes a serious and concrete threat to big business (usually in the call for substantial redistribution of resources, wealth and power). Yet this threat, though significant, is short-lived, owing to repression and incorporation. After such social movements, American radicalism is relegated to a defensive posture, that is, trying to preserve its victories by defending extensions of American liberalism.

If this crude historical scenario has merit, the major role of the law in progressive politics is threefold. First, past victories of social movements encoded in the law must be preserved in order to keep alive the memory of the past, struggle in the present, and hope for the future. Second, this preservation, though liberal in practice, is radical in purpose, in that it yearns for new social motion and movements that can threaten the new social stability of big business and cultural conservatism long enough to enact and enforce more progressive laws before repression and incorporation set in. In this regard, radical American legal practice is a kind of Burkean project turned on its head. It fosters tradition not for social stability, but to facilitate threats to the social order; it acknowledges inescapable change not to ensure organic reform but to prepare for probable setbacks and defeats of social movements. Third, the new memories and victories inscribed in new laws are kept alive by the defensive work of progressive lawyers in order to help lay the groundwork for the next upsurge of social motion and movements.

The interplay between the work of progressive lawyers and social change is crucial. In some cases, it is a matter of life or death for charismatic leaders or courageous followers. In other instances, it is a question of serving as the major buffer between the unprincipled deployment of naked state power and "principled" use of the courts against social movements. Such a buffer may prolong these movements and increase their progressive impact on society and culture. The *moral* character of these movements is important precisely because it may make repressive attackers less popular, and will more than likely help sustain the memory of the movement more easily. One of the reasons the civil rights movement led by Martin Luther King, Jr. is remembered—more than, say, other equally worthy ones like the CIO-led unionization movement or the feminist movement—is that its *moral* vision was central to its identity and accented by its major spokesperson. Needless to say, this vision appealed to the very ideals that define the national identity of many who opposed the movement.

How do progressive lawyers articulate ideals that may subvert and transform the prevailing practices legitimated by limited liberal versions of these ideals? Progressive legal practice must put forward interpretations of the precious ideal of democracy that call into question the unregulated and unaccountable power of big business; it also must set forth notions of the precious ideal of liberty that lay bare the authoritarian attitudes of cultural conservatism. This two-pronged ideological strategy should consist of an unrelenting defense of substantive democracy (in a decentralized, nonstatist fashion) and all-inclusive liberty (as best articulated in the Bill of Rights). This defense is utopian in that it tries to keep alive the possibility of social movements; it is realistic in that it acknowledges the necessity of liberal legal practices for radical lawyers to preserve the gains after social movements have been crushed and/or absorbed.

The possibility of social movements in the 1990s looms large. Eastern Europe has put the spirit of revolution—the quest for substantive democracy and all-inclusive liberty—back on the political agenda. Courageous Chinese students erected a goddess of democracy not to imitate the Statue of Liberty but to build on the tradition of liberty. The end of colonial rule in Namibia, negotiations in

South Africa, electoral activity in Brazil, the reemergence of some semblance of democracy in Chile and free elections in Nicaragua (a country wrecked primarily by an illegal, US-sponsored war waged on military and economic fronts)—all partake of this spirit of revolution.

Even in the popular music of the United States during this period of economic decline and cultural decay, a progressive concern for the ill-fed, ill-clad and ill-housed has surfaced. With solid yet insular academic left subcultures, eager yet sober black, brown, Asian and red lefts, a battered yet determined labor movement (especially organized public-sector workers), beleaguered yet bold feminist and womanist progressives, scarred though proud gay and lesbian lefts, and the growing number of green and gray activists, united social motion and movements are in the making. What is needed is neither a vanguard party nor purist ideology, but rather a coming together to pursue the common goals of radical democratic and libertarian projects that overlap. Jesse Jackson's rainbow politics has enlivened the idea of this coming together. Now it must be enacted—especially locally and regionally—not simply within electoral politics. Democratic leadership of and by ordinary citizens in extraparliamentary modes must flower and flourish. The social stability of the conservative administrations must be bombarded and shaken by democratic demands and libertarian protections. The profits and investments of big businesses should be scrutinized for public accountability and civic responsibility. The xenophobia and jingoism of cultural conservatives have to be morally rejected and judicially checked. A new world is in the making. Let us not allow the lethargy of American politics, the predominance of big business and the pervasiveness of cultural conservatism to blunt the contributions we can make. Especially if some of us choose the law as the vocational terrain for progressive politics.

Explaining Race

16

Race and Social Theory

> In this field of inquiry, "sociological theory" has still to find its way, by a difficult effort of theoretical clarification, through the Scylla of a reductionism which must deny almost everything in order to explain something, and the Charybdis of a pluralism which is so mesmerized by 'everything' that it cannot explain anything. To those willing to labour on, the vocation remains an open one.
>
> Stuart Hall

We live in the midst of a pervasive and profound crisis of North Atlantic civilization whose symptoms include the threat of nuclear annihilation, extensive class inequality, brutal state repression, subtle bureaucratic surveillance, widespread homophobia, technological abuse of nature and rampant racism and patriarchy. In this essay, I shall focus on a small yet significant aspect of this crisis: the specific forms of African American oppression. It is important to stress that one can more fully understand this part only in light of the whole crisis, and that one's conception of the whole crisis should be shaped by one's grasp of this part. In other words, the time has passed when the so-called race question can be relegated to secondary or tertiary theoretical significance. In fact, to take seriously the multi-leveled oppression of peoples of color is to raise fundamental questions regarding the very conditions for the possibility of the modern West, the diverse forms and styles of European rationality and the character of the prevailing modern secular mythologies of nationalism, professionalism, scientism, consumerism and sexual hedonism that guide everyday practices around the world.

My strategy in this essay will be as follows. First, I will examine briefly the major conservative, liberal and left-liberal conceptions of African American oppression. Second, I shall point out the distinctive strengths of adopting a refined Marxist methodology and analytical perspective. I then will sketch four influential Marxist attempts to understand African American oppression. Last, I shall argue that if we are to arrive at a more adequate conception of African American oppression, we must build upon and go beyond the Marxist tradition with the help of neo-Freudian investigations (especially those of Otto Ranke, Ernest Becker and Joel Kovel) into the modern Western forms of isolation and separation, as well as through poststructuralist reflections (by Jacques Derrida, Paul de Man, Michel Foucault and Edward Said) on the role and function of difference, otherness and marginality in contemporary philosophical discourse. I will sketch such a genealogical materialist position.

Conservative Views of African American Oppression

We begin with conservative conceptions of African American oppression primarily because we live in a country governed by those who accept many of these conceptions. Conservative perspectives focus on two terrains: *discrimination in the marketplace* and *judgments made in the minds of people*. It is no accident that conservatives tend to valorize neoclassical economics and utilitarian psychology. The basic claim is that differential treatment of black people is motivated by the "tastes" of white employers and/or white workers. Such "tastes," for instance, aversion to black people, may indeed be bad and undesirable—that is, if it can be shown that such "tastes" are based on faulty evidence, unconvincing arguments or irrational impulse. Yet it is possible that such "tastes" may be rational choices made by white people owing to commitments to high levels of productivity and efficiency in the economy, or due to evidence regarding the inferior capacities and/or performances of blacks.

There are three basic versions of conservative views of African

American oppression: the *market* version, the *sociobiologist* version
and the *culturalist* version. The market version—best represented
by Milton Friedman's classic *Capitalism and Freedom* (1962) and
his student Gary Becker's renowned *The Economics of Discrimination* (1957)—holds that it is not in the economic interests of white
employers and workers to oppose black employment opportunities.
Friedman and Becker claim that such racist behavior or "bad taste"
flies in the face of or is an extraneous factor mitigating against
market rationality, that is, the maximizing of profits. In this way,
both understand "racist tastes" as the irrational choice of white employers and workers that sidetracks market rationality in determining
the best economic outcomes. The practical policy that results from
this market perspective is to educate and persuade white employers
and workers to be more rational or attuned to their own self-interests.
The underlying assumption here is that "pure" market mechanisms
(as opposed to government intervention) will undermine "racist
tastes." Another basic presupposition here is that market rationality,
along with undermining "racist tastes," is in the interest of white employers *and* white workers *and* black people.

The sociobiologist version—put forward by Arthur Jensen
(*Harvard Educational Review,* Winter 1969) and Richard Hernstein
(*Atlantic Monthly,* September 1971)—suggests that prevailing evidence leads to the conclusion that blacks are, in some sense, geneti-
cally inferior. Blacks' IQ performance, which allegedly "measures"
intelligence, that is, the capacity for acquiring knowledge and solving problems, is such that the "racist tastes" of white employers
and workers may be justified—not on the basis of aversion to blacks
but due to group performance attainment. Unlike Friedman and
Becker, Jensen and Hernstein consider the "racist tastes" of white
employers and workers as rational choices made on "scientific"
grounds. In this way, African American oppression is not a change-
able and eradicable phenomenon, but rather part of "the natural
order of things."

Last, the culturalist version—as seen in Edward Banfield's *The*

Unheavenly City (1965), and Thomas Sowell's *Race and Economics* (1975)—holds that the "racist tastes" of white employers and workers can be justified on cultural rather than biological grounds. They argue that the character and content of African American culture inhibits black people from competing with other people in American society, be it in education, the labor force or business. For Banfield and Sowell, the necessary cultural requisites for success—habits of hard work, patience, deferred gratification and persistence—are underdeveloped among African Americans. Therefore African American oppression will be overcome only when these habits become more widely adopted by black people.

Although these three versions of conservative views of African American oppression differ among themselves, they all share certain common assumptions. First, they view market rationality (or marginal productivity calculations) as the sole standard for understanding the actions of white employers and workers. Second, this market rationality presupposes an unarticulated Benthamite felicific calculus or Hobbesian psychological egoistic model that holds self-interest to be the dominant motivation of human action. Third, this calculus or model is linked to a neoclassical economic perspective that focuses principally upon individuals and market mechanisms, with little concern about the institutional structure and power-relations of the market and limited attention to social and historical structures, for instance, slavery, state repression and second-class citizenship. Last, all agree that government intervention into the marketplace to enhance the opportunities of African Americans does more harm than good.

Liberal Views of African American Oppression

Liberal conceptions of African American oppression are under severe intellectual and political assault, yet they remain inscribed within our laws and are still, in some ways, observed. It is crucial to acknowledge that liberal viewpoints adopt the same neoclassical economic perspective and egoistic model as that of conservatives. Yet unlike conservatives, liberals highlight racist institutional barriers which result from the "racist tastes" of white employers and workers. Liberals reject mere persuasion to change these "tastes" and attack genetic inferiority claims as unwarranted and arbitrary. Liberals focus on two domains: *racist institutional barriers in the marketplace* and *inhibiting impediments in African American culture.* Those liberals who stress the former can be dubbed "market liberals"; and those who emphasize the latter, "culturalist liberals." Market liberals, such as Gunnar Myrdal and Paul Samuelson, claim that African American oppression can be alleviated if the state intervenes into racist structures of employment practices and thereby ensures, coercively if necessary, that fair criteria are utilized in hiring and firing black people. Of course, what constitutes "fair criteria" can range from race-free standards to race-conscious ones. Furthermore, culturalist liberals like Thomas Pettigrew hold that government programs should be established to prepare people, especially blacks, for jobs. These programs can range from educational efforts such as Head Start to direct training and hiring to the now defunct Job Corps projects. School integration efforts going back to the gallant struggles of the NAACP decades ago are part of this culturalist liberal position. In fact, it is fair to say that the vast majority of black public officials are culturalist and/or market liberals.

As I noted earlier, both conservatives and liberals subscribe to market rationality as the primary standard for understanding and alleviating African American oppression. Both groups assume that "rough justice" between blacks and white Americans can be achieved if black productivity is given its rightful due, namely, if there is close parity in black and white incomes. At the level of public policy, the important difference is that liberals believe this "rough justice" cannot be achieved without state intervention to erase racist institutional barriers, especially in employment and education.

Left-Liberal Views of African American Oppression

It is important that we do not confuse left-liberals with liberals—just as we should not confuse conservatives with neoconservatives (the latter tend to be market liberals and culturalist conservatives). This is so because left-liberals have what most liberals and conservatives lack: *a sense of history.* This historical consciousness of left-liberals makes them suspicious of abstract neoclassical economic perspectives and sensitive to the role of complex political struggles in determining the predominant economic perspective of the day. In other words, left-liberals recognize that classical economic views shifted to neoclassical ones (from Adam Smith and David Ricardo to Alfred Marshall and Stanley Jevons), not only because better arguments emerged but also because those arguments were about changing realities of nineteenth-century industrial capitalism and inseparable from clashing political groups in the midst of these changing realities. Similarly the versions of market liberalism associated with Franklin Roosevelt in regard to state-economy relations and John Kennedy in regard to state-economy-race relations were transformations of neoclassicism in the face of the Depression, the rise of organized labor and the struggles of southern blacks under evolving capitalist conditions. Left-liberals understand African American oppression as an ever-changing historical phenomenon and a present reality. They locate the "racist tastes" of white employers and workers and the racist institutional barriers of American society within the historical contexts of over two hundred years of slavery and subsequent decades of Jim Crow laws, peonage, tenancy, lynchings and second-class citizenship. It is no surprise that left-liberals remain in dialogue with Marxist thinkers and, in many cases, are deeply influenced by sophisticated forms of Marxist historical and social analysis.

Left-liberals such as William Julius Wilson (*The Declining Significance of Race,* 1978) and Martin Kilson (*Neither Insiders nor Outsiders,* forthcoming), who think seriously about African American oppression, are usually Weberians or followers of contemporary Weberians like Talcott Parsons and Robert Merton. The major theoretical models they adopt and apply are not those of neoclassical economics but rather structural-functionalist sociology. This difference is not as broad as it may seem, but the historical orientation of left-liberals radically separates them from most liberals and conservatives. In fact, this sense of history constitutes a kind of "crossing of the Rubicon" by left-liberals. After such a crossing there can be no return to ahistorical conceptions of African American oppression.

Left-liberals tend to be a rather eclectic lot who borrow insights from conservatives (for instance, a stress on black self-reliance and the need to acquire efficacious habits for black upward social mobility) and from liberals (for instance, the necessity for government action to regulate employment practices and enhance African American cultural deprivation). They acknowledge the crucial structural social constraints upon African Americans and, like Weber, conceptualize these constraints in terms of groups competing for prestige, status, and power over scarce economic resources. For left-liberals, strata and social position supersede class location, and financial remunerations at the workplace, that is, income, serves as the basic measure of societal well-being. The major index of African American oppression for left-liberals is that black incomes remain slightly less than 60 percent of white incomes in the USA. The public policies they support to alleviate African American oppression focus upon full employment, public works programs and certain forms of affirmative action.

Marxist Views of African American Oppression

We come now to Marxist conceptions of African American oppression. And one may ask, given the conservative tenor of the times, why Marxist theory at all? Is not Marxism an outdated and antiquated tradition that: (1) has tragically produced widespread unfreedom in the communist East; (2) utterly failed to attract the working classes in the capitalist West; (3) primarily served the purposes of anticolonial mythologies in the Third World that mask the butchery of present-day national bourgeoisies in parts of Africa, Asia and Latin America; and (4) is presently overwhelmed by information, communication and technological revolutions as well as nonclass-based movements like feminism, gay and lesbian rights, ecology, and the various movements among people of color in the First World? These questions are serious indeed, and must be confronted by anyone who wishes to defend the continuing vitality and utility of the Marxist tradition.

I shall begin by making some basic distinctions between *Marxist thought* as a monocausal, unilinear philosophy of history which accurately predicts historical outcomes; *Marxism* as it is exemplified in diverse "actually existing" communist regimes in the Soviet Union, China, Cuba, Poland, and so forth; and *Marxist theory* as a methodological orientation toward the understanding of social and historical realities. Needless to say, I readily reject Marxist thought as a monocausal, unilinear, predictive science of history or a homogeneous, teleological narrative of past and present events. Such infantile Marxism has been subjected to persuasive criticism by Karl Popper, John Plamenatz, John Dewey and Raymond Aron from outside the Marxist tradition, and by members of the Frankfurt School (Adorno, Horkheimer, Marcuse), Raymond Williams and Antonio Gramsci from within. I also reject, although not without sympathy for, the undemocratic regimes which regiment and dominate their peoples in the name of Marxism. As a democratic and libertarian socialist, I find these regimes morally repugnant, yet I wish to stress that detailed historical analysis of why they evolved as they have is required if we are to grasp their tragic predicament. Such analysis does not excuse the atrocities committed, yet it does give us a realistic sense of what these regimes have been up against.

Despite rejecting Marxist thought as a philosophy of history, and Marxism as it has appeared in diverse "actually existing" communist regimes, I hold that Marxist theory as a methodological orientation remains indispensable—although ultimately inadequate—in grasping distinctive features of African American oppression. As a methodological orientation, Marxist theory requires that we begin from two starting points.

First, the *principle of historical specificity* impels us to examine the various conditions under which African American oppression emerged, the ever-changing structural constraints under which African Americans have accommodated and resisted multiple forms of oppression, and the crucial conjunctural opportunities (for instance, those in the 1870s, 1920s and 1960s) which African Americans have either missed or seized. This historicizing approach entails that we highlight economic, political, cultural and psychosexual conflicts over resources, power, images, language and identities between black and other people as among black people themselves.

The second starting point for Marxist theory is the *principle of the materiality of structured social practices over time and space*. This principle maintains that extradiscursive formations such as modes of production, state apparatuses and bureaucracies, and discursive operations such as religions, philosophies, art objects and laws not only shape social actions of individuals and groups but possess historical potency and effectivity in relation to but not reducible to each other. Marxist theory is materialist *and* historical to the degree that it attempts to understand and explain forms of oppression in terms of the complex relation of extradiscursive formations to discursive operations. Classical Marxists view this relation in terms of a more or less determining base and a more or less determined superstructure, whereas neo-Marxists understand this relation as (in Raymond Williams's famous phrase) "the mutual setting of limits and exerting of pressures." The explanatory power of Marxist theory resides precisely in the specifying of the complex relation of base and superstructure, limits and pressures, extradiscursive formations and discursive operations, that is, in establishing with precision the nature of determination. This problem remains unresolved in the Marxist tradition, while the most impressive efforts remain those enacted in the best of Marx's own textual practices.

Marx's own effort to account for determination highlights the multileveled interplay between historically situated subjects who act and materially grounded structures that circumscribe, that is, enable and constrain, such action. This human action constitutes structured social practices which are reducible neither to context-free discrete acts of individuals nor to objective structures unaffected by human agency. The dialectical character of Marxist theory resides precisely in the methodological effort to view the interplay of subject and structure in terms of dynamic social practices during a particular time and in a specific space. The aim of Marxist theory is to view each historical moment as a multidimensional transaction between subjects shaped by antecedent structures and traditions and prevailing structures and traditions transformed by struggling subjects. As Perry Anderson has recently put it, Marxism is "the search for subjective agencies capable of effective strategies for the dislodgement of objective structures."

Each evolving society then becomes—as an object of investigation—a "complex articulated totality" produced by social practices (including those that constitute the investigation itself) shot through with relations of domination and conflict in an overdetermined economic sphere and relatively autonomous political, cultural, theological and psychic spheres. By "complex articulated totality" I mean that the specific conflicts on the various levels of society are linked to one another, while the specificity of one level is neither identical with nor reducible to a mirror image of the specificity of another level. Yet the articulation of these specific conflicts within and across the various spheres constitutes a "totality" because the relations of these conflicts are not arbitrary or capricious. They are shown not to be arbitrary in Marxist theorists' accounts of them, nor in explanations useful for effectively resisting prevailing forms of domination. These accounts or explanations privilege the economic sphere without viewing the other spheres as mere expressions of the economic. In other words, Marxist theory claims that social and historical explanation must view, in some discernible manner, the economic sphere as the major determining factor in accounting for the internal dynamics (or synchronicity) and historical change (or diachronicity) of human (and especially capitalist) societies. It should be apparent that Marxist conceptions of African American oppression reject the "bad tastes" starting point of conservatives, the "racist institutional barriers" starting point of liberals and the Weberian views about the economic sphere of left-liberals, that is, the stress on strata and status. Nonetheless, there remains considerable controversy among Marxist theorists about how to construe the economic sphere, whether as a mode of production, as merely the forces of production, or as primarily a mode of surplus-extraction or form of appropriation of surplus-value. Consensus has been reached only insofar as all hold that the economic sphere is constituted by conflict-ridden classes characterized by their relation (ownership, effective control or lack thereof) to the means of production.

Unfortunately—and largely due to the European character of Marxist scholarship on race—there exists a paucity of sophisticated Marxist treatments of racially structured societies. Outside the historical work of W. E. B. Du Bois, the grand efforts of Oliver Cox and C. L. R. James, and the pioneering recent writings of Eugene Genovese, Stuart Hall and Orlando Patterson, the richness of the Marxist methodological orientation and analytical perspective in relation to race remains untapped. Instead, Marxist theorists of African American oppression have put forward rather bland and glib views. For example, *class reductionists* have simply subsumed African American oppression under class exploitation and viewed complex racist practices as merely conscious profiteering—or a divide-and-conquer strategy—on behalf of capitalists. Although this view captures a practical truth about racist employers' practices during a particular period in racially fractured capitalist societies, it inhibits more thorough theoretical investigation into other crucial aspects, features and functions of racist practices. Furthermore, it tacitly assumes that racism is rooted in the rise of modern capitalism. Yet it can be easily shown that although racist practices were appropriated and promoted in various ways by modern capitalist processes, racism predates capitalism. Racism seems to have its roots in the early encounter between the civilizations of Europe, Africa and Asia, encounters which occurred long before the rise of modern capitalism. The very category of 'race'—denoting primarily skin color—was first employed as a means of classifying human bodies by François Bernier, a French physician, in 1684. The first substantial racial division of humankind is found in the influential *Natural System* (1735) of the preeminent naturalist of the eighteenth century, Carolus Linnaeus. Yet both instances reveal racist practices—in that both degrade and devalue non-Europeans—at the level of intellectual codification. Xenophobic folktales and mythologies, racist legends and stories—such as authoritative Church Fathers' commentaries on the Song of Solomon and the Ywain narratives in medieval Brittany—were operating in the everyday lives of ordinary folk long before the seventeenth and eighteenth centuries. In fact, Christian anti-Semitism and European anti-blackism were rampant throughout the Middle Ages. In short, the class reductionist viewpoint rests upon shaky theoretical and historical grounds.

The other simplistic Marxist conceptions of African American oppression are those of the *class super-exploitationist* perspective and the *class nationalist* view. The former holds that African Americans are subjected to general working-class exploitation and specific class exploitation owing to racially differential wages received and/ or to the relegation of black people to the secondary sector of the labor force. Again the claim is that this is a conscious divide-and-conquer strategy of employers to fan and fuel racial antagonisms between black and white workers and to "bribe" white workers at the expense of lower wages for black workers. Again, this perspective contains a practical truth about the aims of white employers during a particular period of particular capitalist societies, yet the "bribe" thesis is a weak reed upon which to hang an account of the many levels on which racism works. More important, this position still views race solely in economic and class terms.

The class nationalist viewpoint is the most influential, widely accepted and hence unquestioned among practicing black Marxists. It understands African American oppression in terms of class exploitation and national domination. The basic claim is that African Americans constitute or once constituted an oppressed nation in the Southern Black Belt and, much like Puerto Ricans, form an oppressed national minority within American society. There are numerous versions of this so-called Black Nation thesis. Its classical version was put forward in the Sixth Congress of the Third International in 1928, slightly modified in its 1930 resolution and codified in Harry Haywood's *Negro Liberation* (1948). Subsequent versions abound on the sectarian black left—from Nelson Peery's *The Negro National Colonial Question* (1978), James Forman's *Self-Determination and the African-American People* (1981) to Amiri Baraka's formulations in his journal, *The Black Nation*. More refined conceptions of the class nationalist view were put forward in the form of an internal colony thesis by Harold Cruse in *The Crisis of the Negro Intellectual* (1967) and Robert Allen in *Black Awakening in Capitalist America* (1969); yet even in these two seminal texts of the sixties the notion of African America as an internal colony remains a mere metaphor without serious analytical content. Ironically, the most provocative and persistent proponent of a class nationalist perspective is Maulana Karenga, who arrived at his own self-styled position that infuses a socialist analytical component within his cultural nationalism. His *Essays in Struggle* (1978) and *Kawaida Theory* (1981) stand shoulders above much of the theoretical reflections on African Americans' oppression proposed by the black Marxist left.

On the practical level, the class nationalist perspective has promoted and encouraged impressive struggles against racism in the USA. But with its ahistorical racial definition of a nation, its flaccid statistical determination of national boundaries and its illusory distinct black economy, the Black Nation thesis serves as a misguided attempt by Marxist-Leninists to repudiate the class reductionist and class super-exploitationist views of African American oppression. In short, it functions as a poor excuse for the absence of a viable Marxist theory of the specificity of African American oppression.

Such a theory is, however, in the making. The recent efforts of Howard Winant and Michael Omi to develop a *class racialist* position contribute to such a theory. As I noted earlier, the pioneering work of Eugene Genovese, Stuart Hall and Orlando Patterson is also quite promising in this regard. The Marxist conception of racially structured capitalist societies as "complex articulated totalities" buttressed by flexible historical materialist analysis, looms large in their work. Genovese is deeply influenced by Gramsci's nuanced conception of hegemony; Hall, by Althusser and Gramsci's notion of articulation; and Patterson by Marx's own concept of domination, by a homespun existentialism, and by recent studies of Rytina and Morgan in demography. A distinctive feature of these class racialist (or class ethnic) views is that they eschew any form of reductionism, economism and a priorism in Marxist theory. Furthermore, they attempt to give historically concrete and sociologically specific Marxist accounts of the racial aspects of particular societies. This means that they accent the different forms of racial domination and reject racism as a universal and unitary transhistorical phenomenon, for instance, as a prejudicial proclivity of individual psychology or race instinct.

In this way, recent forms of Marxist theory demystify the *conservative* idea of "bad tastes" by historically situating the emergence of these "tastes" as socially pertinent, functional and potent; they structurally circumscribe the *liberal* notion of "racist institutional barriers" by viewing such mechanisms within the operations of racially fractured and fractioned capitalist modes of production; and they contest the Weberian assumptions of *left-liberals* by linking struggles for prestige and status to changing class conflicts and by stressing peoples' empowerment (participation in decision-making processes) rather than mere increased financial remuneration at the workplace (higher incomes). In stark contrast to vulgar Marxist views, this body of Marxist theory holds racism to be neither a mere conspiracy or ideological trick from above, nor a divide-and-conquer strategy of capitalists, but rather a complex cluster of structured social practices that shape class relations and create a crucial dimension in the lives of individuals throughout capitalist societies. The linchpin in this refined Marxist view is that the economic sphere is the ultimate determining explanatory factor for grasping the role and function of racism in modern societies. My own somewhat hesitant rejection of this linchpin leads me to build upon, yet go beyond, this last incarnation of Marxist theory.

Toward a Genealogical Materialist Analysis

In this last section, I shall set forth a schematic outline of a new conception of African American oppression that tries to bring together the best of recent Marxist theory and the invaluable insights of neo-Freudians (Ranke, Becker, Kovel) about the changing forms of immortality quests and perceptions of dirt and death in the modern West, along with the formulations of the poststructuralists (Derrida, de Man, Foucault, Said) on the role of difference, otherness and marginality in discursive operations and extradiscursive formations.

My perspective can be characterized as a genealogical materialist analysis: that is, an analysis which replaces Marxist conceptions of history with Nietzschean notions of genealogy, yet preserves the materiality of multifaceted structured social practices. My understanding of genealogy derives neither from mere deconstructions of the duplicitous and deceptive character of rhetorical strategies of logocentric discourses, nor from simple investigations into the operations of power of such discourses. Unlike Derrida and de Man, genealogical materialism does not rest content with a horizon of language. In contrast to Foucault and Said, I take the challenge of historical materialism with great seriousness. The aspects of Nietzsche that interest me are neither his perennial playfulness nor his vague notions of power. What I find seductive and persuasive about Nietzsche is his deep historical consciousness, a consciousness so deep that he must reject prevailing ideas of history in the name of genealogy. It seems to me that in these postmodern times, the principles of historical specificity and the materiality of structured social practices—the very founding principles of Marx's own discourse—now require us to be genealogical materialists. We must become more radically historical than is envisioned by the Marxist tradition. By becoming more "radically historical" I mean confronting more candidly the myriad effects and consequences (intended and unintended, conscious and unconscious) of power-laden and conflict-ridden social practices—for instance, the complex confluence of human bodies, traditions and institutions. This candor takes the form of a more theoretical open-endedness and analytical dexterity than Marxist notions of history permit—without ruling out Marxist explanations a priori.

Furthermore, a genealogical materialist conception of social practices should be more materialist than that of the Marxist tradition, to the extent that the privileged material mode of production is not necessarily located in the economic sphere. Instead, decisive material modes of production at a given moment may be located in the cultural, political or even the psychic sphere. Since these spheres are interlocked and interlinked, each always has some weight in an adequate social and historical explanation. My view neither promotes a post-Marxist idealism (for it locates acceptable genealogical accounts in material social practices), nor supports an explanatory nihilism (in that it posits some contingent yet weighted set of material social practices as decisive factors to explain a given genealogical configuration, that is, set of events). More pointedly, my position appropriates the implicit pragmatism of Nietzsche for the purposes of a deeper, and less dogmatic, historical materialist analysis. In this regard, the genealogical materialist view is both continuous and discontinuous with the Marxist tradition. One cannot be a genealogical materialist without (taking seriously) the Marxist tradition, yet allegiance to the methodological principles of the Marxist tradition forces one to be a genealogical materialist. Marxist theory still may provide the best explanatory account for certain phenomena, but it also may remain inadequate to account for other phenomena—notably here, the complex phenomenon of racism in the modern West.

My basic disagreement with Marxist theory is twofold. First, I hold that many social practices, such as racism, are best understood and explained not only or primarily by locating them within modes of production, but also by situating them within the cultural traditions of civilizations. This permits us to highlight the specificity of those practices which traverse or cut across different modes of production, for example, racism, religion, patriarchy, homophobia. Focusing on racist practices or white-supremacist logics operative in premodern, modern and postmodern Western civilization yields both racial continuity and discontinuity. Even Marxist theory can be shown to be both critical of and captive to a Eurocentrism which can justify racist practices. And though Marxist theory remains indispensable, it also obscures and hides the ways in which secular ideologies—especially modern ideologies of scientism, racism and sexual hedonism (Marxist theory does much better with nationalism, professionalism and consumerism)—are linked to larger civilizational ways of life and struggle.

Second, I claim that the Marxist obsession with the economic sphere as the major explanatory factor is itself a reflection of the emergence of Marxist discourse in the midst of an industrial capitalism preoccupied with economic production; and, more important, this Marxist obsession is itself a symptom of a particular Western version of the will to truth and style of rationality which valorizes control, mastery and domination of nature and history. I neither fully reject this will to truth, nor downplay the crucial role of the economic sphere in social and historical explanation. But one is constrained to acknowledge the methodological point about the degree to which Marxist theory remains inscribed within the very problematic of the unfreedom and domination it attempts to overcome.

Genealogical materialist analysis of racism consists of three methodological moments that serve as guides for detailed historical and social analyses.

1) A *genealogical* inquiry into the discursive and extra-discursive conditions for the possibility of racist practices, that is, a radically historical investigation into the emergence, development and sustenance of white-supremacist logics operative in various epochs in the modern Western (Eastern or African) civilization.

2) A *microinstitutional* (or localized) analysis of the mechanisms that promote and contest these logics in the everyday lives of people, including the ways in which self-images and self-identities are shaped, and the impact of alien, degrading cultural styles, aesthetic ideals, psychosexual sensibilities and linguistic gestures upon peoples of color.

3) A *macrostructural* approach which accents modes of overdetermined class exploitation, state repression and bureaucratic domination, including resistance against these modes, in the lives of peoples of color.

The first moment would, for example, attempt to locate racist discourses within the larger Western conceptions of death and dirt, that is, in the predominant ways in which Western peoples have come to terms with their fears of "extinction with insignificance," of existential alienation, isolation and separation in the face of the inevitable end of which they are conscious. This moment would examine how these peoples have conceptualized and mythologized their sentiments of impurity at the visual, tactile, auditory and, most important, olfactory levels of experience and social practice.

Three white-supremacist logics—the battery of concepts, tropes and metaphors which constitute discourses that degrade and devalue people of color—operative in the modern West may shed some light on these issues: the *Judeo-Christian racist logic* that emanates from the Biblical account of Ham looking upon and failing to cover his father Noah's nakedness, thereby provoking divine punishment in the form of blackening his progeny. This logic links racist practices to notions of disrespect for and rejection of authority, to ideas of unruly behavior and chaotic rebellion. The *"scientific" racist logic* which promotes the observing, measuring, ordering and comparing of visible physical characteristics of human bodies in light of Greco-Roman aesthetic standards associates racist practices with bodily ugliness, cultural deficiency and intellectual inferiority. And the *psychosexual racist logic* endows black people with sexual prowess, views them as either cruel, revengeful fathers, frivolous, carefree children or passive, long-suffering mothers. This logic—rooted in Western sexual discourses about feces and odious smells—relates racist practices to bodily defecation, violation and subordination, thereby relegating black people to walking abstractions, lustful creatures or invisible objects. All three white-supremacist logics view black people, like death and dirt, as Other and Alien.

An important task of genealogical inquiry is to disclose in historically concrete and sociologically specific ways the discursive operations that view Africans as excluded, marginal, other, and to reveal how racist logics are guided (or contested) by various hegemonic Western philosophies of identity and universality which suppress difference, heterogeneity and diversity. Otto Ranke and Ernest Becker would play an interesting role here, since their conception of societies as codified hero-systems or as symbolic-action systems which produce, distribute and circulate statuses and customs in order to cope with human fears of death or extreme otherness may cast light on modern Western racist practices. For example, with the lessening of religious influence in the modern West, human immortality quests were channeled into secular ideologies of science, art, nation, profession, race, sexuality and consumption. The deep human desire for existential belonging, and for self-esteem—of what I call the need for and consumption of *existential capital*—results in a profound, even gut-level, commitment to some of the illusions of the present epoch. None of us escapes. And many Western peoples get much existential capital from racist illusions, from ideologies of race. The growing presence of Caribbean and Indian peoples in Britain, Africans in Russia, Arabs in France, and black soldiers in Germany is producing escalating black/white hatred, sexual jealousy and intraclass antagonisms. This suggests that the means of acquiring existential capital from ideologies of race is in no way peculiar to the two exemplary racist Western countries, the USA and South Africa. It also reminds us that racist perceptions and practices are deeply rooted in Western cultures and become readily potent in periods of crisis, be that crisis cultural, political or economic.

The second moment, the microinstitutional or localized analysis, examines the elaboration of white-supremacist logics within the everyday lives of people. Noteworthy here is the conflict-ridden process of identity-formation and self-image-production by peoples of color. The work of Goffman and Garfinkel on role-playing and self-masking, the insights of Althusser, Kristeva and Foucault on the contradictions shot through the process of turning individual bodies into ideological subjects (for instance, "colored," "Negro," "black" subjects), and the painful struggle of accepting and rejecting internalized negative and disenabling self-conceptions (for instance, pervasive lack of self-confidence in certain activities, deep insecurities regarding one's capacities) among people of color, as highlighted in Memmi and Fanon, are quite useful to this analysis.

The third (and last) moment, the macrostructural analysis, deepens the historical materialist analyses of Genovese, Hall and Patterson, with the proviso that the economic sphere may, in certain cases, not be the ultimate factor in explaining racist practices. As I noted earlier, there is little doubt that it remains a crucial factor in every case.

17

The Paradox of the African American Rebellion

The distinctive feature of African American life in the sixties was the rise on the historical stage of a small yet determined petite bourgeoisie promoting liberal reforms, and the revolt of the masses, whose aspirations exceeded those of liberalism but whose containment was secured by political appeasement, cultural control and state repression. African America encountered the modern American capitalist order (in its expansionist phase)—as urban dwellers, industrial workers and franchised citizens—on a broad scale for the first time. This essay will highlight the emergence of the black parvenu petite bourgeoisie—the new, relatively privileged, middle class—and its complex relations to the black working poor and underclass. I will try to show how the political strategies, ideological struggles and cultural anxieties of this predominantly white-collar stratum both propelled the freedom movement in an unprecedented manner and circumscribed its vision, analysis and praxis within liberal capitalist perimeters.

For interpretive purposes, the sixties is not a chronological category which encompasses a decade, but rather a historical construct or heuristic rubric which renders noteworthy historical processes and events intelligible. The major historical processes that set the context for the first stage of the black freedom movement in the sixties were the modernization of southern agriculture, the judicial repudiation of certain forms of southern racism and the violent white backlash against perceived black progress. The modernization of southern agriculture made obsolete much of the traditional tenant labor force, thereby forcing large numbers of black rural folk into southern and northern urban centers in search of employment. The judicial repudiation of certain forms of southern racism, prompted by the gallant struggles of the National Association for the Advancement of Colored People (NAACP) and exemplified in the *Brown v. Board of Education* decision of 1954, was not only a legal blow against tax-supported school segregation; it also added historical momentum and political legitimacy to black struggles against racism. Yet there quickly surfaced an often violent white reaction to this momentum and legitimacy. For example, Rev. George W. Lee was fatally shot in May 1955 for refusing to take his name off the voter registration list. Sixty-three-year-old Lamar Smith was killed in broad daylight in August 1955 for trying to get out the black vote in an upcoming primary election. And most notably, Emmett L. Till, a fourteen-year-old lad from Chicago visiting his relatives, was murdered in late August 1955. These wanton acts of violence against black people in Mississippi, though part of the American southern way of life, reflected the conservative white reaction to perceived black progress. In 1955, this white reaction was met with widespread black resistance.

The greatness of Rev. Dr. Martin Luther King, Jr.—the major American prophet of this century and black leader in the sixties—was his ability to mobilize and organize this southern resistance, such that the delicate balance between the emerging "new" black petite bourgeoisie, black working poor and black underclass was maintained for a few years. The arrest of Rosa Parks on December 1, 1955 in Montgomery, Alabama—as a result of one of a series of black acts of civil disobedience against Montgomery's bus line that year—led to the creation of the Montgomery Improvement Association (MIA), the adoption of a citywide black boycott and the placement of King at the head of the movement. After nearly a year of the boycott, the US Supreme Court declared Alabama's state and local bus segregation laws unconstitutional. Judicial repudiation of Southern racism again gave the black struggle for freedom momentum and legitimacy.

King is the exemplary figure of the first stage of the black freedom movement in the sixties not only because he was its gifted and courageous leader or simply because of his organizational achievements, but, more important, because he consolidated the most progressive potential available in the black Southern community at that time: the cultural potency of prophetic black churches, the skills of engaged black preachers, trade-unionists and professionals, and the spirit of rebellion and resistance of the black working poor and underclass. In this sense, King was an organic intellectual of the first order—a highly educated and informed thinker with organic links to ordinary folk. Despite his petit bourgeois origins, his deep roots in the black church gave him direct access to the life-worlds of the majority of black southerners. In addition, his education at Morehouse College, Crozier Theological Seminary and Boston University provided him with opportunities to reflect upon various anticolonial struggles around the world, especially those in India and Ghana, and also entitled him to respect and admiration in the eyes of black people, including the "old," black, middle class (composed primarily of teachers and preachers). Last, his Christian outlook and personal temperament facilitated relations with progressive nonblack people, thereby insuring openness to potential allies.

King institutionalized his sense of the social engagement of black churches, his Christian-informed techniques of nonviolence and his early liberal vision of America, with the founding in February, 1957 in New Orleans of the Southern Christian Leadership Conference (SCLC). This courageous group of prophetic black preachers from ten southern states served as the models for young black southern activists. I stress the adjective "southern" not simply because most black people in the USA at this time lived in the South, but also because the core of the first stage of the black freedom movement was a church-led movement in the belly of the violence-prone, underindustrialized, colonylike southern USA. Of course, the North was quite active—especially Harlem's Rev. Adam Clayton Powell, Jr. in Congress and the Nation of Islam's Malcolm X in the streets—but activity in the North was not the major thrust of this first stage.

Like David against Goliath, black activists openly challenged the entrenched, racist, white status quo in the South. Widespread white economic sanctions and physical attacks on black people, fueled by the so-called "Southern Manifesto" promoted in 1956 by Senator J. Strom Thurmond of South Carolina along with over a hundred congressmen, rendered both the Democratic and Republican parties relatively silent regarding the civil rights issues affecting black people. Two diluted civil rights bills (in 1957 and 1960) limped through Congress, and the Supreme Court, owing to congressional pressure, took much of the bite out of its earlier Brown decision. Black resistance intensified.

Inspired by the praxis of King, MIA and SCLC—as well as the sit-in techniques employed by the Congress of Racial Equality (CORE) in the North—four black freshmen students at North Carolina Agricultural and Technical College in Greensboro staged a sit-in at the local Woolworth's on February 1, 1960. Within a week, their day-to-day sit-in had been joined by black and white students from the Women's College of the University of North Carolina, North Carolina College and Duke University. Within two weeks, the sit-in movement had spread to fifteen other cities in Virginia, Tennessee and South Carolina. Within two months, there were sit-ins in seventy-eight cities. By the end of 1960, over fifty thousand people throughout the South had participated in sit-in demonstrations, with over twenty-five percent of the black students in predominantly black colleges participating. In short, young black people (and some progressive white people) had taken seriously King's techniques of nonviolence and the spirit of resistance.

This spontaneous rebellion of young black people against the southern taboo of black and white people eating together in public places exemplified a major component in the first stage of the black freedom movement: the emergence of politicized, black, parvenu, petit bourgeois students. These students, especially young preachers and Christian activists, prefigured the disposition and orientation of the vastly increasing number of black college students in the sixties: they would give first priority to social activism and justify their newly acquired privileges by personal risk and sacrifice. So the young black student movement was not simply a rejection of segregation in restaurants. It was also a revolt against the perceived complacency of the "old" black petite bourgeoisie. It is no accident that at the first general conference on student sit-in activity, which began Good Friday (April 15) 1960, the two keynote speakers— Rev. James Lawson and Rev. Martin Luther King, Jr.—launched devastating critiques of the NAACP and other "old" black middle-class groups. King articulated this viewpoint when he characterized the sit-in movement as "a revolt against those Negroes in the middle class who have indulged themselves in big cars and ranch-style homes rather than in joining a movement for freedom." The organization which emerged later in the year from this gathering—the Student Nonviolent Coordinating Committee—(SNCC)—epitomized this revolt against the political reticence of the "old" black middle class.

The major achievement of SNCC was, in many ways, its very existence. SNCC initiated a new style and outlook among black students in particular and the "new" black petite bourgeoisie in general. Its activist, countercultural orientation even influenced disenchanted white students on elite university campuses. Yet SNCC's central shortcoming was discernible at its inception: if pushed far enough, the revolt against middle-class status and outlook would not only include their models but also themselves, given their privileged student status and probable upward social mobility.

The influence of SNCC's new style was seen when James Farmer departed from the program directorship of the NAACP to become National Director of CORE. Within six weeks, he announced that

CORE would conduct "Freedom Rides"—modeled on the 1947 Journey of Reconciliation led by CORE—to challenge segregation in interstate bus depots and terminals. On May 4, 1961, seven black people and six white people left Washington, D.C. Within ten days, one of the buses had been burned to the ground and many riders had been viciously attacked in Birmingham and Montgomery. This "Freedom Ride" was disbanded in Montgomery on May 17. A second "Freedom Ride" was initiated by SNCC, led by Diane Nash, composed of white and black people from CORE and SNCC. Violence ensued again, with twenty-seven people arrested and given suspended two-month sentences and fines of two hundred dollars. They refused to pay and were taken to Parchman Prison.

These two "Freedom Rides"—though responsible for the desegregation of bus and train stations on September 22, 1961, by the Interstate Commerce Commission—served as a portent of the two basic realities which would help bring the initial stage of the black freedom movement to a close: first, the slow but sure rift between SNCC and King, and second, the ambiguous attitude of Democratic Party liberals to the movement. Both aspects came to the fore at the crucial August 1961 staff meeting at SNCC at the Highlander Folk School in Tennessee. It was well known that the Kennedy administration had called for a "cooling off" period, motivated primarily by its fear of alienating powerful Southern Democratic comrades in Congress. At the meeting, Tim Jenkins, a fellow traveller of the Democratic Party, proposed that SNCC drop its emphasis on direct action and focus on voter education and registration. The majority of the SNCC staff opposed Jenkins's project, owing to its connections with the Kennedy administration and the open approval of it by King's SCLC. In the eyes of many SNCC members, the "Establishment" against which they were struggling began to encompass both the Democratic Party's liberals and the SCLC's black activist liberals. This slow rupture would result in some glaring defeats in the civil rights movement, most notably the Albany (Georgia) Movement in December 1961, and also led to the gradual breakaway of SNCC from the techniques of nonviolence.

Yet in 1963, the first stage of the black freedom movement would culminate in its most successful endeavors: Birmingham and the March on Washington. The televised confrontation between the civil rights marchers and the Commissioner of Public Safety, Eugene "Bull" Connor, as well as the dramatic arrest of King, gave the movement much sympathy and support throughout the country. And the use of hundreds of black children in the struggle reinforced this effective histrionic strategy. Despite the bombing of the black Gaston Hotel, of King's brother's home, and black spontaneous rebellions in Birmingham, the massive nonviolent direct action—including over three thousand people imprisoned—proved successful. The city of Birmingham, often referred to as the "American Johannesburg," accepted the black demands for desegregation and black employment opportunities. Furthermore, President Kennedy responded to the Birmingham campaign with a televised address to the nation in which he pledged his support for a comprehensive civil rights bill. However, the assassination of Medgar Evers, state executive secretary of the Mississippi NAACP, only hours after Kennedy's speech cast an ominous shadow over the Birmingham victory.

The famous March on Washington in August 1963—the occasion for King's powerful and poignant "I have a dream" speech—was not the zenith of the civil rights movement. The movement had peaked in Birmingham. Rather the March on Washington was the historic gathering of that coalition of liberal forces—white trade unionists, Christians, Jews and civil rights activists—whose potency was declining, whose fragile cohesion was falling apart. The central dilemma of the first stage of the black freedom movement emerged: the existence and sustenance of the civil rights movement neither needed nor required white aid or allies, yet its *success* required white liberal support in the Democratic Party, Congress and the White House.

The March on Washington exemplified this debilitating limitation of the civil rights movement. With white liberal support, the movement would achieve limited success, but slowly lose its legitimacy in the eyes of the now more politicized black petit bourgeois students, working poor and underclass. Without white liberal support, the movement could raise more fundamental issues of concern to the black working poor and underclass, yet thereby render the movement marginal to mainstream American politics and hence risk severe repression. It comes as no surprise that the March on Washington witnessed both the most powerful rhetoric and the most salient reality of the civil rights movement: King's great speech and the Kennedy administration's supervision of the March.

In summary, the first stage of the black freedom movement in the sixties—the civil rights struggle—began as a black response to white violent attacks and took the form of a critique of everyday life in the American South. This critique primarily consisted of attacking everyday cultural folkways which insulted black dignity. It was generated, in part, from the multifarious effects of the economic transformation of dispossessed southern rural peasants into downtrodden industrial workers, maids and unemployed city dwellers within the racist American South. In this regard, the civil rights movement prefigured the fundamental concerns of the American New Left: linking private troubles to public issues, accenting the relation of cultural hegemony to political control and economic exploitation.

The major achievements of the civil rights movement were noteworthy: the transformation of everyday life (especially the elimination of terror as a primary mode of social control) of central regions in the American South; the federal commitment to the civil and voting rights of African Americans; and the sense of confidence among black people that effective mobilization and organization were not only possible but imperative if the struggle for freedom was to continue. The pressing challenges were immense: transforming the power relations in the American South and North, obtaining federal support for employment and economic rights of the underprivileged, sustaining black organizational potency in the face of increasing class differentiation within the black community, and taking seriously the long-overlooked specific needs and interests of black women. The first stage came to a close principally because the civil rights struggle achieved its liberal aims, namely, absorption into mainstream American politics, reputable interest-group status in the (soon to falter) liberal coalition of the Democratic Party.

The second stage centered primarily on the issue of the legitimacy and accountability of the black political leadership. Like the first stage, this historical movement was engendered by a sense of black resistance and rebellion, and led by black petit bourgeois figures. Yet these "new," black, middle-class figures had been highly politicized and radicalized by the strengths and weaknesses of King's movement, by the rise of the New Left movement among white privileged students and by the revolutionary anticolonial struggles in the Caribbean (Cuba), Africa (Ghana and Guinea), Latin America (Chile and Bolivia) and Southeast Asia (Vietnam). The transitional events were the Mississippi Freedom Summer in 1964, the Democratic National Convention in Atlantic City, late August 1964, and the Selma campaign of 1965. The Freedom Summer brought to the surface the deep cultural and personal problems of interracial political struggle in America: white attitudes of paternalism, guilt and sexual jealousy, and black sensibilities of one-upsmanship, manipulation and sexual adventure. The Atlantic City convention illustrated the self-serving machinery of the Democratic Party, whose support even King at this point solicited at the risk of white-controlled compromise. Finally, King's Selma campaign, initiated by SNCC years earlier, was sustained primarily by federal support, escort and legitimacy. In short, the bubble was about to burst: the vision, analysis and praxis of significant elements of the black freedom movement were to move beyond the perimeters of prevailing American bourgeois politics.

The Watts explosion in August 1965 revealed the depths of the problem of legitimacy and accountability of black political leadership. The rebellion and resistance (especially in northern urban centers) could no longer find an organizational form of expression. In the cities, it had become sheer anarchic energy and existential assertion without political direction and social vision. The Watts rebellion was a watershed event in the black freedom movement, in that it drew the line of demarcation between those who would cling to liberal rhetoric, ties to the Democratic Party and middle-class concerns, and those who would attempt to go beyond liberalism, expose the absorptive role and function of the Democratic Party and focus more on black proletarian and lumpenproletarian interests.

The pressing challenges of the second stage were taken up by Martin Luther King, Jr. His Chicago campaign in 1966—though rejected by most of his liberal black and white comrades in SCLC—pushed for the radical unionization of slum-dwellers against exploitative landlords. His aborted poor people's campaign of 1967 to 68, initiated after his break with President Johnson and the Democratic Party, which had been precipitated by his fierce opposition to the Vietnam War, was even more attuned to black, Latino and white working poor and underclass concerns. Yet, despite his immense talent, energy and courage, it became clear that King lacked the organization and support to address these concerns. Notwithstanding his 1968 murder—preceded by intense FBI harassments and threats—the widespread ideological fragmentation and increased class and strata differentiation in African America precluded King from effectively meeting the pressing challenges. His new focus on the urban poor led to black middle-class abandonment of his movement; his nonviolent approach perturbed black committed leftists who welcomed his new focus; his Christianity disturbed black secularists and Muslims already working in urban ghettoes; and his integrationist perspective met with staunch opposition from black nationalists who were quickly seizing hegemony over the black freedom movement. In other words, King was near death politically and organizationally before he was murdered, though he will never die in the hearts and minds of progressive people in the USA and abroad.

Ironically, King's later path was blazed by his early vociferous critic, Malcolm X. Even as a narrow black nationalist under the late Honorable Elijah Muhammad, Malcolm X rejected outright white liberal support and ties to the Democratic Party, and he highlighted the plight of urban black working poor and unemployed people. More than any other black figure during the first stage, Malcom X articulated the underlying, almost visceral, feelings and sensibilities of black urban America—North and South, Christian and non-Christian, young and old. His early rhetoric was simply prescient: too honest, too candid, precisely the things black folk often felt but never said publicly due to fear of white retaliation, even in the early sixties. In fact, his piercing rhetoric had primarily a cathartic function for black people; it purged them of their deferential and defensive attitudes toward white people.

Although Malcolm X moved toward a more Marxist-informed humanist position just prior to his assassination by rival Black Muslims in February 1965, he became the major symbol for (and of) the second stage of the black freedom movement in the sixties. What were accented were neither his political successes nor his organizational achievements, but rather his rhetorical eloquence and homespun honesty. Malcolm X did not hesitate to tell black and white America "like it is," even if it resulted in little political and practical payoff. This eloquence and honesty was admired at a distance by the black working poor and underclass: it expressed their gut feelings and addressed their situation but provided little means or hope as to how to change their predicament. The "old," black, middle class was horrified; they publicly and secretly tried to discredit him. The "new" black petite bourgeoisie, especially black students, welcomed Malcolm X's rhetoric and honesty with open arms. It resonated with their own newly acquired sense of political engagement and black pride; it also spoke to a more fundamental problem they faced—the problem of becoming black leaders and elites with organic, existential and rhetorical ties to the black community.

In a complex way, Malcolm X's candid talk both fueled more protracted black rebellion and provided a means to contain it. In short, his rhetoric was double-edged and functioned in contradictory ways. On the one hand, it served as an ideological pillar for revolutionary black nationalism. On the other hand, his rhetoric was employed by manipulative black petit bourgeois politicians, professionals, administrators and students to promote their own upward social mobility. The adulation of Malcolm X in the black community is profound. Yet an often overlooked component of this adulation among the "new" black middle class was (and is) their subtle use of his truth-telling for their narrow, self-serving aims. The relative silence regarding his black sexist values and attitudes also reveals the deep patriarchal sensibilities in the black community.

The revolt of the black masses, with hundreds of rebellions throughout the country, set the framework for the second stage. The repressive state apparatus in American capitalist society jumped at this opportunity to express its contempt for black people. And the basic mechanism of pacifying the erupting black ghettoes—the drug industry—fundamentally changed the content and character of the black community. The drug industry, aided and abetted by underground capitalists, invaded black communities with intense force, police indifference and political silence. It accelerated black white-collar and solid blue-collar working-class suburban flight, and transformed black poor neighborhoods into terrains of human bondage to the commodity form, enslavement to the buying and selling of drugs. For the first time in African American history, fear and trepidation among black folk toward one another became pervasive. As crime moved toward civil terrorism, black distrust of and distance from the black poor and underclass deepened. And, of course, black presence in jails and prisons rapidly increased.

The revolt of the black masses precipitated a deep crisis—with political, intellectual and existential forms—among the "new" black petite bourgeoisie. What should the appropriate black middle-class response be to such black working poor and underclass rebellions? This complex response is best seen in the internal dynamics of the Black Power movement. This movement, more than any other at the time, projected the aspirations and anxieties of the recently politicized and radicalized black petite bourgeoisie. From Adam Clayton Powell, Jr.'s Howard University baccalaureate address of 1966, through the Meredith March, to the Newark Black Power Conference, the message was clear: beneath the rhetoric of Black Power, black control and black self-determination was a budding, "new," black, middle class hungry for power and starving for status. Needless to say, most young black intellectuals were duped by this petit bourgeois rhetoric, primarily owing to their own identity crisis and self-interest. In contrast, the "new" black business, professional and political elites heard the bourgeois melody behind the radical rhetoric and manipulated the movement for their own benefit. The rebellious black working poor and underclass often either became dependent on growing welfare support or seduced by the drug culture.

The second stage was primarily a black nationalist affair. The veneration of "black" symbols, rituals, styles, hairdos, values, sensibilities and flag escalated. The "Black Is Beautiful" slogan was heard throughout the black community and James Brown's "Say It Loud, I'm Black and I'm Proud" became an exemplary—and healthy—expression of the cultural reversal of alienating Anglo-American ideals of beauty and behavior. Yet this cantankerous reversal (like the black rediscovery of jazz) was principally a "new" black middle-class phenomenon.

The working poor and underclass watched as the "new" black middle class visibly grappled with its new identity, social position and radical political rhetoric. For the most part, the black underclass continued to hustle, rebel when appropriate, get high and listen to romantic proletarian love songs produced by Detroit's Motown;

they remained perplexed at their idolization by the "new" black, middle class, which they sometimes envied. The black working poor persisted in their weekly church attendance, struggled to make ends meet and waited to see what the beneficial results would be after all the bourgeois "hoopla" was over. In short, the black nationalist moment, despite its powerful and progressive critique of American cultural imperialism, was principally the activity of black petit bourgeois self-congratulation and self-justification upon reaching an anxiety-ridden, middle-class status in racist American society.

To no surprise, the leading black, petit bourgeois, nationalist groups such as SNCC (after 1966), CORE, Ron Karenga's US and Imamu Amiri Baraka's Congress of African People were viewed by black proletarian and lumpenproletarian organizations as "porkchop nationalists" who confused superficial nation-talk with authentic cultural distinctiveness, middle-class guilt with working-class aspirations, and identity crises with revolutionary situations. The late Honorable Elijah Muhammad's Nation of Islam, though petit bourgeois in intent, was staunchly working poor and underclass (and especially strong in American prisons) in composition. Devoid of leading black intellectuals yet full of eloquent spokesmen, the nation of Islam put to shame the "porkchop nationalists," not only by being "blacker than thou" in both mythology and ideology, but also by producing discernible results in the personal, organizational and financial life of its members and the black community.

The Black Panther Party (founded in Oakland, California, 1966) was the leading black lumpenproletarian revolutionary party in the sixties. It thoroughly rejected and consistently struggled against petit bourgeois nationalism from a viewpoint of strong black leftist internationalism. Yet it was overwhelmed by the undisciplined character of black underclass life, seduced by the histrionic enticements of mass media and crushed by state repression. The only other major national response of black progressives against black petit bourgeois nationalism was George Wiley's Fannie Lou Hamer's National Welfare Rights Organization (founded in August 1967).

But it was unable to sustain broad membership, and thereby control encroaching bureaucratic leadership. The League of Revolutionary Black Workers (founded in Detroit, Michigan, 1969), though regional in scope, was the most important revolutionary group among black industrial workers in the country. It eventually split over the issue of the role of black nationalism in a Marxist organization.

The rift between black petit bourgeois nationalists and black revolutionary leftists was best illustrated in the American response to James Forman's historic Black Manifesto. Forman, a former executive director of SNCC, ex-minister of Foreign Affairs of the Black Panther Party, and leader of the short-lived Black Workers' Congress, proposed at the National Black Economic Development Conference in Detroit and later, more dramatically, at New York City's Riverside Church's 11:00 p.m. service, reparation funds of five hundred million dollars from white Christian churches and Jewish synagogues in order to finance the black revolutionary overthrow of the US government. This "revolution" would turn into an "armed, well-disciplined, black-controlled government."

This symbolic gesture represented the peak of the black nationalist moment in the sixties, though it was enacted by a black Marxist. It also signified liberal white America's absorption and domestication of black nationalism. Despite the Manifesto's Marxist critique and demand of American capitalist society—such as the call for a black revolutionary vanguard party and even the call for white progressive people to accept this black leadership—the most salient issue became that of reparations to existing black middle-class groups.

The white American response to these demands on the eccleslastical, educational and corporate levels was widespread. Of course, the major funds were not given to Forman's group (though it received about three hundred thousand dollars), but rather to church agencies, denominational caucuses, minority-oriented programs and, above all, black businesses and banks. Regardless of Forman's naive revolutionary intent, the black petit bourgeois nationalists triumphed. Soon the federal government and even the Nixon administration would openly support such moves in the name of "black self-determination" and "black capitalism."

The hegemonic role of black petit bourgeois nationalism had four deleterious consequences for African America. First, it isolated progressive black leftists such that orthodox Marxism became the primary refuge for those concerned with class struggle and Internationalism. And even in these new Marxist formations the Black Nation Thesis—the claim that black people constitute a nation within the USA—once again became the widely accepted understanding of African American oppression. Second, the machismo lifestyles of black nationalists (of the petit bourgeois and revolutionary varieties) so marginalized black women that the black feminist movement of the seventies and eighties was often forced to sever ties with black male-dominated groups, thereby encouraging an understandable but innocuous black feminist separatism. Third, black nationalism disarmed and delimited a large number of young black intellectuals by confining them to parochial black rhetoric, pockets of "internal dialogues," which resulted in posing almost insurmountable walls of separation between progressive white, brown, red, yellow and black intellectuals. Last, black nationalist rhetoric contributed greatly to the black freedom movement's loss of meaningful anchorage and organic ties to the black community, especially the churches. In short, besides the severe state repression and the pervasive drug invasion, the black petit bourgeois nationalist perspectives and practices were primarily responsible for the radically decentered state of the black freedom movement in the seventies and eighties. This was so principally because they undergirded the needs and interests of the "new" black middle class.

The sixties in African American history witnessed an unforgettable appearance of the black masses on the historical stage, but they are quickly dragged off—killed, maimed, strung out, imprisoned or paid off. Yet history continues and the growing black petite bourgeoisie still gropes for identity, direction and vision. This black middle class is "new" not simply because significant numbers of black people recently arrived in the world of higher education, comfortable living and professional occupations, but also because they achieved such status against the backdrop of undeniable political struggle, a struggle in which many of them participated. And the relation of their unprecedented opportunities and privileges to the revolt of the black masses is quite obvious to them. This is why the "new" black middle class will more than likely refuse to opt for political complacency. Its own position hangs on some form of political participation, on resisting subtle racist practices, housing policies and educational opportunities. Only persistent pressure can ensure a managerial job at IBM, partnership in a Wall Street firm, a home in Westchester or a slot at Harvard College, whereas in the past little resistance by the "old" black middle class was required to service the black community, live in the Gold Coast of Washington, D.C. or send the kid to Howard, Fisk or Morehouse. The roots of the "new" black middle class are in political struggle, in SCLC, SNCC, CORE, in the values and sensibilities these groups generated.

The major challenge of the "new," black, petite bourgeoisie is no longer whether it will take politics seriously (as posed in E. Franklin Frazier's classic *Black Bourgeoisie* in 1957). Rather it is what kind of politics the "new" black middle class will promote in the present national context of austere economic policies, declining state support of black rights and escalating racist violence and the prevailing international context of the crisis of capitalism, the nuclear arms race and anti-imperialist struggles. Like any other petite bourgeoisie, the "new" black middle class will most likely pursue power-seeking life styles, promote black entrepreneurial growth, and perpetuate professional advancement. Yet the rampant racism in American society truncates such life-styles, growth and advancement. The "new" black middle class can become only a "truncated" petite bourgeoisie in American society, far removed from real ownership and control over the crucial sectors of the economy and with intractable ceilings imposed upon their upward social mobility.

Presently, there are three major political options for this "truncated" black middle class: electoral politics in the bosom of the centrist Democratic Party or conservative Republican Party; social democratic and democratic socialist politics on the margin of the liberal wing of the Democratic Party (for instance, the Democratic Socialists of America) and inside grass-roots, black leftist, nationalist, preparty formations (for instance, the National Black United Front); or orthodox revolutionary politics far removed from both bourgeois American politics and black grass-roots groupings. The effects of the second stage of the black freedom movement in the sixties—beneath and between the endless ideological debates about violence versus nonviolence, the viability of black-white coalitions, reform versus revolution—primarily consisted of an oscillation between the first and third options, between vulgar realpolitik and antiquated orthodoxy, bourgeois politics and utopian rhetoric, with no mediating moment, hence little acknowledgment of the historical complexity of the prevailing African American predicament.

The prospects of galvanizing and organizing renewed black resistance are open-ended. The major tasks are repoliticizing the black working poor and underclass, revitalizing progressive black proletarian and petit bourgeois organizations, retooling black organic and traditional intellectuals, and forging meaningful alliances and beneficial fusions with progressive Latino, Asian, Native American and white groups.

Despite the historical limitations of the "new" black petite bourgeoisie, the African American predicament dictates that this group play a crucial role in carrying out these tasks. This is principally because the black middle class—preachers, teachers, lawyers, doctors and politicians—possess the requisite skills and legitimacy in the eyes of the majority of African Americans for the articulation of the needs and interests of African America. This unfortunate but inescapable situation requires that the politicized progressive wing of the black petite bourgeoisie and stable working class incessantly push beyond the self-serving liberalism of major black leaders and raise issues of fundamental concern to the black working poor and underclass. In short, the "new" black middle class must not be prematurely abandoned or denigrated. Rather, black progressives must keep persistent pressure on, and radical fire under, their liberal reformism until more effective political mobilization and organization emerge among the black working poor and underclass.

The repoliticizing of the black working poor and underclass should focus primarily on the black cultural apparatus, especially the ideological form and content of black popular music. African American life is permeated by black popular music. Since black musicians play such an important role in African American life, they have a special mission and responsibility: to present beautiful music which both sustains and motivates black people and provides visions of what black people should aspire to. Despite the richness of the black musical tradition and the vitality of black contemporary music, most black musicians fall far short of this crucial mission and responsibility. There are exceptions—Gil Scott-Heron, Brian Jackson, Stevie Wonder, Kenneth Gamble and Leon Huff—but more political black popular music is needed. Jamaican reggae music and Nigeria's Fela Anikulapo Kuti can serve as inspiring models in this regard. The radical politicization of black popular music, as best seen in Grandmaster Flash and the Furious Five's "The Message" and "New York, New York" (despite their virulent sexism) in the early years of rap is a necessary, though not sufficient, condition for the repoliticization of the black working poor and underclass. Black activists must make black musicians accountable in some way to the urgent needs and interests of the black community.

The major prerequisite for renewed organizational black resistance is the political revitalization of existing black groups—fraternities, sororities, lodges, trade unions and, especially, black churches. Without black religious participation, there can be no widespread black resistance. The prophetic wing of the black church has always been at the center of the black freedom movement.

Without a strong organizational base with deep organic connections in the black community, there can be no effective renewed black resistance. Only the political revitalization of black prophetic churches can provide this broad organizational base—as Rev. Herbert Daughtry's African Peoples' Christian Organization and other such groups are attempting to do.

The role of black intellectuals—organic ones closely affiliated with the everyday operations of black organizations or traditional ones nesting in comfortable places geared toward theoretical and historical analyses, social visions and practical conclusions—is crucial for renewed black resistance. Without vision, the black freedom movement is devoid of hope. Without analysis, it lacks direction. Without protracted struggle, it ossifies. Yet the vision must be guided by profound, not provincial, conceptions of what it is to be a human being, an African human being in predominantly white, postindustrial, capitalist America, and of how human potential can be best realized in an overcoming of existing economic exploitation, racial and sexual oppression. Likewise, the analysis must be informed by the most sophisticated and cultivated, not self-serving and cathartic, tools available in order to grasp the complexity and specificity of the prevailing African American predicament on the local, regional, national and international levels. Last, the political praxis, though motivated by social vision and guided by keen analysis, must be grounded in moral convictions. Personal integrity is as important as correct analysis or desirable vision. It should be noted that while black intellectuals deserve no special privilege and treatment in the black freedom movement, the services they provide should be respected and encouraged.

It should be obvious that African Americans cannot fundamentally transform capitalist, patriarchal, racist America by themselves. If renewed black resistance is to achieve its aim, alliances and coalitions with other progressive peoples are inescapable. Without such alliances and coalitions, African Americans are doomed to unfreedom. Yet, the more consolidated the black resistance, the better the chance for meaningful and effective alliances and coalitions with others. Of course, each alliance and coalition must be made in light of the specific circumstances and the particular contexts. The important point here is that any serious form of black resistance must be open to such alliances and coalitions with progressive Latino, Asian, Native American and white peoples.

In conclusion, the legacy of the black freedom movement in the sixties still haunts us. In its positive form, it flows through our veins as blood to be spilt if necessary for the cause of human freedom, and in the visions, analyses and practices that build on, yet go beyond, those in the sixties. In its negative form, it reminds us of the tenuous status of the "new" black petite bourgeoisie—its progressive potential and its self-serving interests, its capacity to transcend its parochial past and its present white subordination. The challenge of the black freedom movement in the late twentieth century is neither a discovery of another Rev. Martin Luther King, Jr.—though it would not hurt—nor a leap of faith in a messianic black working class or underclass—though the role of both is crucial. Rather the challenge is a fusing and transforming of indigenous forms of American radicalism—of which black resistance is a central expression—into a major movement which promotes workers' self-management, cultural heterogeneity (including nonracist and nonsexist ways of life) and individual liberties.

Notes

The author gratefully acknowledges permission to republish these essays, some of which appear here in revised versions.

"The New Cultural Politics of Difference," *Out There,* ed. Russell Ferguson, Martha Gever, Trinh T. Minh-ha, and Cornel West (Cambridge: MIT Press, 1990), pp. 19–36; "Minority Discourse and the Pitfalls of Canon Formation," 1:1 *Yale Journal of Criticism;* "Horace Pippin's Challenge to Art Criticism," in *I Tell My Heart: The Art of Horace Pippin* (Universe Publishing, 1993), reprinted with the permission of the publisher, © Pennsylvania Academy of the Fine Arts, Philadelphia, 1993; "The Dilemma of the Black Intellectual," *Cultural Critique,* No. 1, pp. 109–24, © 1985 Oxford University Press; "Theory, Pragmatism, and Politics," in *Consequences of Theory,* edited by Jonathan Arac and Barbara Johnson (Baltimore: The Johns Hopkins University Press, 1991), pp. 22–38; "The Historicist Turn in Philosophy of Religion," from *Knowing Religiously* (Boston University Studies in Philosophy and Religion, Volume 7) edited by Leroy S. Rouner, © 1985 The University of Notre Dame Press; "The Limits of Neopragmatism," 63 Southern California Law Review, 1747–1762 (1990); "Lukacs: A Reassessment," *minnesota review,* 1982, pp. 86–102; "Ethics and Action in Fredric Jameson's Marxist Hermeneutics," *Boundary 2* volume XI, Numbers 1 and 2, pp. 177–200, © 1982 Duke University Press; "Reassessing the Critical Legal Studies Movement," *Loyola Law Review,* vol. 34, 1988, pp. 265–275; "Critical Legal Studies and a Liberal Critic," The Yale Law Journal Company and Fred B. Rothman & Company from *The Yale Law Journal,* Vol. 97, pp. 757–71; "Hegel, Hermeneutics, Politics: A Reply to Charles Taylor," Volume 10, Numbers 5 and 6, *Cardozo Law Review* pp. 871–875 (1989); "The Role of Law In Progressive Politics" from *Politics of Law Revised* by Cornel West, ed. David Kairys, pp. 468–477 © 1982, 1990 by Cornel West, reprinted with permission of Pantheon Books, a division of Random House, Inc.; "The Paradox of the Afro-American Rebellion", from *The Sixties: Without Apology,* ed. Sohnya Sayres and others (Minneapolis: University of Minnesota Press, 1984), pp. 44–58; "Race and Social Theory: Towards a Genealogical

Materialist Analysis," from *Year Left*, ed. Michael Sprinker (London: Verso, 1985), pp. 74–90.

3. A Note on Race and Architecture

1. John Summerson, *Heavenly Mansions* (New York: Norton, 1963), p. 111.
2. Charles Jencks, *Modern Movements in Architecture* (New York: Penguin, 1973), p. 51.
3. Aaron Betsky, "The End(s) of Architecture," unpublished essay; James Wines, *De-Architecture* (New York: Rizzoli, 1987), p. 38.
4. Roger Kimball, "The Death and Resurrection of Postmodern Architecture", *New Criterion*, June 1988, pp. 21–31, "Is Modernism the Enemy? The Case of Mies Van Der Rohe," *New Criterion*, May 1989, pp. 67–77.
5. Alan Colquhoun, *Essays in Architectural Criticism: Modern Architecture and Historical Change* (Cambridge: MIT Press, 1981), p. 140.
6. Lewis Mumford, *The Myth of the Machine II: The Pentagon of Power* (New York: Harcourt Brace Janovich, 1970).
7. Alan Colquhoun, *Essays in Architectural Criticism*, p. 13.
8. Quoted from Charles Jencks, *Le Corbusier and the Tragic View of Architecture* (Cambridge: Harvard University Press, 1973), p. 67.
9. For assorted essays on Mies, see *Mies Reconsidered: His Career, Legacy, and Disciples* (New York: Rizzoli, 1986).
10. Robert Venturi, *Complexity and Contradiction in Architecture* (New York: Doubleday, 1966); Robert Venturi, Denise Scott Brown and Steven Izenour, *Learning from Las Vegas* (Cambridge: MIT Press, 1972); Charles Jencks, *The Language of Post-modern Architecture* (New York: Rizzoli, 1977); *Post-modern Classicism* (New York, 1980); James Wines, *De-Architecture*, op. cit.
11. Mark Wrigley, "Deconstructivist Architecture," *Deconstructivist Architecture* (Boston: Little, Brown, 1988), p. 16.
12. Mark Jarzombek, "Post-Modernist Historicism: The Historian's Dilemma," *Threshold:* Journal of the School of Architecture, The University of Illinois at Chicago (New York: Rizzoli), Vol. IV, Spring 1988, p. 96.
13. Charles Jencks, *Le Corbusier and the Tragic View of Architecture*, p. 102.

14. Quoted in Jencks, p. 102.

15. Quoted in Jencks, p. 109.

16. Quoted in Jencks, p. 110.

17. Quoted in Stephen Gardiner, *Le Corbusier* (New York: Viking, 1974), p. 115.

18. The pioneering work of Darell Fields, Kevin Fuller and Milton Curry in their journal *Appendx* is of great significance to race and architecture.

4. Horace Pippin's Challenge to Art Criticism

1. John Dewey, *Art as Experience* (1934), *Later Works,* 10:278, ed. Jo Ann Boydston (Carbondale: Southern Illinois University Press).

2. Ralph Waldo Emerson, "The American Scholar," *Selected Writings of Ralph Waldo Emerson,* ed. William H. Gilman (New York: New American Library, 1965), p. 239.

3. John Dewey, *Art as Experience,* 10:10–11.

4. Ralph Waldo Emerson, *Emerson in His Journals,* selected and edited by Joel Porte (Cambridge: Harvard University Press, 1982), p. 136.

5. Richard J. Powell, *Homecoming: The Art and Life of William H. Johnson* (Washington, D.C.: Smithsonian Institution, 1991), p. 138.

6. Alain Locke, "Horace Pippin, 1888–1946," Horace Pippin Memorial Exhibition, exhibition catalogue (Philadelphia: The Art Alliance, 1947).

7. James Clifford, *The Predicament of Culture: Twentieth Century Ethnography, Literature and Art* (Cambridge: Harvard University Press, 1988), p. 196.

8. Samella Lewis, *Art: African American* (New York: Harcourt Brace Jovanovitch, 1978), pp. 105–6.

9. Michele Wallace, "Modernism, Postmodernism and the Problem of the Visual in Afro-American Culture," *Out There: Marginalization and Contemporary Cultures,* eds. Russell Ferguson, Martha Gever, Trinh T. Minh-ha, and Cornel West (Cambridge: MIT Press, 1990), pp. 47–48.

10. See "The Cultural Politics of Difference," in this volume.

11. E. P. Richardson, *Painting in America: The Story of 450 Years* (New York: Thomas Y. Crowell, 1956), p. 389.

12. Martin Puryear, introduction to Richard J. Powell, *Homecoming*, p. xix.

13. W. E. B. Du Bois, *The Souls of Black Folk* (1903; rpt. New York: Penguin, 1989), introduction by Donald B. Gibson, p. 5.

14. Arnold Rampersad, introduction to *The New Negro*, ed. Alain Locke (New York: Atheneum, 1991), p. ix.

15. For Alain Locke's influence on the intellectual framework that shaped the practices of the William E. Harmon awards for distinguished achievement among Negroes, and the 1928 to 1933 annual Harmon Foundation Exhibitions, see the fine essay by Beryl J. Wright, "The Harmon Foundation in Context: Early Exhibitions and Alain Locke's Concept of a Racial Idiom of Expression," *Against the Odds: African-American Artists and the Harmon Foundation*, ed. Gary A. Reynolds and Beryl J. Wright (Newark, N.J.: The Newark Museum, 1989), pp. 13–25. Leslie Bolling was the only "folk artist"—with no formal art training (though he did attend Hampton Institute and Virginia Union University)—who exhibited with the Harmon Foundation.

16. For Locke's complex development as an art critic—especially his modernist views of African and African American art, see *His Negro Art; Past and Present* (Associates in Negro Folk Education, Albany, N.Y.: The J. B. Lyon Press, 1936). See especially his discussion of the notion of the "primitive" in African and European art, pp. 93–116.

6. Theory, Pragmatisms and Politics

1. John B. Thompson, *Studies in the Theory of Ideology* (Berkeley and Los Angeles: University of California Press, 1984), pp. 5ff.

2. Steven Knapp and Walter Benn Michaels, "Against Theory," *Critical Inquiry* 8, No. 4 (1982), p. 742.

3. John B. Thompson, *Studies in the Theory of Ideology*, p. 6.

4. Arthur O. Lovejoy, "On the Discrimination of Romanticisms," *Essays in the History of Ideas* (Baltimore: Johns Hopkins University Press, 1948), pp. 228–53.

5. Arthur O. Lovejoy, "The Thirteen Pragmatisms," *The Thirteen Pragmatisms and Other Essays* (Baltimore: Johns Hopkins University Press, 1963), pp. 1–29.

6. Hilary Putnam, *Reason, Truth and History* (Cambridge: Cambridge University Press, 1981), pp. 103–26, 174–200. For a brief interpreta-

tion of Putnam that chimes with mine, see Ian Hacking, *Representing and Intervening: Introductory Topics in the Philosophy of Natural Science* (Cambridge: Cambridge University Press, 1983), p. 60.

7. Steven Knapp and Walter Benn Michaels, "A Reply to Richard Rorty: What Is Pragmatism?" *Critical Inquiry* II, No. 3 (1985), p. 470.

8. Frank Lentricchia, *Criticism and Social Change* (Chicago: University of Chicago Press, 1983), p. 34.

9. Ibid., p. 4.

10. Richard Rorty, review of Allan Bloom's *The Closing of the American Mind, New Republic,* 4 April 1988.

11. See Cornel West, "Reassessing the Critical Legal Studies Movement," and "Critical Legal Studies and a Liberal Critic," in this volume, and "On Christian Intellectuals" and "The Crisis in Theological Education," *Prophetic Fragments* (Grand Rapids, Mich.: Eerdmans, 1988), pp. 273–80.

12. Jim Merod, *The Political Responsibility of the Critic* (Ithaca: Cornell University Press, 1988), pp. 191, 261.

13. Cornel West, *The American Evasion of Philosophy: A Genealogy of Pragmatism* (Madison: University of Wisconsin Press, 1989).

7. *Pragmatism and The Sense of the Tragic*

1. Alfred Kazin, *An American Procession* (New York: Alfred Knopf, 1984), p. 114.

2. Sidney Hook, *Pragmatism and the Tragic Sense of Life* (New York: Basic Books, 1974), pp. 1–25.

3. C. I. Lewis, *Collected Papers* (Palo Alto: Stanford University Press, 1970), p. 108.

4. John Dewey, "The Need For a Recovery of Philosophy," *On Experience, Nature, and Freedom,* ed. Richard Bernstein (New York: Bobbs-Merrill, 1960), pp. 25, 26.

5. Josiah Royce, *Sources of Religious Insight* (New York: Octagon Books, 1977), pp. 144, 145–46.

6. William James, *Collected Essays and Reviews* (New York: Russell and Russell, 1969) p. 11.

7. John Dewey, "Philosophy and Democracy," *Characters and Events* (New York: Holt, Rinehart, and Winston, 1929), Vol. 2, p. 843.

8. Josiah Royce, *Sources of Religious Insight*, p. 159.

9. John Dewey, *Philosophy and Civilization* (New York: Peter Smith Edition, 1968), pp. 24–25.

10. Quoted from editor's introduction, Josiah Royce, *Fugitive Essays*, ed. Dr. J. Loewenberg (Cambridge: Harvard University Press, 1920), p. 34.

11. John Dewey, "The Need for a Recovery of Philosophy," p. 27.

12. Josiah Royce, *The Spirit of Modern Philosophy*, pp. 228, 229, 247.

13. Ibid., p. 266.

14. Josiah Royce, *Sources of Religious Insight*, pp. 153–54.

15. Josiah Royce, *The Spirit of Modern Philosophy*, pp. 469, 467.

16. Ibid., p. 469.

17. Josiah Royce, *The World and the Individual*, Second Series (Gloucester, Mass.: Peter Smith Edition, 1976), p. 387.

18. Ibid., p. 407.

19. Josiah Royce, *Sources of Religious Insight*, p. 157.

20. Josiah Royce, *The Spirit of Modern Philosophy*, pp. 461–62, 463, 465.

21. Ibid., p. 470, 471.

8. *The Historicist Turn in Philosophy of Religion*

1. For intellectual explorations in the American grain for philosophy and theology, see John E. Smith, *The Spirit of American Philosophy* (New York: Oxford University Press, 1963): and Randolph Crump Miller, *The American Spirit in Theology* (Philadelphia: United Church Press, 1974). A more contemporary expression and examination can be found in John Rajchman and Cornel West, eds., *Post-Analytic Philosophy* (New York: Columbia University Press, 1985).

2. The major essays on the refinement and rejection of these philosophical distinctions are Carl G. Hempel, "Empiricist Criteria of Cognitive Significance: Problems and Changes" and "The Theoretician's Dilemma: A Study in the Logic of Theory Construction," in his *Aspects of Scientific Explanation and Other Essays in the Philosophy of Science* (New York: Free Press, 1965), pp. 101–22; 173–226.

3. For the persuasive arguments for Quine's epistemological holism and methodological monism, see his classic essay "The Dogmas of Empiri-

cism," in his *From a Logical Point of View* (New York: Harper & Row, 1963), pp. 20–46; and his less rigorous personal reflections in "The Pragmatists' Place in Empiricism," in *Pragmatism: Its Sources and Prospects,* ed. Robert J. Mulvaney and Philip M. Zeltner, pp. 23–39.

4. Goodman's postempiricist antireductionism is best illustrated in his powerful essay "The Test of Simplicity," and his classic piece "The Way the World Is," in his *Problems and Projects* (New York: Bobbs-Merrill, 1972), pp. 279–94; 24–32. Goodman's full-fledged ontological pluralism is put forward in his *Ways of Worldmaking* (Indianapolis: Hackett, 1978). For Quine's critique of Goodman, see *Theories and Things* (Cambridge: Harvard University Press, 1981), pp. 96–99.

5. Sellars's classic statement is "Empiricism and the Philosophy of Mind," in *Minnesota Studies in the Philosophy of Science,* vol. 1, ed. Herbert Feigl and Michael Scriven (Minneapolis: University of Minnesota Press, 1956), pp. 253–329.

6. For a more detailed account of this takeover, see Cornel West, "Nietzsche's Prefiguration of Postmodern American Philosophy," *Boundary 2: A Journal of Postmodern Literature,* Special Nietzsche Issue, Vol. 9, No. 10 (Spring-Fall 1981), pp. 241–70.

7. C. S. Peirce, *The Collected Papers of Charles Sanders Peirce,* 6 vols., ed. Charles Hartshorne, Paul Weiss and Arthur Burks (Cambridge: Harvard University Press, 1933–58), Vol. 1, p. 135.

8. The texts of liberation theology I have in mind are Gustavo Gutierrez, *A Theology of Liberation,* trans. Sister Caridad Inda and John Eagleson (Maryknoll: Orbis Books, 1973); Mary Daly, *Beyond God the Father* (Boston: Beacon Press, 1973); and James H. Cone, *God of the Oppressed* (New York: Seabury Press, 1975).

9. Jeffrey Stout, *The Flight from Authority* (Notre Dame, Ind.: University of Notre Dame Press, 1981). This important book has yet to receive the attention it deserves.

10. On Georg Lukács

1. In his superb book, *Georg Lukács—From Romanticism to Bolshevism* (New York: Schocken, 1979), Michael Löwy writes: "One of the most typical expressions of this *arriviste* enthusiasm for the semi-feudal establishment was the buying of titles through which Hungarian big bourgeois, of commoner or even Jewish origin, were 'ennobled.' To

take but one example, József Löwinger, director of the Anglo-Austrian Budapest Bank and later of the General Credit Bank of Hungary, was ennobled in 1889 and became József 'von Lukács.' As is well known, this was the father of György" (p. 71).

2. Lukács wrote in 1909, "Ady is conscience, and a fighting song, a triumpet and standard around which all can gather should there ever be a fight." Quoted in Ferenc Tokei, "Lukács and Hungarian Culture," *New Hungarian Quarterly* 47 (Autumn 1972), 119. Quoted also in Löwy, p. 79.

3. Löwy, p. 93.

4. Ibid.

5. Note Löwy's comments: "The story is evidently related to the writer's own life: for Irma Seidler, who had a relationship with him in 1908, had just killed herself in 1911 after an unhappy marriage" (p. 103). Löwy fails to add that Lukács's first marriage was an unhappy one.

6. Agnes Heller, "Von der Armut am Geiste: A Dialogue by the Young Lukács," *Philosophical Forum* 3 (Spring-Summer 1972), p. 364.

7. For a pioneering interpretation of Lukács's texts in his early and middle periods, see Fredric Jameson, "The Case for Georg Lukács," in his fine book *Marxism and Form: Twentieth-Century Dialectical Theories of Literature* (Princeton: Princeton University Press, 1971), pp. 160–205. Jameson stresses the link between the quest for totality and the concern with narrative.

8. Georg Lukács, *The Theory of the Novel*, trans. Anna Bostock (Cambridge: MIT Press, 1975), pp. 152–53.

9. Löwy, p. 124.

10. Ibid., p. 130.

11. Ibid., p. 131.

12. Ibid., p. 132. For the Dewey-Trotsky debate (in 1938), see *Their Morals and Ours: Marxist vs. Liberal Views on Morality* (New York: Pathfinder Press, 1975), pp. 13–52, 67–73.

13. Löwy, p. 128. Quoted also in David Kettler, "Culture and Revolution: Lukács in the Hungarian Revolution of 1918/19," *Telos* 10 (1971), pp. 68–69.

14. Löwy, pp. 136–37.

15. Georg Lukács, *History and Class Consciousness: Studies in Marxist*

Dialectics, trans. Rodney Livingstone (Cambridge: MIT Press, 1972), p. 188.

16. Ibid., p. 204.

17. Ibid.

18. On the relation of Lukács's appropriation of Hegel and his surrender to Stalinism, see Löwy, pp. 193–213.

19. Quoted from István Eörsi, "The Story of a Posthumous Work: Lukács' Ontology," *New Hungarian Quarterly* 16 (Summer 1975), p. 106.

20. For a brief treatment of the history of ontology, see Jose Ferrater Mora, "On the Early History of Ontology," *Philosophy and Phenomenological Research* 24 (1963), pp. 36–47.

21. George Lukács, "Hegel's False and His Genuine Ontology," chapter III, Part one of *Toward the Ontology of Social Being,* trans. David Fernbach (London: Merlin Press, 1978), I, p. 78.

22. Ibid., pp. 72–73.

23. Georg Lukács, "Marx's Basic Ontological Principles," chapter IV, Part one of *Toward the Ontology of Social Being,* II, p. 30.

24. Ibid., pp. 60–61.

25. Lukács, "Hegel's False and His Genuine Ontology," pp. 82–83.

26. Ibid., p. 78.

27. Ibid., p. 84. For more on the "epistemology of mimesis" and the "consciously mimetic epistemology of dialectical materialism," see pp. 39–40.

28. Georg Lukács, *Die Eigenart des Ästhetischen* (Halbbände, 1963), I, p. 158. For English translation, see Kenneth Megill, "Georg Lukács as an Ontologist," *Studies in Soviet Thought* 9 (1969), p. 344.

29. Lukács, *Die Eigenart des Ästhetischen,* II, pp. 294–95; Megill, p. 344.

30. Lukács, "Hegel's False and His Genuine Ontology," pp. 53–54.

31. Georg Lukács, "Labor," chapter I, Part two of *Toward the Ontology of Social Being,* III, p. 11.

32. Ibid., p. 35.

33. Ibid., pp. 6, 8, 9–10.

34. Ibid., pp. 87–88.

35. Quoted from Lukács's recently discovered journal for December 15, 1911 in Löwy, p. 107.

11. Fredric Jameson's American Marxism

I would like to extend my gratitude to Jonathan Arac, Stanley Aronowitz, Paul Bové, Fredric Jameson, David Langston, Michael Sprinker and Anders Stephanson for their incisive comments and criticisms of an earlier version of this essay.

1. Fredric Jameson, *Marxism and Form: Twentieth-Century Dialectical Theories of Literature* (Princeton: Princeton University Press, 1971). Further references to this work will be given parenthetically as MF. *The Prison-House of Language: A Critical Account of Structuralism and Russian Formalism* (Princeton: Princeton University Press, 1972). Further references to this text will be given parenthetically as PHL. *The Political Unconscious: Narrative as a Socially Symbolic Act* (Ithaca: Cornell University Press, 1981). Further references to this book will be given parenthetically as PU. I shall include in this "trilogy" *Fables of Aggression: Wyndham Lewis, the Modernist as Fascist* (Berkeley: University of California Press, 1979) since it was originally conceived to be a part of *The Political Unconscious* but was separated, enlarged, and published as an independent work.

2. In the preface to PU, Jameson refers to the "flawed yet monumental achievements . . . of the greatest Marxist philosopher of modern times, Georg Lukács" (13).

3. Fredric Jameson, *Sartre: The Origins of a Style* (New Haven: Yale University Press, 1961).

4. Jameson's treatment of Adorno in chapter 1 of MF is based on an earlier essay that appeared in *Salmagundi*, No. 5 (1967), pp. 3–43.

5. For Jameson's view of Adorno's negative dialectics as an aesthetic ideal, see PU, 52, n.29.

6. The major difference between Adorno and Derrida (or de Man), between a dialectical deconstructionist and a poststructural deconstructionist, is that the theoretical impasse the dialectician reaches is not viewed as an ontological, metaphysical or epistemological aporia, but rather as a historical limitation owing to a determinate contradiction as yet unlodged because of an impotent social praxis or an absence of an effective historical revolutionary agent. For interesting comments on this matter, see Stanley Aronowitz, *The Crisis in Historical Materialism: Class, Politics and Culture in Marxist Theory* (New York: Praeger, 1981), pp. 24–34.

7. See also MF 373, where Jameson states that "we take a point of view not so much *philosophical* as *hermeneutic*."

8. Herbert Marcuse, *Eros and Civilization* (New York: Random House, 1955), p. 29, quoted in MF 113.

9. This traditional hermeneutic strategy is enunciated in the following passage in MF: "Thus the process of criticism is not so much an interpretation of content as it is a revealing of it, a laying bare, a restoration of the original message, the original experience, beneath the distortions of the various kinds of censorship that have been at work upon it; and this revelation takes the form of an explanation of why the content was so distorted and is thus inseparable from a description of the mechanisms of this censorship itself" (404).

10. Note also his remark in PU: "That life is meaningless is not a proposition that need be inconsistent with Marxism, whose affirmation is the quite different one that History is meaningful, however absurd organic life may happen to be" (261).

11. For Jameson's interesting remarks on religion, see MF 116–18 and PU 70, 292.

12. Jameson is one of the few Marxists who explicitly rejects a realist epistemological position. See MF 365–66. Note that he invokes the early work of the then American-style Marxist Sidney Hook at this point. For a persuasive treatment of the "textual idealism" of poststructuralists, see Richard Rorty, "Nineteenth-Century Idealism and Twentieth-Century Textualism," in *Consequences of Pragmatism* (Minneapolis: University of Minnesota Press, 1982), pp. 139–59.

13. PU 139, 226.

14. PU 97, 141. Bloch puts forward this complex notion in "Nonsynchronism and Dialectics," *New German Critique*, No. 11 (1977), pp. 22–38. For Jameson's powerful critique of teleological and genetic forms of Marxism, see "Marxism and Historicism," *New Literary History* 11 (1979), pp. 41–73.

15. MF 402.

16. Fredric Jameson, "Criticism in History," in *The Weapons of Criticism*, ed. Norman Rudich (Palo Alto, Calif.: Ramparts Press, 1976), pp. 31–50.

17. For the Lévi-Straussian language, see PU 167 and for Frye's notion of literature, see PU 70.

18. Yet I remain unconvinced that the cosmic body in Blake's anagogy is even roughly analogous to the individualistic bourgeois body. See Northrop Frye, *Anatomy of Criticism: Four Essays* (Princeton: Princeton University Press, 1957), pp. 119f.

19. Geoffrey H. Hartman, "Ghostlier Demarcations: The Sweet Science of Northrop Frye," in *Beyond Formalism: Literary Essays 1958–1970* (New Haven: Yale University Press, 1970), p. 40.

20. Hartman, "Ghostlier Demarcations," pp. 24–41; J. Hillis Miller, "Tradition and Difference." *Diacritics* 2 (Winter 1972), pp. 6–13.

21. Note Jameson's remarks in MF: "This formal character of the concept of freedom is precisely what lends itself to the work of political hermeneutics. It encourages analogy: assimilating the material prisons to the psychic ones, it serves as a means of unifying all these separate levels of existence, functioning, indeed, as a kind of transformational equation whereby the data characteristic of one may be converted into the terms of other" (85).

22. Jameson explicitly states in PU: "I will argue that the critique [by poststructuralism] is misplaced" (21).

23. For the classic reply to Nietzsche on this matter, though not a thoroughly satisfactory one, see Max Scheler, *Ressentiment,* trans. William Holdheim, ed. Lewis A. Coser (New York: Free Press, 1961), pp. 43–46, 79–89, 95–97, 103–11, 114.

24. Friedrich Nietzsche, *Beyond Good and Evil,* trans. Walter Kaufmann (New York: Vintage Books, 1966), p. 48.

25. Nietzsche remarks repeatedly that modern bourgeois European culture is an amalgam of various traditions, only one of which is the Judeo-Christian tradition. Yet what Nietzsche stresses, and Jameson ignores, is that Christian morality is a weapon of the oppressed against the oppressor, not simply a symptom of impotence. On this point, Jameson follows not Nietzsche but Sartre. "The moral attitude appears when technical and social conditions render positive forms of conduct impossible. Ethics is a collection of idealistic tricks intended to enable us to live the life imposed on us by the poverty of our resources and the insufficiency of our techniques." This passage is an unpublished note of Sartre's quoted by Simone de Beauvoir, *Force of Circumstance,* trans. Richard Howard (New York: G. P. Putnam, 1965), p. 199.

26. This point is made most emphatically by Lucien Goldmann, *Immanuel Kant* (London: New Left Books, 1971), pp. 170–79. Hegel puts for-

ward this critique in *Philosophy of Right,* trans. T. M. Knox (Oxford: Oxford University Press, 1967), pp. 89–103, and *Philosophy of Mind, Part Three of the Encyclopedia of the Philosophical Sciences* (Oxford: Clarendon Press, 1971), pp. 253–91. Jameson clearly grasps this point when he states, "as an ideological field, conceptions of ethics depend on a shared class or group homogeneity, and strike a suspicious compromise between the private experience of the individual and those values or functional needs of the collectivity which ethics rewrites or recodes in terms of interpersonal relationships." Yet, unlike Hegel and Marx, Jameson clings to the notion that the historicizing of ethics results in a "going beyond" good and evil. In the same paragraph quoted he continues, "In our time, ethics, wherever it makes its reappearance, may be taken as the sign of an intent to mystify, and in particular to replace the more complex and ambivalent judgments of a more properly political and dialectical perspective with the more comfortable simplifications of a binary myth." The basic point here is that Hegel, Marx, and Jameson agree that bourgeois ethics cannot do justice to the richness of moral experience without embarrassing equivocation. Yet Jameson believes that this has something to do with the binary oppositions of good and evil, whereas Hegel and Marx rightly hold that such poststructuralist itching does not require scratching but rather getting rid of the source of the itch. The passage quoted is from Jameson, *Fables of Aggression,* p. 56.

27. David Couzens Hoy, "Hegel's Morals," *Dialogue* 20, No.1 (1981), p. 99.

28. For a detailed examination of Marx's critique of Kant and Hegel on ethical approaches, see Cornel West, "Ethics, Historicism and the Marxist Tradition," Ph.D. diss., Princeton University, 1980, pp. 28–74.

29. As Richard Rorty notes, "the non-Kantian *is* a parasite—flowers could not sprout from the dialectical vine unless there were an edifice into whose chinks it could insert its tendrils. No constructors, no deconstructors. No norms, no perversions. Derrida (like Heidegger) would have no writing to do unless there were a 'metaphysics of presence' to overcome. Without the fun of stamping out parasites, on the other hand, no Kantian would bother to continue building." See "Philosophy as a Kind of Writing: An Essay on Derrida," *Consequences of Pragmatism,* p. 108. This is precisely the philosophical "game" Marx ignores, sidesteps and avoids. For Rorty's brilliant historical situating of this

modern "game," see *Philosophy and the Mirror of Nature* (Princeton: Princeton University Press, 1979); for a leftist critique of this text, see Cornel West, "The Politics of American Neopragmatism," in *Post-Analytic Philosophy,* ed. John Rajchman and Cornel West (New York: Columbia University Press, 1985), pp. 259–75.

30. For his brief characterization of the French and American left, see PU 54, 31.

31. Jameson does address the role of the Marxist intellectual in the academy in his essay "Marxism and Teaching." *New Political Science,* No. 2/3. (Fall/Winter 1979/1980), pp. 31–36.

12. Reassessing the Critical Legal Studies Movement

1. These texts are written from different vantage points—Bloom being a Straussian, Jacoby being a neo- or even post-Marxist.

2. For Bloom, looking at the critical legal studies movement through the lens of Leo Strauss and his own creative appropriation of the work of Strauss, critical legal studies would be simply this Nietzschenized left—highly irrational, cantankerous, and rebellious but without real intellectual substance and content.

3. By structures of feelings, I refer to the very immediate levels of the existence in the culture of critical discourse. This "structure of feelings" is a term from the late Raymond Williams. Williams was trying to describe a mode of being in a culture which is different from that which one had experienced before entry into this culture of critical discourse in the academy. See, e.g., R. Williams, *Modern Tragedy* (Stanford: Stanford University Press, 1966).

4. An example is that propositional forms have more status as opposed to narrative forms, and the issue then becomes why stories have less status than propositional forms of argument. Oppositional intellectuals question where that value originates.

5. "Regimes of truth" are the various ways in which distinctions between true and false, and legitimate and illegitimate are put forward, and ways in which these regimes of truth themselves have to be legitimate. Of course, one must then ask the next question: Who is going to legitimate the legitimators? This is ultimately, for critical legal studies, a political question.

6. The work of Robert Cover, a former professor of law at Yale University, was not simply interdisciplinary but de-disciplinizing. The very notion

of "interdisciplinary" assumes that there are still such things as disciplines against which one traverses. De-disciplinizing assumes that one moves toward a problematic view and pulls from whatever sources are instructive, whether those sources be Marx, Old Testament studies, Judaic theology, popular culture, Kafka, Proust or whatever.

7. One danger in "trashing" liberalism is that it discourages historical analysis of liberalism's various forms. For example, although John Dewey was a democratic socialist for sixty-five of his ninety-two years, many think of him as just a liberal. His works, *The Public and Its Problems* and *Liberalism and Social Action,* go unread. See J. Dewey, *The Public and its Problems* (1927); J. Dewey, *Liberalism and Social Action* (1935). The political danger in "trashing" liberalism is that for people attempting to free themselves from institutional and structural forms of evil, liberalism might be a valuable resource they can invoke.

8. This represents a major shift from his earlier work, especially *Knowledge and Politics,* in which he "trashed" liberalism. See R. Unger, *Knowledge and Politics* (New York: Free Press, 1975).

13. Critical Legal Studies and a Liberal Critic

1. See Roberto Unger, *Knowledge and Politics* (New York: Free Press, 1975); R. Unger, *The Critical Legal Studies Movement* (Cambridge: Harvard University Press, 1983); R. Unger, *Politics: A Work in Constructive Social Theory,* 3 vols. (New York: Cambridge University Press, 3 vols. 1987); William Ewald, "Unger's Philosophy: A Critical Legal Study," 97 *Yale Law Journal* 665, 668 (1988).

2. Boyle, "The Politics of Reason: Critical Legal Theory and Local Social Thought," 133 *U. Pa. L. Rev.* 685, 775–76 (1985) (emphases in original).

3. Ewald, "Unger's Philosophy," n. 2, at p. 690.

4. Ibid., pp. 720–22.

5. See R. Unger, *Knowledge and Politics,* n. 1, at pp. 264–65.

6. See Ewald, "Unger's Philosophy," n. 2, at p. 721, n. 215; p. 719, n. 208, p. 721 n. 215; p. 722 & nn. 221–22, p. 723 & n. 223; p. 721.

7. R. Unger, *Knowledge and Politics,* n. 1, at pp. 275–76; p. 272; p. 273.

8. Ewald, "Unger's Philosophy," n. 2, at 722.

9. R. Unger, *Knowledge and Politics,* supra n. 1, at p. 260.

10. See Ewald, "Unger's Philosophy," n. 2, at pp. 722–24.

11. See H. L. A. Hart, *The Concept of Law* (New York: Oxford University Press, 1961), pp. 124–25, 249.

12. See Robert Cover, "Violence and the Word," 95 *Yale Law Journal* 1601 (1986).

13. See Brosnan, "Serious But Not Critical," 60 S. *California Law Review* 259 (1987).

Index